THE COMPLEX
AN INSIDER EXPOSES THE COVERT
WORLD OF THE CHURCH OF
SCIENTOLOGY

Nicola Tallant is a journalist with the *Sunday World* newspaper. She previously owned and ran a news and features agency in Dublin and is a former News Editor of the *Irish Daily Mirror*. She holds a Higher Diploma in Criminology and *The Complex* is her first book.

THE COMPLEX
AN INSIDER EXPOSES THE COVERT WORLD OF THE CHURCH OF SCIENTOLOGY

John Duignan

with
Nicola Tallant

MERLIN
PUBLISHING

First published in 2008 by
Merlin Publishing
Newmarket Hall, Cork Street,
Dublin 8, Ireland
Tel: +353 1 4535866
Fax: +353 1 4535930
publishing@merlin.ie
www.merlinwolfhound.com

ISBN 978-1-903582-84-8

*The names of some individuals in this book have been changed to
protect their identities.*

A CIP catalogue record for this book is available from the
British Library.

10 9 8 7 6 5 4 3 2 1

Typeset by Gough Typesetting Services
Cover Design by Graham Thew Design
Cover image courtesy of istockphotos.com © Lorenzo Puricelli
Printed and bound by CPI Cox & Wyman, Britain

CONTENTS

GLOSSARY

AOSH:	Advanced Organisation Saint Hill.
ASI:	Author Services incorporated – Publishing department of Scientology.
CO:	Cadet Organisation – A program for children aged from 12 years of age, based on the same principals as the Sea Organisation.
CMI:	Central Marketing International.
CO:	Commanding Officer– Highest post available in individual Organisations.
CMO:	Commodores Messenger Organisation –organisation that enforces policies drawn up by the Religious Technology Centre.
CMU:	Central Marketing Unit.
COSRECI:	Church of Scientology Religious Education College Incorporated.
EPF:	Estates Project Force – Scientology boot camp where new recruits are trained to graduate as a Sea Organisation member.
FLAG:	Advanced Organisation used for 'retreats', located at the Fort Harrison Hotel in Clearwater, Florida.
GO:	Guardians Office – The Church's former intelligence unit, disbanded after a major FBI investigation into fraud.
HCO:	Hubbard Communication Office.
IAS:	International Association of Scientology.
KSW	Keep Scientology Working.

LRH: L Ron Hubbard – the former science fiction writer who founded the Church of Scientology.

MEST: Matter Energy Space Time Universe – The physical universe.

OSA: Office of Special Affairs – The Scientology intelligence agency that took over the Guardians Office.

OT: Operating Thetan – A Scientologist who has reached 'Clear'.

OT Levels   Levels achieved after the state 'Clear'.

PAC Base: Pacific Area Command Base– Scientology's West Coast HQ which is also known as The Complex.

PTS: Potential Trouble Source – Someone who is connected to or is being influenced by a Suppressive Person.

RPF: Rehabilitation Project Force – A programme set up by the Church of Scientology to 'rehabilitate' Sea Org members which involves hard labour, large study loads and heavy auditing.

RTC: Religious Technology Centre.

SMI: Scientology Missions International – Serves as the ruling Church of all Mission churches.

Sea Org: Sea Organisation – An association of elite Scientologists who dedicate their lives to the Church and manage Organisations.

SP: Suppressive Person – A term used in Scientology to describe 'enemies' of the Church and often those who speak out or criticise it in any way.

The Complex: See Pacific Area Command Base.

Thetan: The spirit of a person that is distinct and separate from the physical body or the brain.

TRs: Training Routines – A system of training drills used in the application of Scientology.

ACKNOWLEDGEMENTS

I found the process of writing this memoir to be a difficult one; it stirred long-buried, painful memories and I experienced degrees of psychological pain and stress that both surprised and disturbed me. This has, however, been both a cleansing and healing experience. I am not sure that I would have seen the project through if it were not for the intense love that I share with my partner, Rosemary Morris. Her unusual intelligence, care, love, incisive wit and warm nurturing nature have been of incalculable value in the rebuilding of a new life and planning of a fulfilling future.

My co-author, Nicola, provided me with the system I needed to distance myself from the material and thus allowed me the space I needed to view and co-write this book dispassionately.

While all of my large close and extended family have played important roles in this new life, the most significant has been that of my foster parents. Frank and Catherine Garvey have been a constant in my life since my return home two years ago. They not only provided me a safe place when I needed it most, but also allowed and enabled me to reconnect with my childhood. Catherine – while providing endless cups of tea and plates of delicious homemade brown bread – helped me with the filling in of gaps in my memories and of familial details I could not otherwise have known. Frank, meanwhile, rekindled my love of the sea, dragging me off to help him sail his 24ft sloop around my beloved Roaringwater Bay. In doing so he also helped me rekindle my desire to live.

Lastly, to my former comrades and the many dear friends I have left behind in the Sea Organisation. These same people are bound to reject me at any given opportunity, as I am now considered truly an enemy of the group. I am here for you when you, as you inevitably will, begin your own journey out of the web of lies and deceit that will forever be personified in the building we know only too well as The Complex.

John Anthony Duignan
September 2008

When I signed the dotted line to co-author The Complex I could never have known just how apt that title was going to be. I was soon to discover that Scientology is not a simple topic at all – in fact it has been one of the most difficult ones I have ever tackled in my career in journalism.

On that note I would firstly like to thank John for his patience and attention to detail in what must have been a difficult process to go through. We often spoke for hours, as he painstakingly re-lived the last 22 years of his life.

I want to thank my husband Fintan for all the evenings he spent alone and his constant ability to give the right advice, my daughters Daisy and Layla for not messing TOO much before going to bed at night and my mum Pauline for all her encouragement and endless babysitting!

To Neil Leslie, Managing Editor of the *Sunday World* newspaper, for giving me the push I needed to do this book in the first place. He has 'never lost it' when it comes to spotting a good story.

Finally, our editor Aoife Barrett at Merlin for producing the structure this book so badly needed and Managing Director Chenile Keogh for all the counselling!

Nicola Tallant
September 2008

PROLOGUE

Dublin, June 2006

I could feel my heart pounding in my chest as I sat in Dublin Airport, scanning the sea of faces in the Departures lounge. Above my head the monitor indicated that my flight to Cork was still delayed. The flight attendant at the boarding desk was telling another passenger that it looked like we were going to be there for a good while.

Every minute was torture and my body was wet with perspiration. Over the last few hours I had played a terrifying game of cat and mouse and I needed this delay like a hole in the head.

I knew the team from the Office of Special Affairs had probably been deployed to secure my return by now. A senior Sea Org member like me was simply not allowed to leave the Church of Scientology.

Three weeks in hiding in Birmingham had left me mentally exhausted, painfully thin and at breaking point. Just hours before, for the first time since my disappearance, I had popped my head above water in my hunting ground, in a very risky attempt to throw them off my scent. I had no idea whether it had worked and now I feared they were on my trail to Dublin.

Home was my only haven now and I longed for its comforting smells. My brother Maurice had booked and pre-paid for my flights after convincing me to come back to Ireland.

I checked the monitor again. Even in this most public place I was at risk. I knew exactly what fate awaited me if the Office of Special Affairs caught up with me. I'd be taken back to the HQ of the Church of Scientology in Britain and subjected to the Rehabilitation Project Force (RPF). It is a programme designed to completely re-indoctrinate a member of the elite Sea Org group of scientologists and is the most feared of all penalties. I didn't think I would survive the brutal regime which is similar in many ways to Stalin's Gulags. RPF consists of a rigorous schedule of heavy and often brutal physical work and a long drawn out indoctrination in the writings and lectures of our founder, L Ron Hubbard.

It takes an average of five years to complete. On it, I would be forced to spend all my time on a military-style base located in the isolated grounds of a stately mansion, known as Saint Hill, in the West Sussex countryside which serves as the headquarters of the Church of Scientology in the UK.

I would have to do heavy duty physical work from 7am to 3pm every day followed by studies from 3pm to 8pm and work again from 8.30pm to 11pm. I would be placed on one third of the salary of a regular Sea Org staff member which would mean earning about five pounds a week. There would be no liberties. All telephone calls are monitored and there are no holidays or visits to families. The work is harsh. Jobs are the filthiest and heaviest imaginable. An RPFer has to live and work exclusively within the programme and is totally isolated from anyone outside it. Those who are married cannot see their wives or children and have only the most curtailed communication with non-RPF staff. Conversation with a person outside the RPF programme is only permitted in a dire emergency.

I knew people who had been on this regime for over 15 years, or even longer. Most of them had become psychotic and suicidal.

The RPF member is controlled by the threat of further loss of already minimal privileges and by being sent to the RPF's RPF. This is an even harsher regime. Those who fail are excommunicated or in the case of Alice, one girl I knew quite well, suicidal

Alice was brought up in the cult from childhood and spent three years in the Sea Org. She was a very intelligent woman and she was highly conversant in Hubbard's counselling techniques. She was working as a Public Relations Officer for a front line operation and engaged to be married to a fellow Scientologist.

Her crime was sleeping with her fiancé, an act that is forbidden in the sexually repressive world of Scientology.

Alice was assigned to the RPF and her fiancé was sent to an RPF abroad so they would not distract each other. Alice decided to leave but the Church suggested that she 'route out' a process of extensive and intrusive vetting, confessions and signing of a number of non disclosure bonds. She was put on the RPF's RPF.

Six months into it and subjected to a course of intensive daily interrogations, she could see little hope for the future

One afternoon I arrived at Saint Hill and saw an ambulance and a lot of activity around the gym area.

I soon found out that Alice had walked out of the

RPF course room, gone to the workshop, found a tin of paint thinner, swallowed it and made her way on to the gym roof where she jumped.

Alice lived but is crippled for life. Her lower intestine is ruined and she carries a colostomy bag. She was a very attractive and energetic 19-year-old when she decided to take her life.

To the best of my knowledge she is still cared for by her mother, a top level Italian Scientologist who has never complained about her daughter's treatment by the Sea Org.

Thinking about Alice brought the reality of my own situation home to me. I really needed to get to Cork but there was no sign of our plane arriving. I knew my disappearance had the Church's security arm in overdrive. I had gone missing three weeks previously and had been hiding out in Birmingham in a truck stop motel in Tisley, an industrial wasteland outside the city, while I frantically tried to work out what to do next.

My foster parent's home back in Cork was already under siege. My Aunt Cath had been deeply troubled when two men, with a British registered car, had parked up across from their house a few days earlier.

Every so often one of the men had pointed a device, which was most likely a mobile phone tracking receiver, towards her house. Maurice had warned me not to call the house.

At one point, they had approached her and asked her did she know where I was. They'd even asked if I'd gone back to the Aran Islands where they knew I had once gone for a brief holiday.

Before I disappeared I had wiped my computer, in an attempt to mask my trail, I had erased what I could of the traces that could lead them to the people who were helping me. I had bought myself some time by telling the Church I had to return to Ireland for a week to see a dying relative. I had survived hiding in Birmingham for three weeks, on a diet of cigarettes, coffee and crackers. But the game was up as soon as I failed to return to the office on Ethel Street, colloquially known as Birmingham Organisation.

A skilled examination of that hard drive would reveal my agonised path through the lies, half-truths and factual distortions that made up the Scientology myth I had swallowed, hook, line and sinker, 22 years before.

That first Monday morning my mobile phone had started ringing as soon as the staff arrived at the office and realised that I had failed to show up. Then the texts had come and within hours the Church of Scientology had issued a full blown code red.

In Tisley I had disguised myself as best I could, cut off my hair, grown a beard and cast aside my neat two-piece suits in favour of nondescript black jeans, a jumper and a baseball cap.

I'd spent my days hounding government offices trying to get myself a social security number so I could register for housing and claim some sort of benefit to keep me going.

For the previous 22 years nobody knew I existed, as I had never been registered anywhere but in the ranks of the Church of Scientology.

In the evenings I'd sat in my shabby Stg£30 a night room, smoking and trying to make some sense of it all. Fragmented memories tormented me.

I had not suffered from asthma since I was a child but it was back now in full force and the tightness in my chest scared me.

Dermot Fortune had provided the money I needed to get out. His brother Odhran had made national news in Ireland back in the 1990s. Odhran was a fellow Sea Org member, based in Copenhagen and when he went home to visit his family, during Christmas 1997, they were horrified by his emaciated appearance.

The family had got in touch with an exit counsellor and Odhran agreed to stay at home and leave behind his life in Scientology. But just when they thought he was doing so well, he disappeared one night from the family pub with two men wearing suits and they hadn't seen him since. He later issued a statement, supposedly of his own volition, saying he didn't want anything to do with his family.

Mike Garde, a cult expert based in Dublin, had put me in touch with Dermot as I planned my escape.

After three weeks on the run, the money he'd wired had run out and all the Birmingham authorities had offered me was accommodation in a homeless shelter. I'd started to feel like my attempts to exist outside Scientology were futile and I was getting desperate. Then Maurice had convinced me to come home and so here I was in Dublin Airport, with all my worldly possessions stuffed into a holdall bag.

That morning I had woken early, packed up, settled my bill and headed for the shopping centre in Central Birmingham where Roger, a senior Sea Org member and former colleague, religiously went for his lunch. I'd wanted to make sure the Office of Special Affairs guys weren't waiting for me when I arrived in Cork.

I was relieved when Roger had walked in the doors at his usual time and headed for the escalator. I'd then very purposely, stepped onto the opposite escalator making sure he couldn't miss me.

Roger had spotted me immediately and started calling out for me to wait for him. By the time he had barged his way to the top and started the back down, I'd been ducking and diving through the crowds and out the front door of the centre.

I'd run to Moore Street Station across the road, knowing he was following me. Out of breath, I'd ducked into the public toilets and tore off my suit and pulled on the black jeans and jumper. Then I'd headed for Platform 4 and the train to Tisley.

My chest had tightened again and I'd prayed that Roger had lost sight of me and turned back to inform the Office of Special Affairs that I was in Birmingham.

If I had succeeded they would have pulled out of Cork by the time I arrived.

If I had failed, the full force of Scientology was now hot on my trail and I would be lucky to make it out of Dublin Airport.

By the time I'd arrived in Dublin I was utterly exhausted. In the Departures lounge I'd checked my watch then scanned the monitor to make sure my Aer Arann flight to Cork was leaving on time.

I could feel my heart sink again as the word Delayed came up on the screen once more.

Beside it, the arrivals monitor showed that the next flight in from Birmingham was landing in 20 minutes...

ONE

THE ROAD TO
THE TRUTH

Stuttgart, Germany: June 1985

I stared at my results. They were all along the bottom of the sheet in the zone that stated, 'URGENT ATTENTION REQUIRED'.

Danny, the tester who had drawn up my graph, couldn't speak English. I suppose it is fortunate that I hardly understood a word he said. From what I could gather, he was telling me that I was a complete failure but that 'Dianetics' could help me with that.

I wasn't surprised. I knew my life was a bit of a mess and I was deeply unhappy in myself. I had been in town shopping, but my mind was miles away when I was approached by a blonde-haired German girl and asked: "Haben Sie ein gutes Gedächtnis?"

I'd asked her to repeat the question in English as I simply hadn't had the energy to translate her heavy

Schwäbisch dialect.

"Do you have a good memory?" she'd repeated.

The obscure question may as well have been left in German for all the sense I had made out of it. While I was still searching for an answer, she'd taken me by the arm and guided me across the street.

"My name is Sabina," she'd told me. "I'm promoting a thing called Dianetics. Would you be interested in a Free Personality test?"

With that, she had led me up the stairs and straight into what I later found out was the Church of Scientology Stuttgart Mission office. It was contemporary, clean-looking and was positioned over two floors above a shop. Posters on the walls and books that lined the shelves made no mention of Scientology.

Sabina had directed me towards a table and chair and introduced me to a small Indian girl called Priha, who, she said, would conduct the test on me – a test I was told that would usually cost me a few hundred quid and which would measure my IQ and various personality characteristics such as communication skills and happiness.

When I was settled in, Sabina had wished me luck and gone back to her position on the street outside.

Priha had handed me The Free Personality Test that was made up of 210 questions set out over a folded A3 sheet. For each question I was to tick a 'Yes', 'No' or 'Maybe' answer and would be scored accordingly.

"When you've completed the test, an evaluator called Danny will calculate your answers, draw up a graph and discuss it with you," Priha had explained.

The questions were fairly innocuous and had ranged from anything from whether or not I liked to browse though railway timetables to if I liked spreading gossip about work colleagues.

As I'd sat there that day and ticked off each question, other staff members had busied themselves around me. They were extremely friendly and each had a large smile for me if they caught my eye. I'd felt very welcome there and relaxed in the warm environment. The test instructions had emphasised that I must answer each question with regard to how I was feeling at that moment in time. I didn't know it then but the test is designed to pick out people like me. That day in the Mission office I was feeling down, isolated from my family and very open to offers of any sort of help.

After a half an hour, I'd handed back my tests and sat browsing through some brochures about Dianetics while Danny had drawn up my graph.

I wasn't shocked by the results. I had been concerned about my mental health for quite a few months. I was depressed again and this time it was particularly bad. As I turned the pages of the brochures I'd wondered if it was sheer luck or even fate that a group of mental health experts had found me that day and were willing to help me. I was thankful to be there and really hoped that this was where I was going to find the help that I so desperately needed.

After Danny had finished trying to explain my results, he led me out to a couch and handed me a big paperback book with a volcano on the front of it. The book, written in English, was called 'Dianetics: the Modern Science of Mental Health' and the author was L Ron Hubbard. I was offered a cup of coffee and left alone as I started to read through the pages of the book. It instantly engrossed me.

The book is, in fact, the classic introduction to Scientology. It was first launched in 1950 by the science fiction writer and hypnotist Lafayette Ron Hubbard (LRH) who developed it by merging hypnotic techniques with research abandoned by Freud years previously. In it, Hubbard describes a collection of pictures in our minds which are the recorded experience of traumatic events from current and past lives as well as pre-natal experiences. According to the book my mind had recorded everything that had happened while I was in the womb. It explained that if my father had sex with my mother while I was in there, then I would have been hurt and possibly even rendered unconscious. I would have contracted a whole series of 'engrams' associated with this painful incident. Hubbard stated that the time in the womb was not the calm, safe and nurturing experience that we had been led to believe was the case – it was actually a time of fear, pain, frustration and danger. During moments of stress or pain, the mind often shuts down because it can't cope and instead records a kind of movie of them which he called engrams.

These memories, he said, are the cause of all psychological and physical problems we have. Erasing the engrams, through a system of therapy called auditing, would free an individual from all compulsions, obsessions, neuroses and depressions. It would even liberate them from physical conditions, including everything from stuttering to heart trouble and even leukaemia.

I was sitting at a little table by the window. I could see that shops were beginning to close up for the day but I kept reading. Auditing, or counselling in layman's terms, would re-file these memories in the mind through a one-on-one therapy session. An auditor would observe and record responses and repeatedly return to an experience of pain until it is identified, confronted and processed. He promised that with his system of psychotherapy, this old mind could be erased and that in this way, human kind could attain perfection. He described how a patient would eventually reach this 'State of Clear', a place devoid of these engrams and thus all compulsions, pains and psychoses. Auditing seemed to offer a straight-forward path back to full sanity, 20-20 vision, perfect hearing, a deep masculine voice and an ever increasing IQ.

Not having read or studied psychology I had nothing against which to gauge the claims he was making. It all sounded really good to me and for the first time in my life, as I browsed through the book, I was being given a black and white explanation and cure for the insecurities and depressions that had shadowed me since childhood. The brash and simple language which Hubbard used to express his beliefs seemed to break through that wooliness I had been feeling in my head for quite some time.

After my first few hours at the Stuttgart Mission Office, I reckoned that Hubbard's Dianetics was definitely for me. I approached the counter, paid for the book and arranged to come back the following day for my first consultation. I was quite excited as I headed down to the Hauptbanhof to catch the train back to my flat in Leonberg.

That night I stayed up well into the early hours, smoking hash and reading 'Dianetics: the Modern Science of Mental Health' and all about Hubbard's wonderful idea of 'Clear'. To me the subliminal message was that all that horrible pain of my childhood would finally be gone, all the depression I would so often suffer from would be gone and the sense of restlessness that had dogged my life would slide away, through what appeared to be a simple and sensible technique. For some reason the Dianetics stuff turned on a light in my head. It appeared scientific rather than mystic or religious. It made my confusing mind seem uncomplicated. Hubbard gives a simple explanation to mental problems and a simple solution. There is no room for critical thinking or analysis and everything he says is a statement of fact.

As I read on, I became more engrossed and convinced by this basic psychology. In the book Hubbard likens the mind to a computer and makes it become a very graspable and a very fixable commodity. In a nutshell 'Dianetics: the Modern Science of Mental Health' was offering me an insight into this mysterious thing that was causing me pain and offering me a whole bunch of counselling to fix it.

By the following morning I had bought the sales pitch. I was hungry for Hubbard's wonderful painkiller that was going to make me better.

I was bang on time for my appointment with the Mission Executive, Daniella, that morning. She needed to do little to convince me that I badly needed Dianetics auditing.

I soon found myself sitting in a tiny little auditing room with Peter. He told me he was going to get me to close my eyes and look back into my mind. I was not going to remember incidents from my past, rather, I was going to re-experience these things. I was directed to find a moment of pain and describe it to him. He told me his cue for ending the session was to snap his fingers, at which point I was to open my eyes again.

We got started after that. I had to close my eyes and concentrate hard on his voice and nothing else. It took a considerable time for me to go under.

During the session he asked me over and over again to remember a time or a moment that I had injured myself. I did try but I couldn't come up with anything. Once Peter clicked his fingers, I came out of the trance.

I found the auditing frustrating, I was not really sure about what he wanted. I do recall getting very heavy-headed during my first session which would be a feeling that later repeated itself many times during auditing. It was like being really dopey, almost painfully dopey. Physically, I was very lethargic but mentally, I felt as though I had been drugged. I was glad to be finished.

Not sure I wanted any more of this auditing, I was about to go home, but Daniella quickly appeared at my side.

"John, wait. Don't worry about that session. It'll get better," she reassured me.

With her encouragement, I put the unpleasantness of the experience down to being a beginner. Everyone else seemed to have a knowing smile and a look in their eye that told me I would soon find the 'Bridge to Total Freedom'. I asked them what that meant and Daniella pointed to the last chapter in the *Dianetics* book. I skimmed through it there and then. Hubbard described how Dianetics is like 'A Bridge' that would help me move away from the bad place I was in, so that I could reach a better place – a place called 'Clear'. I found the idea of a simple and well laid out path over the chasm of my own internal pain and depression very exciting.

Over the following few days I went back for more of these auditing sessions and each time sank into a deeper state of hypnosis.

Frustratingly, I couldn't find these incidents that Peter was looking for and it started to annoy me. I eventually told him that this wasn't going anywhere so he took me to Daniella. She smiled and said that I was probably not doing well in auditing because I had been taking drugs – something I had told them in the first interview. She suggested that I should do the Communications Course instead. According to the results of my Free Personality Test, I was not communicating very well.

Antonio was running my Communications Course and got me started the very day I signed up for it. Antonio told me that the course should take one week if I came in every evening for two or three hours.

The course room was small and sparsely furnished. It was located on the third floor of the Stuttgart building. I was rapidly introduced to my 'twin' who was an American military guy. He had joined a couple of days after me. He was a big guy from Maryland who introduced himself as Rick and told me he worked in the big US military base, Robinson Barracks, as a naval intelligence liaison officer. Antonio was a very witty Italian and he had us relaxed fairly quickly with his funny comments. He gave us little orange booklets and showed us the purpose of the course. We read the first page and learned that: "It's your ability to communicate, not just talk, but really communicate that determines success in life."

The booklet informed us that there were a set of definite aspects to truly skilled communication. The course would teach us how to make ourselves understood, initiate and steer conversations, keep a discussion on a point, how to avoid going 'dead' and to end a dialogue smoothly. We were also to learn how to resolve upsets.

Antonio had us sit and face one another with our eyes closed. We were not to move or react in any way. I found this difficult and had to struggle to suppress my natural desire to be aware of what was going on around me. It is not easy to sit in a room with a stranger and keep your eyes closed.

We eventually got that bit and Antonio ticked off our papers. We then had to sit facing each other with our eyes open. The idea was to sit perfectly still and not even blink your eyes, while staring at this other guy without as much as flinching. You are supposed to just remain in the present and not think of anything else but being right there in that moment of time.

We kept cracking up, and as the day progressed both of us started to act a bit like we were slightly drunk, giggling at little things. When we did this, Antonio would jump in and say 'Flunk' and we would have to start again. We were told our aim was to rid our minds of all thoughts and impulses to move or react in any way. It took a few days for both of us to get it right. I remember eventually sitting there and blocking out everything else and going into a form of trance. My eyes were wide open and I could see and hear everything that was going on around me, but I could not move my body. It was as if it did not exist and I was just my conscience staring out through my eyes. Antonio seemed pleased and said: "That's it. Pass."

Rick jumped up but I could not move my body. I sat there in the same position staring out in front at the space where my co-student had been. I could not contact my body; I could not even think any thoughts.

Antonio looked nervous and he came up close to

me. He snapped his fingers and said again: "That's it."

I remained in the exact same position, unmoving and unblinking. Then I watched as he raised his hand and slapped my face.

I suddenly came back.

"You ok John?" he asked concerned.

"I am fine; I will go for a coffee," I said and left the building.

I sat down across the street at a coffee shop and slowly began to get a grip on myself. As I sipped my coffee, all I could think was: 'Wow that was weird.' It felt quite trippy and made me want to experience more. Just a few weeks previously, I would have gone straight to my girlfriend Jutta to tell her all about it. But since the first day that I'd walked into the Stuttgart office our relationship had all but finished. I hadn't even seen her. We had been growing apart for some time as my depression deepened and then my infatuation with this new self-help group had absorbed all my time and interest.

My American twin didn't show up the next day, nor did he show up the day after that. Antonio had me call him at work in Robinson's Barracks.

When he answered he was angry. "I work in Intelligence. I'm in big trouble with my superiors for being involved in Scientology and for allowing you to call me. Do not talk to me again," he warned me before he slammed the phone down.

I was a bit shook up but Antonio told me that he was under the influence of the 'psyches'. I didn't know what Antonio was talking about but I was reassured by his calm handling of the situation. As for the 'psyches', it would take me another while to learn that it was a reference to Scientology's arch enemies, the psychiatric profession.

Antonio took Rick's place, as there were still no other students to match me up with. The course moved up a level and for an entire day I had to ask over and over again 'Do Fish Swim?' I had to get the affirmative answer "yes they do" or "of course they do" and not accept anything else.

Antonio would try to lead me off track by saying silly things like "No, they fly" or make other non-related comments. My job was to repeatedly get the right answer, without any reactions, like laughing or getting angry, until I passed.

I did pass, eventually. The use of this repeater technique is just one of the methods used to induce an altered or trance-like state in the study of Scientology. There is no doubt that key words and directions are implanted into the mind during these sessions to make an individual more susceptible to direction.

After finishing that section of the course, I was given little drills to complete. I had to go out onto the street and talk to people to test my new communication skills. My brief was to bring the conversation to a pleasant conclusion and to achieve a sense of 'win'.

I went out to the Square near the train station and spotted a pretty girl sitting on her own. She was my first target. I started a conversation by saying a few innocuous things to her. One of my missions on that drill was to make sure that she smiled at me and that I got my point across very quickly. I got her to laugh and then ended the conversation. I was very pleased with myself. Then I went to a market stall and engaged a woman in conversation about her fruit and vegetables. I made sure we had a pleasant conversation and I held her attention while other customers were waiting to be served. Again I felt that I had got a 'win' doing this little drill. I felt quite elated going back to the centre on Hirsch Strasse.

When I got back I simply signed off that section of the check sheet and Antonio counter-signed it. I was then routed to an area of the building known as 'Exams', to verify that I had successfully completed all aspects of the course. This is where I had my first introduction to the E-Meter. The electro psycho-meter, or E-Meter for short, is used extensively in Scientology auditing. However it is rarely introduced to those recruited through Dianetics until they move on to the Scientology courses. Hubbard claimed to have been the real force behind the development of the E-Meter for use in the therapeutic context.

The examiner hooked me up to the E-Meter and stared at the dial for a few moments.

"Would you like someone else to achieve the knowledge you now have?" he asked me.

I had enjoyed going out and talking to people, and felt that the course had helped me to do that so I replied: "Yes, I would."

I was happy to attest to the completion of this first important step in what would turn out to be my Scientology career.

I had no particular reaction to the E-Meter, although I did feel an electric tingling sensation in my hands. As far as I was concerned, this was all a classic example of what a brilliant man Hubbard was. After all, he had invented a machine that could read thoughts.

On my way out of the examination room I was congratulated by other staff members and very purposely guided back to reception where the Registrar immediately offered me another course. I was low on money but the Registrar was very insistent that I at least buy something. I felt pressured, but also felt that I owed them something more than just the cost of the course I had completed, so I bought a book.

Anke, who headed up the Communications Office, called me in to talk to her before I left the building with my book under my arm.

"Congratulations on your course, John," she said, "but to see results you really have to stick with it."

"It's just that I don't have much money to continue my studies," I told her.

"Then you should join the staff, as that way you get your courses for free."

I liked the atmosphere in the office and was flattered by her offer of a job. I had little to lose as I could keep up my factory job on shift work.

"Ok then, I'll do it," I replied.

"Great, we'll have a contract drawn up for you by the end of the week," Anke replied.

There and then, I signed up to the Dianetics Auditor Course and happily went back to my flat.

On my way home on the train through the Schwabish countryside, I felt a sense of belonging that I had not experienced in a long time. In fact I hadn't felt it since that dreadful afternoon in September 1974 when my childhood was shattered.

I hoped against hope that I had finally found the one thing that just might help me heal my broken past.

Two

Troubled Times

My mother was pregnant with me when my father told her that he had put poison in her cup of tea. She made herself vomit so it wouldn't get into her bloodstream but she was very scared. Shortly after that he disappeared. My mother was left alone with Kate and Jeremy to support and with no means of feeding them or paying the rent. Scotland was a fairly unforgiving place for a pregnant single mum in the early 1960s. She had little option but to get out and do what she could to feed her children. Desperate times meant desperate measures. To feed Kate and Jeremy my mother used to go out to the fields late at night and scavenge for the potatoes that the pickers had left behind.

I was born on October 29, 1963 and my earliest memories are of being alone in my cot and crying. I had nightmares as a very young child, two of which remain etched in my mind. In the first my Gollywog rag doll had grown to adult size and was on its hands and knees staring at me through the bars of the cot. I screamed and cried but no one came. I spent most of my childhood terrified of black people. In the other nightmare my mother's shoes were walking down the stairs towards me.

Our desperate state of affairs only came to light when Granny Cotter arrived from Ireland to help with me – the new baby. She was taken aside by the old lady next door who described how she could hear 'that poor girl' crying deep into the night.

My mother had never known poverty before she met my father. He suffered from bi-polar disorder. Between fits he was a witty, eloquent, charming and engaging man and a wonderful father. During his bad periods he displayed no emotion except rage against my mother. He attempted to kill her several times, although he was never physically violent towards her.

My parents met at a Legion of Mary gathering in 1955, when she was a 21-year-old trainee midwife and he was just 17. He was AWOL from the army after he'd tried to commit suicide in the parachute regiment. They fell in love straight away. At the time, he didn't really know what he wanted to do but was toying with the idea of studying at third level and going into teaching. Ever the impetuous dreamer, my father wanted to get married then and there but she made him hold off for a couple of years while they got on their feet. He got a job as an auxiliary teacher in one of the rougher schools in Glasgow while they saved for university fees. They married in late summer 1960. He was 22 and she was 26. It wasn't long until my mother found out that she was pregnant with Kate.

They didn't have a bad start. My father was earning a few pounds to pay the rent on a two-storey stone house they were living in near the Bridge of Allan, just north of Stirling in Scotland. Dad managed to get through first year and second year in college before his illness began to rear its head again.

By the time my mother had Jeremy things must have been very bad. My father was highly unbalanced and would often slip, without warning, into cold rages and threaten to kill my mother. Afterwards he would be apologetic and get very depressed. She never mentioned anything to Granny Cotter, probably not wanting to admit that her mother's initial foreboding about the marriage was right. As a devout Catholic she also believed that such travails were sanctioned by God to test her faith.

I found out later that when my mother became pregnant with me, my father sank into a deeper depression. He said that he felt terrible about the pregnancy and overwhelmed at the financial challenges that a third child would pose. He felt as if his world had fallen in on him and totally lost control, trying to do away with both of us. After the incident he got a job in a forestry project while she went to Ireland for a month or so to take stock of the increasingly life threatening situation that her marriage had become. When she got back, he had disappeared.

I was born into all that confusion and upset.

News of my father came in sometime later. He was living in Oxford with a young nurse called Judith. He had suffered a total mental breakdown and seemed to think that he was living in the early days of his marriage before any children came along. On some advice from The Legion of Mary organisation in Oxford, he had been committed to a psychiatric hospital. He was in and out of hospital for the next two years, remaining an outpatient for a further three.

In the meantime we moved out of our rental home. We qualified as severely disadvantaged and were granted Council housing in Bannockburn, a town just south of Stirling. We were allocated a small terraced house on Duke Street. My father would come there on his day and weekend releases from hospital. He was a total stranger to me when he first visited but I grew to like him. I have few memories of him then but I do recall one day walking with him to the shop and holding his hand. He was wearing a trench coat and seemed very big to me. He was eventually deemed healthy enough to return to normal life and moved home full-time. He got a job working with Stirling County Council as an administrator. I remember the year he came home because we got Christmas presents.

Maurice was born in July 1966 and I think that the new addition to our household meant that we needed a bigger home. I remember the day we moved to Randolf Crescent, a post-war Council housing estate of two-storey semi-detached houses. It backed onto a rubbish-strewn glen, not far from Duke Street. I was about 3 and a half at the time and enjoyed all the hustle and bustle of packing and finding toys behind cupboards. One of my earliest memories was when my father took the three of us over to the new house the day before we moved in. We slept on the floor, in sleeping bags with candles for light.

Relatives described later how after Maurice came along, my father's moods went from being coldly unemotional, to raging uncontrollably and then to being warm and loving. One day my parents had a row over my tendency to spend hours in my room curled tight and rocking to and fro.

My father loved the countryside and hated the idea that his kids were being brought up in such a built-up area. He wanted us to have the freedom of wide open spaces and longed to move out of Randolf Crescent. I have a memory from when I think I was around five years old, of my father taking myself, Kate and Jeremy on a long hike across a wild Scottish bog. I can still smell the peat. I hitched a lift on my father's back as we walked. He always made a huge effort and really wanted us to enjoy those outings with him.

I remember one summer he took me, Kate and Jeremy youth hostelling to the Isle of Arran and it was magical. Declan and Maurice were toddlers at the time and my mother was pregnant with her sixth and last child, Ann Christine, so opted to stay home. We boarded the train in Stirling and took the ferry over to the island. I remember being in awe of the smartly uniformed Captain and Officers.

We hired bikes soon after we arrived and cycled from Brodick to Whiting Bay. I was the smallest and while I tried really hard to keep up with the others, they wouldn't slow down for me. I was hot and fed up, so I drove my bike into the drainage ditch that ran alongside the road. I knew they'd have to stop then. I remember my father coming back along the road and laughing his head off when he saw me covered in brambles and the back wheel of the bike sticking out of the ditch.

Another time he took us to a lovely house he had come across in some woodlands and told us it was going to be our new home. We were so excited but when we got back to Randolf Crescent my mother vetoed the plan. Looking back I can see why. My father was a dreamer. At the time he was barely making ends meet and she was working nights at an old people's home while raising her six children during the day. There followed long nights of loud arguments and accusations between the two of them and I was often quite frightened.

Our own disappointment on losing out on the house in the forest soon faded into the background when he came up with an even more exciting plan. It was around 1971 and he had applied for a posting on the remote islands of Tristan da Cunha in the South Atlantic Ocean. The islands had been annexed by the UK at some point during the early 1800s and had a colourful history. A small local Council, staffed by UK civil servants, ran all of its administration. Now a post had come up and my father seemed certain he would get the job. I remember him coming home with brochures and showing us pictures of island life from a book he'd borrowed from the library. It looked like a huge adventure. The little ones were too young to grasp what it was all about but us older ones were very excited. We couldn't stop day-dreaming about running around sandy beaches and finding shipwrecks.

Again, my mother vetoed the plan. Her health had been breaking down with the stress of raising six children with a mentally ill husband. At the age of only 39, she actually looked a withered and malnourished 60. The iron supplements she had been prescribed had little effect. Asthma, a condition she suffered from as a child, had returned with a vengeance and it got so bad that some days she could barely move. Uprooting to a volcanic island just wasn't on.

Once more, the arguments had raged back and forth. When they blew up, Kate used to scuttle out of the house. Jeremy would go into his own little world. I was terrified by the fighting. I regularly collapsed and vomited on the floor. Often this stopped the arguments as both my mother and father would turn their attentions to me and forget their row for the time being. My school work was abysmal. Eventually the fighting stopped and my father had never mentioned Tristan da Cunha again.

Somewhere in the midst of all this hardship, another woman came along. I recall that my father seemed to be relapsing again and my mother was having difficulty coping. He would disappear for days at a time and it was pretty clear that he was having an affair. I remember one day my mother sat me down.

"If your father was to go off and marry another woman, would you stay with me or go with him?"

I knew I was going to upset her.

"I'd go with Dad because he takes us out walking in the hills," I replied.

She looked like she was about to cry and then walked away.

After another period of very heavy drinking and depression, dotted with absences from home, he eventually got some help. From what I recall the Council had been fairly sympathetic towards him and he had largely managed to show up for work, even on his darkest days. He had certainly never lost his job and off the drink he started to concentrate on local politics. He worked closely with his friend and Labour candidate Dennis Canavan and threw himself into backing him.

I have a memory of him sitting at the kitchen table, with his glasses on top of his nose and a pen and paper in front of him, writing out speeches. Dennis seemed confident of gaining the Stirlingshire seat. I'm not sure if it was just another of my father's fantasies, but he was talking to us of our imminent move to a house near Westminster. We were very excited about moving to London and were delighted with the prospect of leaving Bannockburn behind.

Over the next few months, thanks in part to developments in psychiatric drugs, my father had seemed to recover some kind of stability. My mother was told that he was in remission and that if he stayed stable over the following seven years he could be considered to have overcome his illness. Mum seemed more upbeat than she had been in a very long time. He was able to focus himself and things started looking up for him. This had a rippling effect through the whole family and we were happier than we had been in years.

In 1972, he got a promotion to a short-term posting. It was better paid than anything he had done before. It involved the down-sizing of Social Services and brought with it a brand new sky blue Vauxhall Viva. I still remember the number plate – AMS 801K. It was the best car by far on the estate and we were very proud. For him it brought both freedom and a badly needed boost to his self-esteem. The car had opened up a whole new world to us. He would bundle myself, Kate and Jeremy in and take off for the mountains. We'd hike across bogs and examine all the birds and wildlife.

With my father in good form, and a little bit more money from his new job, we'd experienced a period of relative normality. At the tail end of the summer, we'd even gone on a holiday up to a little cottage by the sea near the Mull of Kintyre. Granny Cotter came over for a few days and we just loved it. Everyone seemed to be smiling – even my mother.

I've one very clear memory from that week. One evening Kate, Jeremy and I were walking along the strand telling one another ghost stories. Suddenly we got scared and bolted for home. We climbed over an old wooden stile at the back of the cottage and tumbled in the door. Our father was sitting at the table and my mother was grilling up a huge pile of cheese on toast. He took one look at our white faces, smiled and went out into the yard and howled like a banshee. We hid under the table and I remember him coming back in, laughing. Then he pulled me up and tickled me.

Three weeks later he would be dead.

Coming back from the holiday a huge pile of post had awaited us, with one letter looking the most urgent. My father had picked it up and started to read. His mood changed immediately. His employment had been terminated. I remember him saying very sarcastically over and over again, in his broad Scottish accent: "That is great. That is just great. That is just what I needed."

My heart sank and I could sense the same thing was happening with my brothers and sisters.

During that late August and early September 1973, his mood turned very black. He was either silently raging or argumentative and bitter.

He went off to work three weeks later and never came back.

They found him, up at the Karen Valley Reservoir, a lovely silent stretch of water bordered by forested hills in North Lanarkshire. He was collapsed in front of the car.

The police report indicated that he had committed suicide by breathing in fumes directly from the car exhaust. At some point, it seemed, he'd had second thoughts and tried to crawl away from the car. But there was so much carbon monoxide in his lungs that he had no hope.

My father was just 35 years old when he died.

I came home from school as normal, expecting to have a glass of milk sitting in front of the television, but instead the living room was full of women crying. I recognised some of them but others were strangers to me. I scanned the room but couldn't see my mother. My cat, Mr Spock, was sitting on the huge old sideboard. I felt a sick feeling at the pit of my stomach and I knew something was very wrong.

A close friend of my mother, Mrs Masterson, stood up and took me by the hand and told me: "John, we are going to have dinner in my house."

I walked with her out of our house and down to her bungalow at the end of the road.

"Your Daddy has had an accident and your Mummy is up at the hospital," she said.

I spent the afternoon with her watching television. Later that evening, when my mother got back from the hospital, we went back up to the house. My brothers and sisters were there too.

Mum was crying. "Your Daddy is dead," she told us.

"Did you see him? What does he look like?" I blurted out.

"He looked very peaceful John," she said.

The next thing I remember was the police dropping off some of his stuff – the tartan rug from the car, papers and a thermos flask.

I buried the real pain deep down inside of me. I didn't cry at the funeral but I did cry at home later, lying on my parents' bed. When Kate, in her own pain and grief, made fun of me, I stopped.

In the weeks after his funeral my mother seemed bowed and tired. She cried a lot. I think if the truth be told, she lost her will to live. Her asthma attacks became progressively worse and shortly afterwards she was taken to the hospital with a particularly severe bout. The doctor gave her some tests and they told her that her immune system had practically collapsed.

I started to avoid coming home and started to hang around with some of the rougher lads in the neighbourhood. We often spent hours throwing stones at dilapidated buildings and breaking windows. Kate became very withdrawn and morose. I saw very little of Jeremy so he must have been finding solace with friends too. We were all worried about our mother but we didn't know what to do.

Eventually, we'd been sent back to school. Home was very gloomy and by and large I'd still tried to stay away. I don't even remember that Christmas. My mother seemed to just struggle through each day. The locals pitched in but she wasn't coping at all with my father's death.

One night, six months after he died, I was upstairs reading a book when I heard Kate shouting. I just knew something was terribly wrong by the urgency in her voice. We ran down and piled into the kitchen. We all stopped still when we saw our mother. Maurice and Declan were standing just behind me, wide-eyed and in their pyjamas. Her head was lying on the table. Her skin looked paper thin and was tinged green. She wasn't breathing.

Kate shouted something at us and Jeremy and I ran outside and started banging on the next-door neighbour's door. Mr Cameron had been an ambulance driver and he immediately dialled the emergency services.

I was completely numb as I watched her body being stretchered into the back of the ambulance. Our family friend, Mrs Masterson, took us in again.

At some point that night she tearfully told us that our mother had died before the ambulance arrived.

It was March 13, 1974.

I was utterly stunned and couldn't take it in. I think I just shut down emotionally. It was too much.

The next day Granny Cotter had arrived, along with Uncle Tony and Auntie Julia. Uncle Tony did what he could to keep us cheered up. He hired a car and took us out. I remember we went to Wimpy's one night for dinner. It was my first time in a restaurant and I was thrilled with the huge burger and chips. Meanwhile Granny Cotter and Auntie Julia had organised the funeral.

I remember the day vividly. I was totally numb and never shed a tear. The big black funeral car had more of an impact on me than watching my mother's coffin being lowered into her grave.

By the end of that first fortnight it was decided that we were going to Ireland. The six of us were split up among my mother's brothers and sisters. This was far better than the other option which was an orphanage near Edinburgh. The youngest two, Declan and Ann Christine, went to Uncle Tony and Aunt Pearl in County Wicklow. Maurice went with Auntie Julia and her husband Tom who were living out near Dublin Airport. Kate went to live with Granny Cotter in Douglas in Cork and Aunt Cath and Uncle Frank agreed to take Jeremy and me.

I didn't really know Aunt Cath or Uncle Frank. She'd been to Scotland to visit once or twice over the years but that was all I had seen of her. When we arrived at their home in Kilmony we'd discovered a rambling old house, set in the countryside outside Carrigaline in Cork. Much of the land attached to it was taken up with a wooded river valley that fell steeply behind it and gave it spectacular views. Their oldest child, Coleman, was nine when we came to live with them and Celine was just a year or two younger. Claire was five and Dan was a toddler. Frankie and John Paul would come along a bit later.

Our arrival had caused a whirlwind of activity and introductions. Aunt Cath was only 35 and she'd been pretty much as shocked and stressed as we were by the new arrangements. Our broad Scottish accents seemed to highlight the fact that we were outsiders in this close-knit family unit that we had been parachuted into. Things were going to be difficult and even as a child I remember being painfully aware of that.

A few days after we arrived, I'd tried to run away. I walked out the drive and ran down the road toward the village. I wanted to run all the way back to how things were before. I wanted to run back to my parents. One of the neighbours passed up the road, saw me crying and put me into their car. They brought me back to Kilmony but by the time I got there I had stopped crying and said nothing at all. There was a lot of concern and worry in the house about me that evening. But with six mouths to feed and care for, there wasn't time for much else. I gradually pulled myself together again. I must have been so lost in my own world that I don't even remember how Jeremy settled in.

Within a few weeks of our arrival Uncle Frank had decided it was high time we started back at school. He was the Principal and head teacher of a two-roomed

National School in Ballingarry which was in the middle
of nowhere. It was the kind of old country school where
a cow would put its head through the window on a
summer's day. The heating system was an old stove
in the middle of the room. The school had a catchment
area of about 20 miles of remote farmland, a rural
community that had not been touched by modern life.
My schoolmates were farmers' children. Their accent
was broad rural Cork and I couldn't understand a word
they were saying. Likewise, my Scottish accent meant
I was utterly foreign to them.

I remember at lunchtimes sitting on the school wall
in the playground surrounded by a sea of freckly faces
with rosy cheeks.

"Where you 'froam?" one would pipe up.

"I'm fee Scoat-laand," I'd reply.

"Wats dat?" he'd ask and that marked the end of the
conversation because I had no idea what 'Dat' meant.

I spent most of my time with my step-brother
Coleman and Jeremy.

With his suddenly expanded brood, Frank had to
replace his Fiat with a huge old Ford Cortina estate car.
Cath and Frank were by no means wealthy and two
additional children did not help matters at all. When
the exhaust fell off the Ford, it didn't get repaired for
months. This acted as a great early warning system
for us children. It was particularly useful on Tuesday
nights when Frank conducted and Cath sang soprano at
the local Carrigaline choir practice. The village church
was about two miles from Kilmony but we always
knew when they were on their way home because we
could literally hear the car start up down at the church
car park.

After a short two months in school, summer arrived

and with it the holidays. We went back to Scotland for a week but I felt nothing there. When we came back the whole family went out to Inchadonney, a beautiful sandy peninsula in West Cork. Uncle Tony and Aunt Pearl, Auntie Julia and Granny came too. It was an incredibly hot summer and it was just fantastic playing in the dunes and enjoying the sunshine. I loved seeing Maurice, Kate, Declan and Ann Christine again too. I felt so far away from Scotland and all its nightmares. Then one of Auntie Julia's kids complained about us and she said something about 'those Duignans'.

In that instant my brief feeling of happiness and belonging drained away. I felt like an outsider. It really stung. I was an incredibly sensitive child and it seemed when my defences were down it wasn't very hard to unleash all that inner pain. I was overweight too and Jeremy and Coleman were very quick to remind me of it. All the other kids seemed to excel at something as well. Coleman was great with the horses and driving tractors. The other kids were incredibly musical and very fast learners but in my view I was fat and couldn't learn like they did. That sense of difference added to a growing inferiority complex that was to dog me for the rest of my life.

Cath and Frank were wonderful and they tried really hard to include us in everything and to make us feel like we belonged. But they were also realistic enough to know that they could not replace our parents. They focused on doing their best to create a safe and stable home for us, ensuring that we mucked in with our new foster brothers and sisters.

Frank had kept horses and I enjoyed being around them. I loved filling buckets of barley mash for Annie, the big, gentle Irish draught mare, when she was in foal. Sometimes I would take her on a hack, gripping the reins or her mane and riding bare back. I used to hang on for dear life.

Sturdy, the gorgeous old Collie, would run around with us, as myself, Jeremy and Coleman explored the wooded glen and the fields after school. He seemed to always keep one eye on us. He would also accompany me on my solitary expeditions which I did a lot and he was a true friend. I was terribly confused and unsettled by the huge changes that had happened almost overnight. Alone with Sturdy, I felt most at ease. When he started to slow down from old age about a year later I was really upset. I hated the thought of him leaving me. I sat in beside him in the old stable block and stroked his soft, golden coat as he died.

Uncle Frank included us in everything his own children did. Later during that first summer, he introduced us to sailing. He had a 24-foot Folk boat and would take us all down to Crosshaven and bring us out to the mouth of Cork harbour, then head up the coast to Baltimore, Glandore or Bantry. I loved sailing, especially the feeling of the wind in my face and the boat crushing through the waves.

The most obvious signs of my emotional trauma had subsided as I learned to cut logs, plant trees, muck out stables and, with Coleman and Jeremy, herd escaped cows back to our fields. Cath had somehow always managed to feed us. She would cook up huge big pots of food and bulk buy muesli. I remember being sent across the valley to Riordan's farm every day, with big gallon drums for milk.

The second summer was fantastic. Uncle Brian, Frank's brother, a psychologist who lived in Canada, came over on an extended holiday. He owned a lovely old schooner called *The Polaris*, built in Kiel, Germany, in 1916. She was moored at Kilmacsimon Quay and rented out as floating accommodation. The tenants were supposed to maintain the ship but when Brian took us to inspect her he found that she had been badly neglected. As well as the general disrepair, they had filled the fuel tanks with water, ruining the engine. I have never since met someone who could swear and curse with such fluency and eloquence as Doctor Brian Garvey and he spared nothing on the occupant of his beloved *Polaris*. I'd watched with some awe as the tenant cowered under Brian's invective, before slinking back down below deck to pack his bags. The boat was towed down the estuary and into the busy fishing and leisure port of Kinsale for an extensive refit.

Brian had aimed to sail *The Polaris* back to Nova Scotia and use her as part of a therapeutic system he was developing there. The idea was that some of his patients could get away from the stresses of life by taking hands-on cruises in the fine old ship. But there was a lot of work to get done in order to get *The Polaris* in good enough shape to make the transatlantic crossing and it wasn't hard to persuade Brian that he needed our help.

The project had kicked off almost immediately. At that time Jeremy was in secondary school and was off from the beginning of June. Coleman and I did not get out of our primary until July. I do not know how we made it through that month. We were green with jealousy as Uncle Brian and Jeremy headed off together each morning while we remained trapped in the classroom. I remember feeling fit to explode when I was eventually released to join them.

By the time we reported for duty, Uncle Brian had

recruited a fantastic crew of misfits and blackguards, all of them engineers and craftsmen. Shay, the chief engineer, was a wiry Derryman who drove a beaten up MG. He'd told us that he was a bomb-maker by profession and on the run from the British Army. I'd believed him. In reality he had just finished a Masters in electrical engineering.

At that time there was a bunch of abandoned tugs and tenders moored further up the river. They had been used during the salvage operation of the *Titanic's* sister ship, *The Lusitania.* It had been torpedoed off the Old Head of Kinsale during World War I. We often raided them for rope and winches. Clambering down into those ships' holds, cutting huge lengths of rope and scavenging the decks for useful material was the closest I ever got to feeling like a pirate smuggler. It was a magical summer and I'd dreaded the day when Brian had to go back to Canada.

Aunt Cath spent her time driving us here, there and everywhere. She never failed to send us on our way with stashes of sandwiches as we cycled off down to Crosshaven for dingy races or headed off camping in Oysterhaven. At the end of that heady summer of 1977 I'd been uniformed up for secondary school – Colaiste Mhuire in Crosshaven where Jeremy was already a student. Although I was a year younger than Jeremy we hung out together and shared friends.

We got on with life but the past held a tight grip on all of us. Declan and Ann Christine weren't able to adjust and they had great difficulties trying to settle in with Tony and Pearl in Wicklow. Ann Christine developed fairly severe epilepsy and was re-fostered with relatives in Blackrock, Cork two years after we left Scotland. Around the same time Declan moved down to

Kilmony with us. Maurice was having great difficulty too over at Auntie Julia's. He was taking his anger, grief and loss out on his foster parents and doing badly at school. Jeremy was battling his own demons and Kate had been sent to boarding school by my Granny Cotter. We often met up at weekends.

My own problems had begun to re-manifest themselves with a vengeance as I matured into my teens. I suffered bouts of depression and rage. This, along with the typical teenage problems, made it a time of pain and confusion for me. Looking back, I think I was clinically depressed, something I believe I may have suffered from since I was a young child. Life often seemed grey. I'd go to bed with a positive plan for the next day but when I woke up I would be overwhelmed by negativity.

My depression had taken a sinister turn during the late spring of 1978. I was in bed, just drifting off to sleep with David Bowie's 'Ashes to Ashes' playing on the radio, when I went into what I can only describe as a trip-like state. I felt myself disassociate from my body and move into a huge multi-coloured universe. I could actually feel my conscience leaving my body and slowly move further away from it while the music seemed to fade out. The colours that surrounded me were wonderful, yet I felt frightened. I had a sense that if I kept going I would not be able to come back. I pulled back and found myself lying, facing the wall, with the DJ talking over the fade out of the Bowie track.

Even looking back, the experience was unnerving. I'd ended up writing a long letter to my Uncle Brian. He had his own private practice and was a celebrated psychologist, so I'd reckoned if anyone could tell me what had happened to me he could.

Uncle Brian had written back immediately. He'd told me he was very worried about my experience and would talk to me when he came over. In the meantime, he'd advised me to take care and to try not to re-experience this event as it was potentially very dangerous.

I'll always be grateful that when Brian arrived in Ireland, along with wrapping up business with *The Polaris*, he spent a lot of time with me.

He had described what my mind had done: "John, what has happened to you is something I have seen before. It is the psychosis of disassociation, a condition that can lead to a state of catatonia. I had friends in medical school that started experiencing the same thing and they are still in mental hospitals 20 years later. To try to put it simply what is happening to you is the result of the trauma you had in your childhood when you lost both your parents."

I hadn't been that surprised when he linked it to my mother's and father's sudden deaths.

"Do you know if your Dad was a manic depressive?" he asked me.

"I think so," I replied and added that he suffered from schizophrenia too.

"Then it is all the more vital for you to overcome the desire to go back to that place, John," he told me gently. "Your mind is simply shutting down. It cannot cope. When that happened to you it was running away from the world into a little universe where nothing could get at you and where there would be no pain."

To manage the condition, he'd advised me not to read upsetting news, to try to keep myself located and anchored in the real world around me and under no circumstances to take any kind of drugs.

Within weeks, Brian had headed back to Canada but not before giving Cath and Frank advice on things to watch out for me and warning them not to let me get too stressed.

I'd left school after doing my Inter Cert. I wanted to be an artist. Cath had advised me to get a trade or some practical skills under my belt first. The following September I'd begun a trade experience course in St John's on Saw Mill Street, Cork. We started with an introduction to metal work, then carpentry and mechanical drawing. Then we were sent out on work experience. Mine was in mechanics and I got a placement down by the Marina but it didn't really grab me.

Trying farming had been next on the list. I'd landed a job at the nearby Noonan farm which was comprised of a big old mansion and acres of rich pasture at Crosshaven Estuary. It was a beautiful farm and I'd liked the work but it didn't blow me away. The lack of direction in my life meant that those same old feelings of dissatisfaction and depression began to manifest themselves again.

At that time I would babysit for family friends, Michael and Rapheala, at least twice a week. Michael was CEO of an animal feed business. He kept a hen house on the property and I would also earn a few quid every now and again helping him clean it up.

I remember one day we were talking about the quality of food when Michael asked me: "John, would it not be true that if a salmon left the river of its birth and swam the seas of the world before returning and getting caught, that it would taste far richer than a similar salmon that had never left the river but stayed in a dark pool all its life?"

I had to agree and the little parable got me thinking about spreading my own wings outside Cork.

Not long after that I was wandering around town when I'd bumped into Rapheala. "John did you know there is an American Christian Drama group, called the Covenant Players, performing in the Community Hall this Thursday evening? If you would like to go along I could get you a free ticket," she said.

"Who are they then?" I replied.

"They are a professional theatre company that send touring troupes around the world to communicate the essential Christian message through the medium of drama. Go along, sure you might find it interesting," she said.

I found the plays, which were all scripted by the group's founder, Chuck Tanner, challenging. There was no fancy lighting or backdrops, just simple props, basic costuming and strong emphasis on characterisation. Afterwards the MC, Pamela Dennison, had announced that they were offering two year commissions to people who felt they could endure travelling the world doing drama. Training, board and weekly pocket money would be provided. I'd suddenly known what I wanted to do – it was my moment to become a tastier salmon.

I hate to think of the impression I made on Pam that evening. I had shoulder length scraggly brown hair, I wasn't very well-dressed and I was never any good at expressing myself. But she accepted me, and after she talked with Aunt Cath it became official. I became a trainee member of The Covenant Player Repertory Theatre Company and left Cork without any regrets. I was looking forward to my future adventures on the road.

After a few months touring with my new troupe, we set up at the CP United Kingdom office. It was a lovely old Methodist Church in Ilford, Essex. Covenant Players had the use of the big housing wing and we set up an office and rooms to sleep in.

We headed for Nuremburg in Germany after that which I was really excited about. At that stage I had only been on the European continent once before, on a school trip to Paris. I was looking forward to spending a year travelling throughout Western Europe. Furt is essentially a huge area of American military bases, interspaced with fairly small housing developments. I remember I was thrilled by it all – the smells, the snow and all the military trucks, tanks and helicopters. We lived communally in a big old farmhouse, next to a barn on the very edge of Furt. I met Larry, a Texan who more or less ran all logistics for Covenant Players in Germany, and his fiancée Annie from California. I also met Greta Jo, a pretty blond from New England and we fell in love almost immediately.

Our neighbours were two migrant workers from Pakistan. Anjib was the older and better educated, a very decent man. His friend was a bit sleazy-looking and spoke poor English and little German. One night Anjib invited Greta Jo, Annie and me to dinner, to celebrate the end of the month of Ramadan. We were treated to delicious traditional fare, including a wonderful korma.

"That is the recipe from my home town," Anjib proudly told us.

I was really enjoying my night when his friend turned to Annie and said: "Come on. I need some help in the kitchen."

I felt nervous because I hadn't liked him from the

moment I laid eyes on him and I definitely didn't trust him.

"I don't think that is a good idea," I said but Anjib reassured me that everything was ok. Annie got up and took some dirty plates with her.

About five minutes later they hadn't come back and I got very worried. Anjib tried to placate me, but I wouldn't listen and began banging on the kitchen door. It was locked.

Shortly after, Annie came limping out, tear-stained and her clothes were in a mess. "We've got to go," she told us.

I knew something terrible had happened and I was so angry at myself for not trusting my instincts and breaking the door down. Greta Jo and I followed Annie out the door.

Later that evening we watched the police take Anjib and his friend away. The furore had brought us out onto the street and Larry came over to me.

"I'm disgusted at you John. I'm sickened that you let this happen. She was raped at knifepoint," he said and walked away.

I was devastated. I knew I could have done something about it but I hadn't followed my instincts. I was 18, the youngest there, but I had been the responsible male that night.

Some days later, Anjib had tried to apologise for his friend. "Please forgive me. My friend is a stupid, ignorant man," he said.

I couldn't even talk to him.

Annie went back to America after that. I think she returned to give evidence in his trial. The incident is something that has haunted me all my life and I have always used it as a stick to beat myself with whenever

I am feeling low. It made me feel like a complete failure and it was one of the things that I hoped Scientology would help me move on from.

I'd spent the next 18 months travelling the Continent, delivering drama workshops to school kids in Holland and Switzerland, doing Sunday performances in churches and living with people from a wide and varied mix of nationalities and philosophies. One German guy, Joachim, became one of my closest friends. He was from a village near Stuttgart and we just hit it off immediately. We had the same sense of humour and shared a lot of laughs. As my Granny Cotter had spent time teaching me German, I picked up the language very quickly and Joachim helped me out whenever I got stuck.

I did a tour with the US military as well. CP had a contract with them and I spent three months working with army groups all over Germany. It was like being in another country. We'd stayed in military housing, shopped in military shopping complexes known as Post Exchanges, and worked from military offices, while performing in American Schools and churches. We even went on manoeuvres, being driven up to encampments high in the mountains. It was an exciting experience initially but all the bases were more or less identical. They paid no homage to the wealth of culture and richness of life just outside the gates. I rapidly tired of military life and had asked to be assigned back to non-military touring.

In June 1982, I'd transferred to the United States. We spent the summer in Woodland Hills in California doing intensive drama workshops. A small number of us went to Chuck's lunchtime lectures and question and answer time once a week. It wasn't long until I first came across his concept of the lifetime commitment. There was an unstated implication that those that made the lifetime commitment were somehow more purely dedicated to the mission than those of us who had signed up for only two years. We were warned that the decision was not to be taken lightly. If we broke our commitment then we would be considered *persona non grata* and would no longer be allowed to communicate with anyone actively in the group. Other cultish aspects like this had begun to filter into the group around this time. But it took another ten years before a Californian court case forced the group to acknowledge to its members that certain practises were cultish in nature.

I held off on making the decision for some time, but then during a very emotional group moment, after an extremely powerful play, I'd felt compelled to sign up for the lifetime commitment. I'd wanted to stand with the most dedicated.

The Covenant Players has, I believe, become more fundamentalist over the years. At the time I was there, the thinking was more liberal. The whole experience was healthy for me, not just the extensive travel, but having to get up there on stage and act. I ended up as a unit manager in British Columbia, Canada. The job came with a Dodge van and I fell in love with driving around the wild Rocky Mountains.

During the tour, however, I'd discovered that I was not going to swallow some of the more extreme expressions of Christianity that were being manifested in the Churches we visited. I had also seen signs of this extremism beginning to influence the Covenant Players group.

The tour had ended just before Christmas 1983 and I decided that I wanted out. I had to move on. I'd sent the others back to their homes and stored the various materials with a Covenant Players contact point in Maple Ridge, just north of Vancouver. As the 1979 Dodge was beginning to show signs of fairly severe wear and tear, I'd sold it and deposited the money into The Covenant Player's bank account.

I'd boarded a Greyhound bus bound for my Uncle Brian in Halifax, Nova Scotia at 6am on a cold, snowy December Morning. I remember feeling relieved to have left behind the Players and my lifetime commitment.

Brian and his wife Sue were very laid back. I'd spent about two months with them in the little village of Canning, jutting on to the Bay of Fundy. I was delighted to be there and working with my hands again on Brian's boats. They had a gorgeous Labrador dog who I spent all my time with. I had the use of a big jeep and I'd drive it out over the snowy fields until we came to the coast. I would then walk for hours, along stunning beaches with nothing but my own thoughts. I'd also thrown myself into work on *The Polaris* which had been through the mill. After leaving Kinsale, Brian had sailed to the first stop on the transatlantic crossing which was in the Azores. Three masts had come loose during a storm on the next leg of the voyage and *The Polaris* had to return to port. It took another year before Brian had the time and money to repair *The Polaris* and sail on to the port of Halifax.

Early in the morning Uncle Brian and I would head off on the 70km trip to where she was docked. I would dig off the snow from the decks and hatches while Brian would go below and make us both huge steaming mugs of black coffee laced with a generous dose of rum. I could work all day, in freezing conditions, on that wonderful concoction.

I dearly loved living on Canada's eastern seaboard; it bore many similarities to Ireland. I'd decided I would try to get a visa to stay there and study as a Marine Diesel Engineer. But despite pleas to the Immigration Authorities over at Kentville, without qualifications I simply couldn't get a study or work permit to stay in Canada.

I'd eventually given in to the inevitable. With a heavy heart and a sense of foreboding about my future, I'd boarded the plane for Ireland.

I landed in Shannon on a crisp February morning, hired a car and headed for Kilmony. Everyone was thrilled to see me and wanted to hear all about my adventures. Ireland, however, was in the middle of a very serious recession in 1984. I was lucky when, within a few weeks, I got a job on a farm. The pay was rotten but I stuck it for two months while I looked for something else. Eventually I landed a job in a restaurant in Cork as a floor manager. I was 20 years old but I still didn't really know what I wanted to do. I started to feel very depressed again.

After eight months I realised I wasn't going anywhere and decided that I wanted to head back to Germany, where the economy was booming. I managed to persuade my brother Maurice to come along too.

Joachim, my friend who had also left the Covenant Players, had stayed with us while he was on a trip through Ireland. He promised to look after us when we arrived in Germany. We headed out to the University of Ludwigsburg where he was on his final year of a BA degree. Initially, we'd stayed in a student residence but we knew we had to get work. Times were so bad that one night Maurice had gone into a laundrette and managed to pry the Deutschemarks out of one of the machines so that we could eat. Eventually we both got jobs but Maurice didn't like being away from home so he headed back to Cork after two months.

I still saw nothing for myself back in Ireland. I was soon glad I'd decided to stay on and make a go of it. I had a good circle of German friends thanks to Joachim. They were an eclectic bunch and we hung out in a couple of great pubs. We also drove out to the forests at night, lit fires and went night-swimming in lakes. I was working for a big cleaning company and had plenty of money in my pocket. I was also well on my way to becoming fluent in German. When I got a nice apartment over in the little village of Wiesach, I began to really enjoy life.

After I'd been in Germany for three months, I'd met Jutta at the local Lutheran Church where she was running a children's playgroup. We'd fallen in love and more or less moved in together, although she ostensibly continued living at home with her mother. Life with Jutta was very pleasant for the first three months. I was a virgin, and so was she, so we learned from each other. Jutta's mother was very fond of me and used to insist on doing all my laundry. Her brother worked as an engineer over at the local Porsche development and testing works and he sold me his Porsche-tuned VW Beetle. I had great fun taking the car over to the Black Forrest. I loved testing its new suspension and tuned-up engine on the curving Alpine-like roads.

For Christmas, Jutta had gotten me a present of a load of hash and, despite those warnings from my Uncle Brian, I began to enjoy smoking it.

Not long afterwards, the depression had kicked in again. I could feel a growing sense of anxiety and confusion in myself. That whole winter I had felt uncomfortable in my own skin. I was sleeping badly and felt that my life was spinning out of control.

I had moved to the bigger town of Leonberg in February and started working as a spray painter in the local Leonberg Iron Works. I was in a lot of pain emotionally and, as the months passed, Jutta was finding it more and more difficult to get through to me. We had split up a number of times. I began enjoying a concoction of stronger hash, washed down with Jim Beam or Jack Daniels bourbon. Wim Wenders' film 'Paris Texas' came out around the same time and had a profound impact on me. I identified with Travis, the lost and burnt-out character played by Harry Dean Stanton. I knew then that I desperately wanted to go back to America. I suppose I was gradually slipping away from reality.

That day I went to Stuttgart I was feeling particularly lost and had split from Jutta again. Meeting Sabina felt like fate and I really believed that 'Dianetics: the Modern Science of Mental Health' was going to signal a fresh start for me. I thought it was an opportunity to sort out all the baggage I was carrying around from my past.

Being offered a job at the Scientology centre was like the cherry on the pie and I was eagerly looking forward to starting working there – a place where I truly believed I would find inner happiness.

THREE

POTENTIAL TROUBLE SOURCE

I had seen little of Jutta over the first few weeks of my involvement with Scientology. When we did meet again I told her that I was going to start working for the organisation and was doing a few courses. She was alarmed and told me to be careful. She must have talked to Joachim because a few days later he came out to see me at my place.

"You need to get out, John. This is a cult and it has been all over the paper recently," he pleaded with me.

"I saw something recently about The Children of God cult but I haven't heard anything about Scientology being a cult," I replied. "A cult! It's definitely not a cult. "

Joachim was still concerned. "You need to look up the papers and find out what you're getting involved in," he insisted.

He explained that the German government had been very careful about monitoring cults for about the last 10 years. When the Church of Scientology had done a huge expansion across the country to cash in on Germany's economic boom, they had put themselves on the Government's radar.

He went on to tell me about how he had read articles and seen TV shows about people who he claimed were drawn into it: "I saw families interviewed on TV appealing to their sons and daughters to get out or asking them to get in contact because they'd totally cut their parents off after getting tangled up in the Church. Their loved ones had become strangers to them because they were dedicating their whole lives to Scientology."

I was a bit taken aback by Joachim. The centre certainly didn't come across as a cult and I couldn't understand why he thought it was. I was adamant that I was under no pressure and was making my own decisions when it came to buying into Dianetics.

Joachim didn't agree. He told me he had recently read one article about the Scientology founder L Ron Hubbard and how he had always advocated very strict methods to deal with critics of his Church and to keep members totally committed.

"The article said that even the slightest criticism has to be heavily handled," he said. "Scientologists have to inform on their colleagues who make any complaints about Hubbard, his teachings or the Church and there are all sorts of discipline techniques in place to urge most members to keep their thoughts to themselves. Did you know this John?"

He went on to describe how the article told of the

policies Scientology used to harass, sue and destroy members of the public who criticised the Church. There were other stories, he cited, from ex-members and others who he said had been labelled 'Suppressive Persons' and who had been targeted by what the Church called the Fair Game policy. Many had been dragged through the courts or silenced in other ways. "Is this really something you want to get into?" he asked me.

"I really don't think you are right about this, Joachim," I said. "I think this is helping me."

I didn't want to be having this argument. Joachim was very insistent about what he was telling me but I felt convinced that Scientology was right for me.

With that he took a newspaper out of his bag and showed me the front page. A bold headline stated an exclusive about a 'Cult' breaking up families. I took the paper from him and began to read.

It started with an interview with a family who were claiming that their daughter hadn't spoken to them in three years since she became involved in Scientology. The article then went on to describe a fight between the Church of Scientology in the US and Paulette Cooper, an American writer famed for her critiques on the Church. She'd published a book in the early 1970s criticising the Church and over the years they had filed 19 lawsuits against her, from all over the world. They also subjected her to several harassment campaigns, including one known as Operation Freakout, in which the Church sent itself forged bomb threats, purportedly from Cooper. They used her typewriter and paper with her fingerprints on it. According to the article, Operation Freakout aimed to have her 'incarcerated in a mental institution or jail or at least to hit her so hard that she drops her attacks'. The Church had finally agreed to an out-of-court settlement with Cooper that year.

I read on as the article described Hubbard's utter paranoia against his critics, which allegedly led to the setting up of the Guardians Office in 1966. It said it was headed up by his then wife, Mary Sue Hubbard. It compared it to the KGB or CIA, explaining that it acted as an intelligence agency and as an internal police force whose name apparently struck terror in most Scientologists. I'd never heard of it and certainly nobody in the Stuttgart Centre had mentioned it to me.

The article seemed very sensational and totally over the top to me. I couldn't make any connection between these allegations and my experience of the modern office in the middle of downtown Stuttgart, staffed by bright young people.

A breakout on the two-page spread explained Operation Snow White – a bid by Hubbard to purge unfavourable records about Scientology and Hubbard from government agencies, foreign embassies, consulates and private organisations in the 1970s. Headed up by Mary Sue and her Guardians Office, a team of upwards of 500 Church members stole from more than 130 institutions, including the Internal Revenue Service. The journalist wrote that it was the largest single infiltration of the United States government in its history.

In the article there was also a reference to a book by Jon Attack, 'The Total Freedom Trap'. He was quoted as saying: 'The Guardians Office was modelled on Nazi spymaster Gehlen's system. GO agents stole medical files, sent out anonymous smear letters, framed critics for criminal acts, blackmailed, bugged and burgled opponents, and infiltrated government offices, stealing thousands of files including Interpol files on terrorism and files on the interchange of intelligence material between the US and Canada.'

After FBI raids on their offices a court case ensued and Mary Sue and ten of her officials were imprisoned. The raids had also uncovered documents relating to the harassment of Cooper and the FBI investigations into her were dropped. According to the article, following the scandal the Church tried to distance itself from the Guardian's Office, dissolved it and replaced it with the Office of Special Affairs. Hubbard went into hiding in the LA desert and continued his writings and dictates from there.

I handed Joachim back his paper and told him that I would certainly think about the content of it. He told me there was a lot more information for me to read up and suggested I do more research myself. Although we didn't part on bad terms I knew that his attempt to dissuade me from my chosen course had driven a huge wedge between our friendship.

That evening I went for a long stroll and I thought about what he had told me and the newspaper article. But I simply couldn't connect what he was saying or what I'd read in the paper to my personal experience of Scientology. There was no way I was being duped by this group who were offering me nothing but help. There was no way I believed that Sabina, Daniella and Anke could possibly be part of this criminal conspiracy and what that article claimed was one of the most powerful and well organised cults in the history of mankind.

I was more perplexed than concerned when I went to Daniella the following morning and told her about my conversation with Joachim and his strong warnings.

Daniella nodded knowingly and told me that I now had what was called a PTS situation. I asked her what this meant and she said I was a Potential Trouble Source and I needed to see Anke, my boss. I was puzzled and thought that sounded a bit scary.

Anke was my recruiter but she was also the Hubbard Communications Office secretary and her functions covered all internal and external communications lines, Ethics and Personnel.

The PTS situation fell under the Ethics department's jurisdiction. I was given a 'Student to Ethics' routing form and went to her office. She sat me down and began to show me what Hubbard had said about psychiatrists and how they were basically an evil lot.

"The German government," she said, "are strongly influenced by psychiatrists and funded by them. Thus they are anti-Scientology because LRH has found a way to liberate and free people's minds and spirits without the use of psychiatry."

She said that the newspapers were all tools of the Government-backed psychiatrists who had infiltrated them when Hitler came to power in the 1930s.

It felt like she was bringing me in on some top secret intelligence information gathered against mental health doctors. It sounded incredible but I really wanted it to be true. I really wanted Scientology to work for me.

She began telling me stories about the kind of things psychiatrists were doing as regards electric-shock treatment and lobotomies and she showed me a Scientology booklet containing pictures of this. One picture was of Brock Chisholm, the former Head of the American Psychiatric Association, electric-shocking somebody.

"If you can't get Joachim and Jutta to see this, then you need to disconnect from them," Anke said.

Maybe it was the Training Routines that I had done on my Communication Course, but I had no thought of questioning her, no thought of challenging where this information came from.

I just accepted it as stated. In my mind I decided immediately that I was going to have to leave Joachim and Jutta behind so that I could make this incredible journey to recovery and enlightenment.

I was immediately routed onto another course called the Ups and Downs in Life Course. It was laid out like a comic book with badly drawn pictures. The images showed how this person, a scowling, moustached fellow in a 1970s business suit, called the Suppressive Person, was ruining the lives of everybody around him. He was invalidating them and making them fall off ladders and he was grinning evilly at their misfortune. He was also shown to be doing shady deals with dubious looking characters.

It became clear from the little course that both Joachim and Jutta were both under the influence of this evil conspiracy and that I had to disconnect. Since Scientology seemed to be responsible for my feeling so much better, feeling needed and important – the choice was a foregone conclusion.

I attested to the Ups and Downs in Life Course and Anke immediately produced my staff contract which was for a two and half year commitment.

I didn't really read what it said, except that pay was a percentage of total weekly organisation income. I could continue my courses and would not have to pay for them.

The day before I embarked on my new career as a Scientology Staff member Daniella called me into her office. She pointed to a large chart on the wall, "This is the Bridge to Total Freedom, John," she said, standing back to allow me a full view of the glossy chart in front of us.

It was in a gold frame, printed in red ink on white paper and was divided into two halves. On the left was the 'Training Bridge' and on the right side, 'Processing'. Each side outlined about 25 complicated looking steps, in ascending order. These were the grades and levels of achievement and certification that I would pass through on my way along Scientology's road to total freedom.

"Hubbard's 'Dianetics' book evolved from its humble beginnings to something far greater," said Daniella, eyeing me closely.

The 'technical training levels' started at the bottom of the chart on the left with the Communications Course that I had recently completed. They advanced on up through various other courses and then on to auditor training levels, which were called the Academy levels.

"On the right side is your auditing route to full Operating Thetan, John. You are not your body; your body is just meat. You are a spirit, or as L Ron Hubbard said 'A Thetan'. On the OT levels you are operating outside of your meat-body and eventually you will not need it," she said, looking at me intently.

I scanned the chart and then Daniella handed me a pamphlet. It told how my capabilities were unlimited, that my experiences extended well beyond this single life time.

One statement struck me with particular clarity: Once the spirit or 'thetan' was in good enough condition, it could "fix up, repair or alter its own body at will". While I was buying into this notion that my body was 'just meat' I still had some real issues with this 'meat' body that I had to live in. I was embarrassed by my malformed teeth, had a pronounced squint, was prone to asthma and didn't like my hair. I was sure that Hubbard's wonderful technology could cure these ills. I counted the steps that would take me from 'raw meat' to fully-fledged 'Clear', the state that Ron described as Homo Novis, the 'New Man'.

'State of Clear' was marked in bold red ink halfway up the right side. Next to it was the statement of 'gain' which outlined what an individual would get out of it. The chart stated that this is where I would be: 'Free from all psychosomatic ills, free from cruel impulses' and 'A well and happy human being free from the effects of the Reactive Mind'. The very top of the chart showed Operating Thetan Levels from I to VIII. OT VIII looked very exciting. There I would handle the 'primary reason for amnesia on the whole-track'.

I decided to set my sights realistically. I focused on a goal half way up the chart, in the section around the 'State of Clear'. This was the fabulous achievable state promised by Hubbard in the book 'Dianetics' which I had read over and over. Hubbard wrote about a 'Reactive' mind and I knew more than anything else that I had it. I so much wanted the 'Analytical' mind that he promised – the perfect 'calculating Machine' that could not produce a wrong answer. With the 'Bridge to Total Freedom' laid out in front of me, it was obvious that all the hard work had been done by L Ron Hubbard. All I had to do was to work out how to avail myself of this wonderful new 'technology of the human mind'.

As I scanned the chart, the door opened and Daniella introduced me to Susanna, who I was told was the Chief Registrar.

She wasted no time at all. "Do you want to go Clear, John?" she asked.

"Yes, I do. It is just what I need," I replied.

She handed me a brochure which laid out the hourly costs of professional Scientology counselling, or auditing, up to the 'State of Clear'.

"How many hours would I need?" I asked.

"That is impossible for me to answer," she said. "You will need to get a technical estimate from the Director of Processing. I can give you a rough estimate, a ballpark figure, but the technical division would moderate it based on your own case."

She sat down with a pen and paper and did some calculations. Then she handed me a piece of paper. The total figure took me aback. It worked out at what would be something like €30,000 today.

I shook my head. "I just don't have that kind of money," I told her.

"Well, do you have any property or do your family have any property?" she asked.

I told her it was unlikely that I could get any of that.

"What if you demanded your inheritance from your family now?" she queried.

"I don't want to go there Susanna," I replied.

"Well then as a full-time staff member at the Stuttgart Mission you will be eligible for discounts on the professional rate, or the other way to go Clear is to train and you can get the training at no cost as a staff member. But you would need to buy materials, meaning books, course packs, an E-Meter and some other items."

She took the time to work out the total cost of the materials I would need to train all the way up to audit or counsel someone to the 'State of Clear'. At that point I would be Clear myself and auditing others to that state. It sounded exciting and I watched eagerly as she added and subtracted some figures. But the cost of the materials was still quite stunning. For what she described as 'The Academy Levels Package' worked out at what would be about €12,000 nowadays.

"I'll have to see what I can do," I said, not wanting to sound put off by the money. "Look John, it could take a long time but it is possible to Clear in exchange for being on staff full-time," she said.

I followed her to the Hubbard Communications Office where we met Anke. She had my contract ready.

As I signed Anke told me: "You should be Clear by then and then you can make lots of money and live well."

I had to rush off to catch my train after that. As I watched the lights pass by the window, my feelings were mixed but the one thing I was sure about was Scientology and achieving Clear. I had firmly fixed the layout of the chart in my mind and was determined to reach my goal.

My first day as a staff member was simple enough: locate reception, find your mail box in the communication centre, locate the building on a map and introduce yourself to your 'senior' or department head.

I was assigned to 'the expeditor pool'. This meant that I was under the Personnel Office until such a time as I was assigned a specific 'post'. By the end of my first week, the Stuttgart Mission had made a big sale so we all had a night out at a classy restaurant called the 'Movenpeck'. I got about the equivalent of €150 pay and I expected that this would be the normal course of events but I was wrong.

By my second week I realised that the reality of being a Scientology Staff member revolved around statistics. Unless we continued the success of that exceptional week we were not going to see anything like that kind of pay again.

Everyone in Scientology has what is known as a 'hat' which is a specific job in the organisation. Performance of this job is rated on statistics – a term that soon become a hugely important part of my life. Every Thursday, at 2 pm, the statistics have to be in and that will be the measure of your week's performance. Every Scientology office around the world has to report these statistics to HQ once a week. If your statistics are up, you get the cookies and cream. If they are down, you are literally going to have to work every waking hour the next week to get them back up. Every job in the organisation is run under this constant pressure of statistics, be it selling books, recruiting new members or even cleaning tables. As I was told all of this, I thought back to my own introduction to the Scientology office. I would have been a very important statistic for Sabina that day. Her role as a body router was literally to bring people like me in from the streets and hand them over to the tester in charge, which was Priha. My completion of the Free Personality Test would have been a statistic for Priha. When I signed up for the Communications Course Antonio would have been awarded two vital statistics, one for getting the money and one for starting me up, and so on.

The following week was bad for statistics and so was the next. Very shortly I began having difficulty paying the rent on my two-bedroom flat. It became clear that the other staff were having similar difficulties. Daniella asked if she and her boyfriend Kei could share my place for a few months and half our rents in the process. Of course I agreed, innocently letting them close the circle further around me.

One evening I was walking out of the building when I saw a book on the shelf called 'Have You Lived Before This Life?' I was stunned at the very idea. It shook me to the core.

I picked up the book and made my way to Daniella's office.

"What's this book about?" I asked her.

She gave me a mysterious grin and said: "I can't tell you. Why don't you find out for yourself?"

It is made up of 41 case histories of reincarnations and past life experiences. These were collected from auditing with an E-Meter during the mid-1960s at Hubbard's mansion and 'research' centre, Saint Hill Manor in East Grinstead, West Sussex, UK. It was an incredible collection of stories from subjects who claimed to have visited their previous lives, many on different planets in far flung parts of the universe. One man told how he was captured by a 'psychiatrist' running a planetary system, lobotomised and then assigned to a military unit. Some stories involved torture and death during the Inquisition and others involved the experiences of Roman Soldiers.

I was unnerved and excited and that night I slept fitfully. All those things my Uncle Brian had warned me not to do were coming back to haunt me. Here I was spending lengthy periods of time in trances and under hypnosis. I had started doing this while in a state of depression and consuming a lot of hash. Now I was getting very upset by a concept that really scared me.

I woke up at 6am, to a feeling that I had separated from my body and was literally floating, just outside the skylight, above my bed. It was both a strange and unnerving feeling. When I realised where I was, my body suddenly jolted and I woke up.

Although I was back in my head, I felt very odd and confused.

I somehow managed to get myself up and made my way into the Mission. On the way, I didn't feel connected to my body and, in fact, I wanted to kill it. There was a noise in my head and the light, the sounds of the cars and the voices of people grated on me. I felt helpless and I alternated between crying and feeling utterly numb. I had obviously had a major mental breakdown just as Brian had warned me might happen. But there was no way I was going to get any medical assistance. In the Founder's hatred of the medical profession and in particular the psychologist and the psychiatrist, Hubbard made it holy writ that no Scientologist was to receive any form of psychiatric help. The answers to all mental health issues were contained in the voluminous writings and recorded lectures of his extensive works. He claimed that only he had the answer to all psychological ills.

I was told that I was 'Out Int' meaning that my mind was 'keyed into' a previous death. I was put under 24-hour 'watch' to ensure that I did not succeed in killing myself. Meanwhile a highly trained auditor was brought in from Switzerland.

I found out later that at least 50 percent of the Scientologists I know have experienced this dangerous level of psychosis at some point in their Scientology training and auditing. Most, however, experience it at a much later stage of advanced Scientology counselling. A culmination of things were responsible for the rapidity of my demise. Firstly, I was away from home and all the security it brought. Secondly, I was living in a foreign country and had just been ordered to disconnect completely from my friends and my girlfriend. Thirdly, I was also being cut off from my last anchor to reality which was everything I knew before Scientology. Combined with the levels of hash I had been smoking and the hypnosis I was undergoing, my mind had snapped. My cure was called the Introspection Rundown Course and Antonio was assigned as my minder.

Little did I know, as I embarked on my cure, that a new recruit called Lisa McPherson was just joining the Church. Ten years later in 1995, while she was on the very same Introspection Rundown Course, she died. At the time she was under the care of the Flag Service Organisation. Flag is located in the spectacular-looking Fort Harrison Hotel in Clearwater, Florida. It is the biggest and most exclusive Scientology centre in the world. Her death, under mysterious circumstances, has remained a major public relations headache for the Church of Scientology. There are constant calls for a full inquiry into what exactly transpired. What is known is that in early February that year, Lisa was involved in a minor car accident. Immediately afterwards she jumped out of her car screaming for help. Lisa then pulled off all her clothes and yelled: "Get them off me; get them off me". Paramedics arrived on the scene, sedated her and took her to a nearby hospital. Under examination, she was found to be physically unharmed but it was recommended she be held overnight and assessed for psychological care. However, that evening the hospital was visited by a group of Scientologists. They said that the 36-year-old had been a Scientologist for years and was against psychiatry and should be released to their care. She consented to being released into their hands and was taken to the Fort Harrison Hotel.

Ten days later she was dead.

Court documents have since discovered that, back at base, Lisa was placed in a room under 24-hour watch, just like I was. A series of 'care logs' that kept a record of the last days of her life showed that she was incoherent and violent. She refused to eat solids and was force fed a concoction of vitamins. Her nails had to be cut so she couldn't injure herself but she damaged her feet and hands hitting the walls. While some of the logs were missing, those that remain suggest Lisa was suffering from a massive mental breakdown and needed urgent psychiatric help. Instead church members from the Office of Special Affairs, who were in charge of her case, ignored medical advice and prescriptions for drugs. She fell into a coma and was bundled into the back of a minibus to be taken to hospital. There were at least three hospitals within a few minutes drive of the Fort Harrison but Scientology staff opted to take her to one where a Scientologist worked, 40 minutes away. Lisa was pronounced dead on arrival.

According to the subsequent Coroner's report, Lisa McPherson was severely underweight and had bruises and cockroach bites on her body.

The actual cause of her death was dehydration. A few days before the car accident, Lisa had told a fellow Scientologist that she wanted to leave the Church and return home to Texas. Within days of her death, all the people directly involved in her 'care' at Fort Harrison were shipped abroad. They were sent to Scientology bases in England, Denmark and Australia.

In 1998, the Church was indicted on two felony charges in her death. By 2000, the criminal charges were dropped when prosecutor Bernie McCabe said the medical examiner could bizarrely not be counted on to confidently testify. Lisa's family went on to sue the Church and individuals involved but came to a settlement in 2004. To this day, nobody has been found responsible for her death. There is a growing wave of anti-Scientology forums demanding a full inquiry into it.

Of course back in Stuttgart in 1985 I knew nothing of this. I started the Introspection Rundown and just trusted my colleagues to help me in my hour of need.

Auditing was to play a huge part of this process, but it was a different kind of auditing to the Dianetics auditing I had done with Peter on my second day at the Mission. The difference between Dianetics and Scientology auditing is the use of the E-Meter. In Scientology auditing you sit opposite an auditor in a quiet room, a fellow scientologist trained exclusively in Hubbard's psychology. You hold a 'can' in each hand that is connected with plastic-coated wire to a gold-plated stereo jack, plugged into the back of an E-Meter. This forms an electrical circuit that travels through your body from the meter and back down into the ultra-sensitive pick up just behind the pointer needle. This moves across the face of a dial and is read by the auditor. The E-Meter guides every auditing session. It is not until the needle floats, in a wide gentle swinging motion across the face of the dial, that counselling ends. The needle reaction indicates that you have no more 'charge' or upset on the area being discussed in a particular session.

Each course or grade carries a very specific end result and a carefully designed list of leading questions to draw the Scientologist back to early experiences and get him to locate and look at memories. Initially, I was brought back to areas of my childhood which I had buried deep within myself. My auditor would start my sessions by asking me to "remember a time" when I couldn't communicate, or had suffered pain, or had a cold.

My auditor, Heinz Kroezchek, had me carry out a series of very specific mental exercises, much of which remain a blur. It was as if I were listening in on a conversation, rather than partaking in one.

For a week I operated like a zombie. I was pumped full of vitamins and minerals, spent hours in auditing sessions and was trailed everywhere by Antonio. I have no idea if an opportunity was taken at this stage to implant key phrases into my brain but have long suspected it was, as a later incident would indicate. At night I would be handed over to the care of Daniella and Kei, who would safely return me to the Mission in the morning.

To this day my knowledge of what actually happened to me during this time is vague. Most of it is totally gone from my memory. I do remember that by the end of the process I was convinced that Scientology worked and that Hubbard was a genius who had discovered the key to all mental illness, unlocking the door to experiencing our past lives.

I once again attested to completion of this process, connected up to the E-Meter. The needle 'floating', with a wide side-to-side swinging motion, indicated that I had no hang-ups or queries on the efficacy of the procedure I had just completed. Once more I affirmed that I would like someone else to have the gains that I had experienced.

The courses of vitamins and minerals continued throughout that July and August and into September, as did my study of Hubbard's works and the hypnotic auditing sessions. Within a month from my routing in, I had become a full blown Scientologist. I had disconnected from my former friends, I was living Scientology from morning until night, seven days a week. If I was not 'on post', I was in the course room studying Hubbard's materials on how to become an exemplary staff member. I was also learning how to write and file knowledge reports on fellow staff members, who failed to rigidly apply Hubbard's dictates.

As a staffer I was working up to 14 hours a day in order to get my work in the Mission done and my statistics up. I tried to keep a few quid coming in with delivery work and whatever else I could get. There was absolutely no free time and no room for anyone else in my world except fellow Scientologists.

In my next course 'Keeping Scientology Working', I ran into real difficulties on my study, even though the texts were in English. The course contained a series of 'Hubbard Communication Office Policy Letters' which, by studying and attesting to them, removed the right to critical thinking. Here I learned that Hubbard had, in a mysterious moment of revelation, discovered the true secret of the universe. He had found the only path out of the desperate state that man is in. He described, at great length, how no other system of therapy can help mankind except Scientology. It is a huge policy letter and I really struggled with it and did so for years afterwards. It caused me mental pain, as it sought to crush and throw out of my mind all that I held to be true about society and all that I held respect for outside of Scientology. I was trying to take it on board but felt as if part of my mind was being repeatedly hit with a hammer. I would often get splitting headaches and fall into a semi-conscious state while grappling with the ideas. The course supervisor would come over to the table where I was studying, and have me find 'MU's' or misunderstood words. There was no possibility of Hubbard's ideas being wrong – it was me that was wrong and who had a misunderstood word or a misunderstood concept. The remedy was to look up in detail, every single word in the policy letter, and 'demonstrate' how the concept worked, using bottle tops, paperclips and little wooden blocks.

It was during this course that I learned that Hubbard aimed to 'Clear the Planet' using Scientology organisations. This would mean every single person on Earth having to receive Scientology auditing and going Clear. This course went into greater detail about the pathway outlined on the chart Daniella had shown me. I knew that when LRH set up the Church in 1953, he stated that Scientology is based on the belief that humans are spiritual beings or Thetans who have lived for trillions of years, constantly reincarnating. Through the use of Scientology, Hubbard explained that practioners could achieve supernatural powers. The first major goal is the 'State of Clear', and the promised higher IQs, no illnesses, no hang-ups, the ability to travel back and forward in time and to operate on a far higher level of existence than pre-Clears and non-Scientologists. Once Clear is reached we were promised a move to the Operating Thetan (OT) levels, where the secrets of the universe are revealed. The purpose of the OT level was to learn how to travel in and out of the body, go back in time, talk to the spirit world and eventually come to a massive realisation about the universe. To 'Clear the Planet', seemed like a fantastic goal, and it seemed that the conditioning I had been subjected to so far made it appear to be an absolutely plausible eventuality.

At home, however, things were not as positive and the tight financial situation was taking its toll. Daniella and her boyfriend Kei were having spectacular arguments. Kei damaged the kitchen cabinets during one such fight when he threw a glass at Daniella. Luckily it missed her, but it took a big chunk out of the solid wood cabinet. Both of these people had reached the state of Clear and I was a bit puzzled why they could not control themselves better.

I took a number of part-time jobs to make ends meet. The first was working with a young Scientologist who ran a successful market stall. He sold leather coats and cowboy boots at open air markets all over southern Germany. I drove his van for him. Then I worked as a courier driver for an Operating Thetan Level V businessman – the level into the studies that Hubbard claimed held the universe's secrets. I was given a new Renault 5 and through the early hours of the morning drove a route between Stuttgart and Munich.

I also had my first encounter with Scientologists who had completed the highest possible auditing level available in Stuttgart at that time – Operating Thetan Level VII. They were two Swedish men who came to Stuttgart to get 'Clears' in the area to buy their 'Bridge to OT'. These men had completed OT VII a few months earlier and were looked on with some awe by both staff and public Scientologists. One of them told us a story about how effective this level was: "I used to have real difficulty when girls wearing miniskirts went by. I was always transfixed by their legs and short skirts. Since completing OT VII, I look, and it is just a pair of legs."

It made me feel more enthusiastic than ever.

In late August the world of Scientology took on a whole new dimension for me when I caught my first glimpse of a Sea Org member. These are the Church of Scientology elite. The Sea Org recruits are trained in countries where there are Sea Org bases. This includes the US, the UK, Australia, Denmark, South Africa, Taiwan, Mexico, Canada, America and now Russia. They are uniformed like naval officers and charged with the most important roles and responsibilities in the organization. They are full-time Scientologists and live and work on Sea Organisation bases. The Sea Org direct everything that goes on in the Scientology world, own the title to every Scientology property and have the sole power to investigate perceived wrongs and administer justice through the Office of Special Affairs. Upon graduation, they sign a billion year contract to Scientology. They agree to work towards 'Clearing' target one, Earth, and to then move on to target two, a series of planets beyond our solar system. One place that only employs Sea Org members is the Flag Service Organisation or FLAG, at the Fort Harrison Hotel where Lisa McPherson met her end.

That Autumn a FLAG tour was hosting a huge event in Münich. All the staff and public Scientologists, from both Stuttgart and Ulm, were invited to join their colleagues in the German headquarters of Münich Org for the event. The Flag Service Organisation members all wore navy uniforms, with different coloured braid around their navy caps. Officers wore stripes and stood to attention to Senior Officers.

I thought they were a bit odd but on questioning my colleagues were told that these were the big wigs of Scientology who would have all successfully passed the brutal Sea Org graduation course.

The event was a briefing on some new Hubbard release. FLAG were actually trying to make money, a necessity because at the time their statistics demanded that they turned over a million dollars a week. During the sales pitch, we were all shown pictures of the beautiful big FLAG base, the Fort Harrison Hotel, basking in the Florida sunshine. We all reckoned it looked like a very nice place to be.

A few days later, I was working on reception one evening when a woman called Linda rang. She was from Stuttgart Mission's corporate management body, Scientology Missions International (SMI). SMI were based at middle management level in a naval style compound known as The Complex in Los Angeles. Missions International holds the license that allows Scientology centres like Stuttgart to deliver the copyrighted works, including auditing and Scientology training. It also has the power to revoke the right of that organisation to use the materials. Scientology Missions International was held in very high regard by the executives and staff.

Linda and I got talking, firstly in German and then in English, and she soon realised that I was Irish which seemed to amuse her greatly. With that, she started recruiting me: "You should come over to LA. Join the Sea Org. With your bilingual skills, you could really go far."

It sounded interesting and it would mean a move back to the US which was something I had been dying to do for ages.

"I'll think about it," I agreed and left it at that.

Linda must have figured that I was a sure thing because a couple of weeks later Gerald, the Scientology Missions International recruiter, was sent to Stuttgart.

Again the hard sell kicked in.

"I owe my girlfriend money for the down payment on our apartment," I told Gerald.

"Is she a Scientologist?" he asked.

When I replied "No" Gerald went quiet for a bit.

"Well you can earn $500 a week if you graduate to work for the SMI office in LA," he eventually said.

He put a big sheet of parchment in front of me. Along the top, embossed in blue foil was the title THE SEA ORGANIZATION with a dove or a gull floating above it. Below this was a laurel wreath, open at the top with a star placed in the centre. I would learn the meaning of these symbols within a few months.

I read the rest of the contract. The bit that got me was that if I graduated I was to dedicate my life to the Sea Org for the next billion years. I found this difficult to conceive of.

"I'm having a hard time getting my head around this billion year part," I told Gerald.

Gerald replied: "You're a 'thetan' with a body. The body is not important as it will die, but you will live on. In your next life and many lives after that you will rejoin the Sea Org in its quest to Clear the universe."

The film 'Star Wars' came to mind, but I didn't tell him that. "So do I at least get a holiday after a billion years?" I joked.

Gerald grinned, but he didn't laugh.

A candidate has to pay his own way to join Sea Org so SMI organised that I got an advance on my wages with the Scientologist-owned Courier Company I was working for. I then bought a ticket for the $1200 flights through to Newark and on to LA.

On October 10, 1985, I packed up my little flat in Germany and said farewell to all my Stuttgart colleagues.

Anke was upset as she had recruited me and I was not replaced. The Hubbard rule was that if a staff member were to move to another organization or to leave staff or even take a holiday, he or she had to have a replacement to take over their duties. Very few people join staff, for obvious reasons, thus it can be impossible to get replaced. Gerald dealt with Anke by telling her that Sea Org orders are senior to what she wanted.

I gave Joachim a ring to tell him I was going and to return some blankets I had borrowed. He came to my apartment with his lovely fiancé a few days later. He seemed sad but resigned and never even sat down as he collected his things. We didn't speak much and just shook hands as he left. It was an uncomfortable parting. I did not see Jutta again.

The flights were long haul and I thought about Jutta and Joachim and all their warnings as we soared above the Atlantic. I was nervous about what lay ahead but I was in this now and I had to trust my instincts and see it through. I hoped I had made the right decision but I reckoned that if it all proved to be a disaster, then at least I was in the US and surely I could get some sort of a job to set myself up.

I was tired out by the time I reached the Californian sunshine. At Los Angeles International Airport, I walked out of arrivals and immediately breathed in the Los Angeles mix of smells; aeroplane fumes and the whiff of dry, aromatic scrub blown down from the surrounding hills by the Santa Ana desert winds.

I hopped in a taxi and told the driver I wanted to go to the Church of Scientology on Fountain Avenue.

As we pulled up outside the huge daunting building the first thing I was struck with was its very bizarre colour. It was painted an azure blue and was out of keeping with the creams and whites of the rest of the buildings I had seen on my way from the airport. The taxi stopped in the middle of the horseshoe drive way outside the foreboding-looking former hospital and I wondered again if I had made the right decision.

I checked my pocket and counted out a couple of hundred dollars which was all I had left in the world. I had no return flight.

I gathered my bags and slowly made my way towards the front door. It was flanked by two beefy-looking security guards.

Their eyes followed me as I stepped inside The Complex.

Four

INSIDE THE COMPLEX

> "I, John Anthony Duignan, do hereby agree to enter into employment with THE SEA ORGANIZATION and, being of sound mind, do fully realize and agree to abide by its purpose which is TO GET ETHICS IN on this PLANET AND UNIVERSE and, fully and without reservation, subscribe to the discipline mores and conditions of this group and pledge to abide by them.
>
> THEREFORE I CONTRACT MYSELF TO THE SEA ORGANIZATION FOR THE NEXT BILLION YEARS."

Gerald had given me a glowing account of the establishment of the Sea Organisation. He charted its fine maritime history and applauded the handful of veteran Scientologists who had taken to the high seas with our leader L Ron Hubbard in 1967. Hubbard had formed the Sea Organisation to give him a safe place 'off the crossroads of the world' where he could carry out his research into the secrets of life and the universe. The belief was that the Sea Org would become the 'sole guarantee for the future well being of mankind on this planet'.

He told me that it had all kicked off when Hubbard first purchased the 40ft steel-hulled ketch *Enchanter*. The Commodore then rapidly expanded his fleet with the purchase of a battered old North Sea trawler that was refitted by his crew. Finally, a huge old Harland and Wolfe built ferry called *The Royal Scotsman* was purchased by 'The Hubbard Exploration Company' in 1968. This ferry was constructed in 1936, by Burns and Laird, and it transported people, goods and cattle between Belfast and Glasgow. Due to her size and considerable passenger capacity, this ferry became the *Flag Ship Apollo*, or 'Flag' as she was known in Sea Org speak.

'Flag' became the focal point for Scientology internationally. It functioned as the main centre for the secret upper levels of Scientology. It was also Hubbard's home as well as the Sea Org management base for the worldwide Scientology network. Their home port became Las Palmas in the Canaries, off the coast of North Africa.

As the Sea Organisation and Scientology itself grew, Hubbard returned the complete operation to land. The Sea Org established a base at Clearwater, Florida and set up the Flag Service Organisation at the Fort Harrison Hotel. This became both the retreat centre for delivery of the upper OT levels and the base from which the Sea Org managed the international Scientology Empire.

In 1977, the Church had bought the old Cedars of

Lebanon Hospital in Hollywood, as a second Sea Org headquarters to be known as The Complex. By 1979, this had become the main management centre of the Church, where, with great speed and efficiency, all Sea Organisation middle and upper management recruits received their training. They also bought up properties in Florida and California, bases from which the mission of Scientology, spearheaded by the loyal and dedicated Sea Organisation, could be carried out with greater speed and efficiency. This is the glowing account of the establishment of the Sea Org that Gerald told me.

Now, less than 10 years later, I was standing at the entrance of The Complex, ready to sign over my life to the Church of Scientology. This is where I hoped to become a fully fledged member of the Church's elite inner circle.

The Complex was an enormous building that stretched along the east end of Sunset Boulevard. Two wings created a V-shape around a central core, giving it a very 1920s institutional look. It had many cracked or broken windows with blankets and sheets in place of curtains. The building looked a bit like I felt, worn out and in need of a good wash after my long transatlantic flight.

I felt a chill despite the Californian sun blazing in the sky above me as I entered. The two security guards, patrolling the building were armed with nightsticks and hooked up to walkie-talkies. Everyone else just seemed to be in a rush, heads down in quasi-military attire – black suits, black ties and lanyards across the shoulders of crisp white shirts. No one was smiling and their faces looked pinched and undernourished.

A huge, gold Scientology emblem, the eight-pronged cross, sat on the wall of the south-facing wing and a sign above the entrance read: Pacific Area Command Base. I passed the security guards and made my way into the entrance hall where cameras were trained on every corner. I was directed to turn immediately right for the Scientology Missions International (SMI) office.

In my head I had an illusion of how smart the office was going to be but in reality it was a far cry from the contemporary look of our Stuttgart base. Everything was old, from the shabby brown furniture to the heavily patterned carpet. It was dimly lit and there was no natural light. The posters that peeled from the walls advertised Scientology mission stuff but looked as tired as everyone in the office. The woman behind the front desk had long brown hair and was in her 50s. Although she was friendly, she could do little to dispel the sinking feeling I was beginning to get in the pit of my stomach.

"Hi, I'm John Duignan. I'm reporting from Stuttgart to begin training for Sea Org," I told her.

She introduced me to the SMI Commanding Officer, Jean Disher, and her Deputy Commanding Officer, Clare Gaiman. Together they ran the office of about 15 Sea Org members and were directly responsible for the effective functioning of some 100 Mission offices worldwide, just like the one I had come from in Germany.

At that time, in the 1980s, the Missions were undergoing a major overhaul. The original concept was that the Missions were to be small city, townland or borough offices which could be franchised at a cost of around $10,000. They were given a special license from the Church of Scientology International to deliver Scientology auditing to Clear and a number of fairly basic courses. The Missions were able to operate fairly independently and many had done so very successfully. Meanwhile a wholly owned and operated Church of Scientology Organisation, called 'Class V' Orgs, delivered higher level services. Class V Orgs existed as the 'big brother' office either in the same city or region. The Missions would bring a recruit up to a certain level of Scientology study before handing them over to the nearest Class V Org. The SMI office provided the services, literature and course material to these Mission offices and in return the Missions had to pay a percentage of their turnover back to SMI.

Everything had been chugging along quite happily, with random inspections from SMI every couple of months. Then, at some point in the early 1980s, it was noticed that a number of people who had bought up Mission franchises were making a hell of a lot of money. The Church decided it wanted a bigger slice of the pie. By the time I joined up, it was in the process of making the Missions less independent and more financially beneficial to itself.

That first day in the office, Jean handed me a huge bunch of forms and told me to make myself comfortable on the sofa while I filled them out. I handed over my passport. I was told this was for safe-keeping but I later learned that this was standard procedure. All passports are held by the Hubbard Communications Officer, not the individual.

One of the first forms was entitled 'The Life History Questionnaire'. It was an incredibly lengthy and detailed form that sought names and addresses of anyone I had ever known; brothers, sisters, friends and former girlfriends. It asked for deeply personal details about my sexual history, schooling and family background. I didn't question why the information was relevant and dutifully jotted down as much as I could recall, including the names and addresses of my extended foster family.

The form would go straight into my ethics file, something I didn't even know existed back then. It is an intelligence file which is kept on every Scientologist. It includes all sorts of data relating to them, as well as confessions and embarrassing admissions made during auditing sessions. Throughout the career of a Scientologist this could involve hundreds or thousands of such write-ups of counselling sessions. The Free Personality Test is the first document in the file and, over time, this is re-visited again and again and results are compared. The ethics files are held by the Office of Special Affairs, the central, secret police force I had heard about within Scientology.

The form took me about three hours to fill in. By the time I was finished, I was seriously exhausted and must have looked it. Jean suggested I go and drop my bags off at my dorm.

"Grab a cup of coffee before coming back to fill in the rest of the forms," she told me. She called over a guy named David and asked him to show me to my berthing area and bring me for something to eat.

We chatted awkwardly, as he led me to the second floor of the west wing of the building.

As we walked, I got my first picture of just how vast The Complex is. The corridors, gloomy and painted in a monotonous off-white, seemed to stretch on for hundreds of metres. Along the corridors I peered through doors into dormitory after dormitory of bunks, some stacked six and eight high. The polished, concrete floors felt cold and echoed with each footstep. It all felt unwelcoming.

We eventually came to a halt outside a Spartan-looking dormitory, packed with stacks of bunk beds, with an old sheet covering the window. Since moving into the old hospital, the Sea Org had evidently done little to decorate it or make it look any less institutional. Old bed stations could still be made out on the walls and the hospital smell seemed to linger in the air. The old, army metal-framed bunks were rusting and unclean looking blankets and sheets covered mattresses of dubious age and origin. There was no wardrobe in the room and my dorm buddies appeared to be living out of their bags.

As I looked around, I got another rising sense of panic but managed to suppress it. I dumped my holdall and followed David down to the canteen where we had an awful cup of watered down coffee and something to eat.

When I had finished, it was straight back to the business of my 'routing in' which I realised the SMI office were relying on as part of their weekly statistics. After filling out another load of forms, I was eventually allowed head off to bed for the night and told to be back by 9am the following morning.

I was groggy and jet-lagged when I woke up. I headed straight for the washrooms to try to brighten up for the day ahead. They stank of damp and mildew. I stood under a large shower head and watched the water make its way towards a communal drain. I realised that no matter how little money I had left, I was going to have to invest in a pair of flip flops if I was in this for the long haul.

On my way down to the SMI office, I noticed lines of uniformed officers standing in formation for role calls throughout the building. The term for this is 'mustering up' and I soon learned that it was required at least four times a day.

I finished off the last of the forms at the SMI office and then made my way, with Jean, over to the Estates Projects Force office. This was where I would remain in training until I graduated as a Sea Org member. There were about 30 of us in total that morning, all in our late teens or early twenties, and mostly from middle-class backgrounds. I was the only Irishman among a bunch of New Zealanders, Canadians and Americans.

A small wiry French man dressed in black trousers, a black tie and white shirt with a lanyard suddenly appeared in front of us. He herded us into an exercise yard.

"Hello, good morning. I am Francois. I'd like to welcome you all to the Estates Projects Force," he barked at us. "I have some forms that you need to complete. Please take one each and collect your uniforms on your way. You must wear your uniforms at all times."

We all filed up and collected more forms and our uniforms which consisted of blue boiler suits, army boots and matching blue baseball caps. We would not be 'berthing', staying over, at the Complex. Instead we would be transported every day from a building off Hollywood Boulevard. Francois went on to explain the daily routine for us EPFs.

Our daily schedule would start at 7am for a 'Muster' or role call. After that, at 7.30am, we would be bussed into the Complex for a 15 minute breakfast at the canteen. At 8am we would start five hours 'Chinese schooling and drilling'. We would then break for a 20 minute lunch followed by another 'Muster' or role call. At 1.30pm we would commence work details which could involve cleaning, painting, sorting the bins or even repair work. At 6pm there was a half an hour for dinner at the canteen but by 6.30pm we had to report at our course room for study until 10pm. At 10pm we would have our final 'Muster' of the day, then board our bus back to our 'berthing'. Lights out was strictly 11pm.

Once Francois was finished explaining our schedule, he ordered us inside to retrieve our belongings from the dorms and change into our new uniforms. We were then segregated into smaller units of five and assigned a Unit Leader. My leader was James, a big black guy from Compton, a poor area of Los Angeles where blacks were constantly at war with 'Spics' or Hispanics. James claimed to be a Vietnam veteran and looked like he could floor you with a simple sweep of his hand.

I liked my team. There was a guy from New Zealand called Paul who was about 24. He had been living over in Redondo Beach, just outside Los Angeles for a few years. He was a qualified mechanic and owned his own car, an old Buick. Julie was a rosy-cheeked beauty from Northern California. Her parents and big sister were Scientologists. Leroy from Texas was a small, skinny and edgy twenty-something. Then there was a 12-year-old child called Maria. Her mother was a Sea Org member in the Advanced Organisation. Maria had just graduated from the Sea Org's childcare operation, Cadet Org, and she seemed a bit lost.

They immediately called me 'Irish' and started making fun of my accent and heritage as only Americans can. We chatted and laughed as we made our introductions. The friendly banter helped expel my earlier anxieties. I found comfort in the fact that no matter how bad this was going to be, we were all in it together. But just as we began to relax, James roared at us: "Muster Up!"

We stood awkwardly in line as he read out our work detail for that morning. We had been assigned clean-up duty at the International Network of Computer Orientated Micro-Management (INCOMM) executive dining room. INCOMM was a computer network group that were involved in the process of computerising the Church of Scientology. They were obviously highly regarded and must have had very high statistics because they had their own dining room, away from the larger canteen area. The remains of their food looked a bit better than the beans and rice I'd had the night before.

We marched in formation behind James to their dining area which was right above the SMI Office, overlooking Catalina Street and the few sad looking palm trees that lined it. The dining room had nautical *décor*. There were pictures of old Sea Org ships on the wood-panelled walls and some boating memorabilia scattered around the place. There was another team ahead of us who seemed to have the job of clearing the tables. We had to scrape the leftovers into the bins and get the plates down to a huge industrial kitchen where they were washed on a big conveyor belt.

James roared orders at us as we went about our task. His face turned an even darker shade as he screamed orders into our faces. Just inches from my nose as I lifted some cutlery, he blasted: "Get it done right, you're not moving fast enough!" He seemed to be getting a huge kick out of the whole thing. Maybe he was imagining himself as a US army drill sergeant or something. Or maybe he just got a kick out of screaming at losers like me.

It was a big job. The place had to be vacuumed,

cleaned and then re-set for the next meal before we were finished. It took us a good few hours to complete. The kitchens were another eye opener to the scale of this compound we were now in. At the time, around 600 people were living there full-time and this was not including other units, like our own, berthing outside it but spending most of their days drilling and studying there.

The Complex operates like a full military base. Men and women sleep in separate dormitories, some horrendously overcrowded. For those who have children there is Day Org, where kids are left in the care of other Scientologists for up to 16 hours a day. All children are part of the Cadet Org, with older kids filling the roles of Commanding Officers and the Executive Structure. When they turn 12 or 13, children, like Maria in our unit, graduate from Cadet Org into the EPF. Their graduation age depends on the childcare laws and legal scrutiny in each country. Each unit is assigned a particular time to eat and depending on its statistics, gets the standard fare of beans and rice. If stats are up, you could expect a varied offering from lumpy soups to mutton stews. We learnt that we got statistics through a process called Cycles of Action. It was based on a Hubbardian concept called 'start, change, stop'. The moment of stop is when the task is completed. That meant any tasks we had would be completed and verified by our unit leader and then we would get a point or a statistic. EPFs, like ourselves, were trained to work on menial jobs. It was not uncommon to see groups of blue uniforms loading trolley-loads of plates onto freight lifts for the kitchens, washing windows or mopping up, all the while being drilled by uniformed officers in Hubbard's way of doing things.

After our first task we were moved outside for sweeping duties, before being mustered up for our uniform and attendance check. Then it was lunch of some disgusting-smelling stew and straight into our course room.

The first course was called Welcome to the Sea Organisation. It was made up of a series of tapes of Hubbard talking to early recruits back in 1967. On the tapes he repeatedly pointed to the fact that the Sea Org member was the elite in Scientology. He spoke about the 'Dukes' and the 'Gentleman Regiment' and how Sea Org members would be 'red-carpeted' wherever they went. He spoke of a 'contagion of abboration' in the 'Wog' World – a term I would become very accustomed to when referring to non-Scientologists.

The big, old yellow school-bus came to collect us after 10pm and it drove uptown to the Hollywood freeway, before turning onto Wilton Avenue which runs parallel with Hollywood Boulevard. We all stared at the building which was to be our home for the foreseeable future. It was an old hotel, or something like that, and we marched in past the old reception. We continued on into the body of the building which had been divided with cheap plywood into very crowded and sorry-looking dorms. The windows were cracked and the place looked tatty.

I turned to Paul and said half-joking: "Are you sure we haven't come here by mistake?"

"No, no," Paul assured me, "this is the EPF berthing."

The building was purely for sleeping in and we were each assigned a bunk. We had just about managed to set ourselves up for the night before the lights went out at 11pm.

The following morning at 7am we were rolled out of bed. We were given 15 minutes to dress and make our beds, before mustering up outside. Then we climbed on our yellow bus and headed downtown to the Complex for a breakfast of scrambled eggs. This meal was shared with around 400 Sea Org members in a huge hall on Catalina Street. Catalina Street is situated in between Santa Monica Boulevard and Sunset Boulevard. It is one of the roads that form a square block of road around the Complex itself.

For the first few weeks, life at the Complex was a shock to the system but we were left with no time or energy to give it any thought. The intense military drilling started the minute we arrived at the Complex in the morning. When the bus pulled in we would file off, march in formation, salute and turn to heel. Under the overbearing James we learned how to stand to attention and turn in a group, before marching in time to the breakfast canteen. Calling it 'breakfast' is being a bit generous – some mornings we were lucky to get soggy toast and a cup of watery coffee. Then it was musters in the EPF yard, along with Chinese schooling. I had found out by then that this was a practice of shouting out, in unison, lines from the commands of the Commodore as they were read out to us and then pointed to in huge charts by Francois, who we nicknamed Frenchie.

Other study involved five hours of listening to the words of Hubbard on scratchy tapes and group chanting his dictates from huge posters on the wall. We would repeat the phrases 'Keep Scientology working' (KSW) or 'Scientology is the only route to freedom', over and over again, while standing rigidly to attention. I recall many days chanting: 'The purpose of the Sea Org is to get ethics in on this planet and the universe.' The schooling also involved deep self-critical examination of our, now meaningless, pre-Scientology lives.

We marched, ran and quick-stepped everywhere in our army boots and blue overalls. All the while we were shouted at by 'unit in charges' who were the same as drill sergeants. Some days we would jog in formation under the hot desert sky, reciting the endless mantra: "Don't think...do. Don't think...do." Then after a not very nourishing lunch of cheap bread and salami, or what passed for cheese, we went to work cleaning the building, painting, emptying bins or in the laundry rooms. There was a correct way to do everything – Hubbard's way. Each of 'Hubbard's ways' had to be painstakingly learnt off.

Dinner was either strange smelling meat or poor attempts at Mexican fare, as the cook was from Southern Mexico. I am not sure what training or qualifications he had. I often sacrificed the break to stand outside and have a coffee and cigarette. After dinner we mustered again and then marched straight to the course room, where we immersed ourselves in the study of Hubbard's dictates.

To get through the Estate Project Force training we had to complete five 'check sheets'. These were courses broken down by each activity we were required to do and there was a space next to it to sign off. When the course was done, two spaces on the check sheet indicated whether another had to verify that you had carried out the assignment. Every course had to be invoiced at its beginning on what were known as 'no charge' invoices. A full record was kept of all our study details so a bill could be produced should we attempt to leave.

The course supervisor was a woman from New

York State. She told us that we would have to redo
our basic study course, redo our basic study manual
and then take the Ethics Course. Ethics involved all
the concepts of Scientology and introduced us to the
theory behind the statistics I had been dealing with in
Stuttgart.

The course was based on Hubbard's world view
of how we should survive on our own, in a group and
in the universe. It gave us eight dynamics of survival
starting with ourselves and grew to everything from
sexual activity, to raising kids or dealing with past
lives. His teachings were all-encompassing. We had
to leave behind all our past education and experiences
and learn everything again from scratch. Everything
from how we should have a shower in the morning,
to how we should think. You learned the materials
exactly. We quickly discovered you were not allowed
to question how it worked. You had to learn the words
and phrases and there was no room for critical thinking
as that was an ethics offence. The course would leave
us with one aim in life, to work for Scientology and to
work towards becoming Clear.

To graduate to Sea Org you are taught to look at
everything in the world through Hubbard's eyes and
there is no room for anything else. Hubbard was fixated
with cleanliness so we also learned how to clean. He
hated dust, chemicals and smells so cleaning had to be
odourless. Certain products were banned. You had to
vacuum a certain way by keeping the engine outside the
room you were working on. Hubbard himself had his
clothes laundered by rinsing them in spring water ten
times. Such luxuries weren't afforded to us but we still
learnt the particular way to do it. Only certain products
passed the Hubbard seal of approval. While washing

windows we would be checked to make sure we knew how to use the old newspapers and vinegar correctly. In personal hygiene also, only odourless products were approved. Simple drawings were used to highlight the fact that men looked better shaved. We were shown different types of uniforms and how to look after them, how to brush our jackets and trousers down, how to polish our shoes, how to clean our fingernails. Every step of the way had to be tested and signed off. We often had to use play-dough to demonstrate what we had learned.

I didn't see anything unusual about this and often role playing these scenarios made them more real than just reading about them in a book or listening to them on a tape. I remember making a clay model which represented a series of figures in a line which represented my own re-incarnation through time. It made the concept very real and I put the end clay figure in a Sea Org uniform.

The last course we completed before graduation was called The Basic Sea Org Member Hat and we had to learn the history of the Sea Org and what was expected of us. It was made up of several taped lectures in which Hubbard cemented the ideology that we were the elite and the most ethical beings on the planet. On the tapes he described Sea Org members as 'the upper tenth of the upper tenth of intelligent life on this planet'. He indicated that we had been re-incarnated from a timeless military unit called 'The Brigade'. The unit, he said, had been fighting for justice through the whole of our galactic history. We were drilled that Sea Org is elite. Our course leaders explained that on one level there are public scientologists and staff and on another level is Sea Org. We were shown images of Sea Org officers, handsome men in beautiful uniforms, berating scruffy-looking staff members.

It felt wonderful and I had a tremendous sense of power as my ego inflated with every word. As far as I was concerned, after my nervous breakdown in Stuttgart, Scientology had healed me. I was completely enthralled by it, completely open to any suggestions made by Hubbard and totally thrilled with this immense sense of belonging I was getting in Sea Org.

Over the duration of the course we received lectures from an OT level VII public member who had been asked to brief us about this upper bridge. On the chart I had seen in Stuttgart they went from OT I as far as OT VIII but I only had a basic understanding of them then. I was now assured that on OT levels I would regain the lost powers that I once had as an immortal spiritual being. I would learn how to operate both inside and outside my body and would be able to cause things to happen in the physical world around me. Most significantly I would learn how to travel through space and time.

I had no idea how long it would take me to get to this state, as the content of the OT levels were a closely kept secret in the world of Scientology – as a Sea Org member it was one of my briefs to protect those secrets no matter what it took.

Mauritzio, who came from Italy and owned the factory which made the cans for the E-Meters, had actually reached OT VII before he joined up with Sea Org. While he was at the same level as us in his training for Sea Org, he was obviously much further up the Bridge than any of us had even hoped to achieve.

During his lectures he mainly tried to encourage us to work hard to get to the OT levels as he was forbidden to describe them or their content. He did, however, give us some anecdotes about just how amazing it obviously was to be OT. "As LRH said, as a Sea Org member you are expected to be cause over matter, energy, space and time. For example I was trying to get hold of my brother one day back in Italy," he said. "But he wasn't at home. I really wanted to speak to him so I just picked up a phone and dialled a number and my brother answered it. That's cause over life."

One day he was quoting from some parts of the course we were studying. "Our job is to make things go right and persist until they do. There is no such thing as failure," he told us, just as LRH had said. "This is what it means to be an OT."

I sat there completely thrilled that this was the future I was facing. I was hoping to soon leave behind my old reactive mind and move towards enjoying the fruits of being fully analytical and Clear.

Each course check sheet had to be star rated and then signed off by a supervisor to make sure you understood it 100 percent. During the process, every scrap of previous education I had received became invalid. Critical thinking was stripped away and replaced completely and utterly with 'Hubbardise'. The effort to suppress any critical thinking was made considerably easier by the immense workload, as well as the drilling and constant bombardment with Hubbard's view of the world. The result is an utter acceptance of what he says, no matter if that means that black is white.

Over the three months I spent on EPF training I was paid $5 a week, just about enough to purchase a few packets of cigarettes. Any step out of line, be that late for musters or slow at work, resulted in a 'chit', a little piece of paper detailing the crime. Frenchie could not say the 'ch' sound. So when he was reading out the offences that warranted a 'chit', each line stated the offence and ended with the statement 'he gets a shit'. Paul, Leroy, Julie and I had a hard time suppressing giggles.

Five 'chits' meant a condition which was included in the ethics file. More than one condition meant disciplinary action. An official form would be posted on the public notice board detailing the misdemeanour and advising that a Court of Ethics was to be held. A Court would immediately be called for more serious misdemeanours like sex outside marriage which was totally banned within the Church. The Court Chairman would then review your case and decide whether or not you were going to try harder. Again, results would be posted in full public view. If the misdemeanour was repeated, or was of a more serious nature, that meant a Committee of Evidence. This was a court of people assigned to adjourn over all sorts of transgressions. The Committee of Evidence are given full access to the ethics file of the accused and all those admissions and confessions from auditing sessions. They will take an admission of guilt, regret or attempts to change behaviour into regard. If the Committee then felt they had come up with sufficient evidence for a severe correction they will recommend the Rehabilitation Project Force or RPF.

Designed to completely re-indoctrinate an intractable member of the elite Sea Org, the RPF was the most feared of all penalties. It was used as an efficacious threat in the total control of a member's lifestyle and thinking. Similar in many ways to Stalin's Gulags, it consists of a rigorous schedule of heavy, and often brutal, physical work and a long drawn out indoctrination in Hubbard's words and lectures. It takes an average of five years to complete. An RPFer does all physical work – no administrative work is allowed – from 7am until 3pm and studies from 3pm until 8pm. Work starts again from 8.30pm until 11pm. They are on one third of the pay sum of the regular Sea Org staff, which means, like us, around $5 per week, as long as the church is allocating a pay sum that given week.

You could never miss the RPF guys in the Complex. Dressed in black and berthed in the rat-infested, dark basements, I noticed them my first week there. The first time I saw them I wondered 'What the fuck?' They do the dirtiest work imaginable – cleaning blocked toilets, sewers or whatever other bodily fluids can be found. They speak to nobody but are assigned a twin and they have to audit one another, often for up to five hours a day. Then they return to hours of the hardest physical labour imaginable. Even in that first week I could see that everybody looked down on the RPFer. They were seen as scum and about as low as a Sea Org member could go.

As I found out more about their life, I vowed that I'd never become one. There are no liberties. All telephone calls are monitored. There are no holidays or visits to family. Any communication from or to others is censored by a Senior Ethics Officer. If an RPFer has to receive a call from a family member, a security person is beside them listening to it. Letters written to others are cross-checked by the 'Master At Arms'. The RPFer must only live and work within the RPF. He does not see his wife or children and has only the most curtailed communication with non-RPF staff. He is not allowed to initiate conversation with anyone outside the RPF, except in the direst emergency. If a non-RPF staff member addresses him, he may answer questions but must address all as 'Sir'.

On our first week at the Complex we studied a policy called 2D Rules which laid out the rules regarding any sexual activity. To hammer home the seriousness of the punishments for infringing these rules, Frenchie pointed out a group of RPFers to us. He told us they were on the regime for over 15 years. Several people had spent the greater bulk of 25 years within the Sea Org doing the RPF program. We heard about three people who were in the regular Sea Org ranks for five years, then spent eight years on the RPF, were off for two years and then spent a further 10 years on the programme. It was really scary stuff and I was terrified to see this punishment being meted out to people before my eyes.

I was quite shocked when I found out that the RPF member is controlled by threat of further loss of already minimal privileges and may be sent to the RPF's RPF. This is, if it can be imagined, an even harsher regime. If this fails, the person is excommunicated by being declared a Suppressive Person (SP). They may never practice Scientology again or speak to anyone still in the Church. This not only includes the close friends made over years but also immediate family – their children, parents, husbands or wives.

I don't recall getting any black marks during my Sea Org training. In fact I was told I was an excellent pupil, dedicated to my study and work and focused on the goal ahead. By January, I had satisfactorily checked out of all my courses. I just had my Kit Course left to pass before I could attend the Fitness Board for assessment for graduation. My records were extensively researched and my statistics examined. I was eventually told that I had passed the Fitness Board and was going to graduate as a Sea Org member.

I was so proud that morning in early January, in my newly purchased black trousers, white shirt and black tie. I stood in front of my former EPF comrades and recited, out loud, the Code of a Sea Org Member:

"I promise to help get ethics in on this planet and the universe, which is the basic purpose of the Sea Org.

I promise to uphold, forward and carry out Command Intention.

I promise to use Dianetics and Scientology for the greatest good for the greatest number of dynamics.

I promise to do my part to achieve the Sea Org's humanitarian objective which is to make a safe environment where the Fourth Dynamic Engram can be audited out.

I promise to uphold the fact that duty is the Sea Org's true motivation, which is the highest motivation there is.

I promise to keep my own personal ethics in and uphold beyond all contemporary honour, integrity and true discipline that is the Sea Org's heritage and tradition.

I promise to effectively lead, care for and train those under my charge and to ensure they keep their own ethics in and if that fails to take action with fair and legal justice.

I promise to take responsibility for the preservation and the continued full and exact use of the technologies of Dianetics and Scientology.

I promise to exemplify in my conduct the belief

that to command is to serve and that a being is only as valuable as he can serve others.

I promise to improve my worth to the Sea Org and mankind by regularly advancing my knowledge of, and ability to apply, the truths and technologies of Dianetics and Scientology.

I promise to accept and fulfil to the utmost of my ability the responsibilities entrusted to me, whatever they may be and wherever they may carry me, in the line of duty.

I promise to be competent and effective at all times and never try to explain away or justify ineffectiveness nor minimise the true power that I am.

I promise at all times, to set a desirable example in appearance, conduct and production to fellow Sea Org members and the area in which I operate.

I promise to demand that my fellow Sea Org members not fall short of the purpose, ideals and spirit of the Sea Org.

I promise to do my part to protect and further the image of the Sea Org.

I promise to come to the defence of the Sea Org and fellow Sea Org members whenever needed.

I promise through my actions to increase the power of the Sea Org and decrease the power of any enemy.

I promise to make things go right and to persist until they do."

My new rank was Swamper and out of respect for my new ranking I was given a day off.

FIVE

DEATH OF A GURU

Just weeks after I graduated the Estates Project Force, I awoke one morning to massive excitement at the Complex. Management had called everyone down to the Hollywood Palladium and it looked like there was a major announcement going to be made. I ironed my black trousers and shirt and battled with my tie before I headed down to the canteen to grab a coffee.

In the canteen nobody seemed to have any idea what it was all about. Speculation was rife that they were going to launch some new OT level or that there was a new policy document from Hubbard.

I bumped into my Kiwi friend, Paul, who had graduated to the Public Relations Office. He knew what was going on but was not at liberty to tell me. "You'll find out" he said mysteriously. One way or another, the general consensus was that the news was going to be massive because the Church of Scientology didn't splash out on the Hollywood Palladium for nothing.

I swallowed my coffee and dashed to the SMI office for muster, where I was sure we would be briefed on the upcoming event. As it turned out, our Commanding Officer was equally in the dark. At muster she simply told us that there would be buses leaving from the American Saint Hill Organisation in front of the Complex at 5pm. Attendance was mandatory and the dress code was to be 'upstat civvies'. We'd been given specific uniforms for particular activities. The full Class A uniform was the full dress naval uniform, with all insignia, buttons and caps. Another uniform, Uniform J, was blue overalls, with a baseball cap and boots. Uniform K was upstat civvies which meant wearing a business suit.

Later in the afternoon I met up with my EPF buddy Julie, whom I had developed a bit of a crush on. She had taken a shine to me too but due to her work in the Office of Special Affairs and my work in Scientology Missions International, we rarely got a chance to meet. We were both thrilled that we were able to arrange to go down to the Palladium together.

I had never been in the Hollywood Palladium but knew it as the famous theatre where Frank Sinatra, Led Zeppelin and the Rolling Stones had all showcased. I was looking forward to seeing the building for myself. I hooked up with Julie and another girl we knew, Michelle, shortly after 4.30pm. We decided to walk the two miles down to 6215 Sunset Boulevard. When we got there a large crowd had gathered and we were ushered to our seating on the upper tiers. On my reckoning there were about 5,000 Scientologists queuing to get through the doors that day.

Inside, the atmosphere was one of tension, as people jostled for seats near the stage and held spaces for friends. Julie and I found a spot with a good view of the stage and planted ourselves there. The place looked almost packed to capacity.

The stage was empty except for a single microphone. A number of large screen monitors hung down overhead.

Eventually there was movement and a hush came over the crowd as a well-groomed David Miscavige strode onto the stage.

I had only ever caught brief glimpses of Miscavige before but I had heard about him. I knew that he was only in his mid-20s and was already one of the Church's top men. He was a short, aggressive young man who chain-smoked and who suffered from severe chronic asthma. He was a second generation Scientologist who had been handed over to the Sea Org by his parents when he was 12. He had spent his teenage years working directly under Hubbard. Miscavige kept a beautiful apartment at the Complex which had been especially renovated with the finest of materials. It was cared for by an organisation called 'The Household Unit', the same operation that cared for Hubbard's residences and needs.

On stage, Miscavige looked very dapper. He was dressed in a navy blue captain's uniform, with a thick gold lanyard across his shoulder. We waited in trepidation as he stepped forward to the microphone. He seemed uptight and a bit on edge. But then he took a breath and in a smooth Philidelphia drawl welcomed us all to the Palladium.

Someone shouted that we could not hear him and he shot the audience a dirty look.

"I am very happy you could all make it to this important briefing this evening," he continued stiffly.

"In 1980, LRH moved off the lines so that he could continue his writings and researches without any distractions. For many years Ron had said that if he were given a time and, that if others wore their Hats, and did their jobs running and expanding the Church, he would be able to concentrate on and complete all of his researches into the upper OT levels, so that the Bridge would be laid out in full for us all."

We shifted in our seats and craned to hear his every word.

"Over the past six years he has indeed been intensively researching the upper bands of OT. You are already enjoying the fruits of some of these researches, most notably solo NOTS [another name for the very upper auditing at OT levels] and more recently you heard in Ron's Journal 39 that he had fully written up OT VIII which would be released at the appropriate time by international management. As you may have surmised, LRH has completed many levels beyond that. Approximately two weeks ago he completed all of his researches he had set out to do."

We cheered uproariously and applauded.

Miscavige smiled tightly and waited for hush before he continued.

"He has now moved onto his next OT level of research, levels beyond anything anyone of us may have imagined. This level is in fact done in an exterior state meaning that it is done completely exterior from the body. At this level of OT the body is nothing more than an impediment and encumbrance to any further gain as an OT."

Julie and I glanced at one another wondering what this was all about. Surely it couldn't mean what I thought it did?

"Thus, at 20:00 hours on Friday, January 24 AD 1986, L Ron Hubbard discarded the body he had used in this lifetime for 74 years, 10 months and 11 days. The body he had used to facilitate his existence in this MEST (Matter Energy Space Time) universe had ceased to be useful and, in fact, had become an impediment to the work he now must do outside its confines."

I blinked and repeated the end of the last sentence. Was Hubbard dead? Is that what Miscavige was saying?

"He felt it was important, as Scientologists, that you were the first to become aware of this fact," Miscavige continued.

You could hear a pin drop in the packed Palladium as we sat stunned and Miscavige stared purposefully at the crowd.

"I can understand that many of you are probably experiencing the effects of a secondary [the shock of death]. However, it is important that you can put this into the proper perspective. LRH defines a body in the tech dictionary as 'an identifying form or non-identifying form to facilitate the control of, the communication of and with and the havingness of the Thetan in this existence in the MEST universe. The body is a physical object. It is not the being himself. The being we knew as L Ron Hubbard still exists. However, the body he had could no longer serve his purposes. This decision was one made at complete cause by LRH. Although you may feel grief, understand that he did not and does not now."

Around the Palladium a sea of faces gazed in shock at Miscavige. The word 'grief' was stripping away any doubts about what we were being told. The news was shattering. A noisy murmur swept through the crowd while most of us just sat stunned by the enormity of it. I was deeply shocked and shaken by it. Years later I would have that same feeling of disbelief as I watched the Twin Towers collapse.

"The rest of this event is devoted to inform you of a few more details of this matter and what LRH's intentions were and also a look to the future," finished Miscavige.

With that he stepped back from the microphone and turned to welcome a heavy-set man in a business suit.

Miscavige introduced him as Earle Cooley and said he was the attorney who handled the matter of Hubbard's passing. He directed Cooley towards the microphone and walked off stage.

We stood up from our seats and applauded eagerly, as the attorney took a pair of glasses from his top pocket and put them on. The cheers continued as he began his pre-prepared speech but a hush soon descended. We had unanimously realised that we wanted to hear what he had to say.

Cooley confirmed that Hubbard had discarded his body but said that he had left specific instructions for its handling and disposal. He told us that the previous Friday he had been furnished with a copy of Hubbard's will. Our Founder had asked for his body to be cremated promptly and his ashes scattered at sea. By 3.40am on Saturday, January 25, less than 24 hours after Hubbard had 'dropped' his body. Cooley said he bore personal witness to the cremation and scattering of his ashes at sea.

To me that sounded very appropriate. Hubbard had been our Commodore and had spent many years living at sea and the whole ethos of our organisation was naval based.

Cooley, with a fitting degree of solemnity continued: "There are several very important matters that I wish to bring to your attention. Firstly the body of L Ron Hubbard was sound and strong and fully capable of serving this mighty thetan for many years had that suited his purposes."

We nodded in agreement. The crowd were convinced by the bizarre tale being played out in front of us.

Cooley then told us that, in his will, Hubbard had provided generously for his wife and a few members of his family. He had left the rest, including, "all money, real estate, tangible personal properties and, of paramount importance, all copyrights, to and for the benefits of Scientology".

The enthusiasm of our applause lifted us from our seats. We hailed our mighty and generous leader.

."Thus, by the decision to continue his work outside the confines of his body, and by the decision to do it now and to make Scientology the principal object of his generosity, LRH has given the ultimate expression of his love for you and his confidence in the present management of the Church. He has, in effect, told us the Church is in good hands."

We cheered again as Miscavige appeared on stage again. He moved to the microphone and thanked Cooley for his contribution. Amid more cheers, Pat Broeker then entered the stage. He was dressed in a similar fashion to Miscavige. The pair shook hands and Broeker stepped up to the microphone in an oddly jovial fashion as Cooley walked off

Broeker immediately roused the crowd by singing the praises of being a Sea Org member and friend to

Hubbard, 'the great thetan'. A born showman, Broeker
kept our attention focused, as he described how he
had lived with Hubbard for the last six years of his
life. He stated that he had been honoured to do so. He
said that Hubbard had actually decided to discard his
body four years previously. This was when he made
a breakthrough in OTVIII and discovered the primary
cause of amnesia. Broeker showed us a document, a
photocopy of a hand-written series of numbers. He
joked about how he had taken the liberty to delete
paragraphs above and below the numbers, something
we would thank him for when we reached OTX. We
laughed along as his speech quickly continued. He
explained that for two years, from 1982, Hubbard had
worked on the upper levels. By summer 1984, LRH
told Pat, and his wife Annie, that he would soon come
to a point that he would have to free himself of his
body. Broeker went on to describe how, at the end of
1984, Hubbard was going to do so but called the whole
thing off. He had decided to go back and polish up the
advanced levels.

"On January 19 he stated that this was it,' Broeker
told us coolly. "He then handled in session those things
necessary so he could completely sever all his ties. Now
we know what they are because he wrote it up."

We applauded, grateful that we would someday be
afforded similar opportunities due to the ever generous
nature of the Founder.

"On January 24, he laid in his bed and left. And
that was it," Broeker told us. He added that Hubbard
had conversed with him before this and told him he
wanted nobody to grieve or mourn his passing. Broeker
then went on to describe how Hubbard had appointed
him as his successor and that David Miscavige would

become 'First Loyal Officer'.

People whistled and clapped. I was too stunned to do anything, as a series of pictures of Hubbard, in pristine naval attire, flashed up on a massive screen over head. Broeker smiled and shook his head fondly at the images.

To me the news was so enormous I couldn't take it in. I had only been in Scientology for eight months. Everything I had read was by Hubbard and every session I had was written by Hubbard. I was in the Sea Org to follow Hubbard, and now he was dead. I was deeply shocked.

The ceremony finished with all of the top brass on stage. I looked closely at Miscavige and, even from where I was sitting, I could feel his nervous aggressive energy. I could see his eyes shifting back and forth. We were urged to 'wear our hats' as LRH would and 'carry out our duties' as Sea Org, Staff and Public. Miscavige wrapped up by saying that despite his 'dropping the body' Hubbard was very much with us and guiding the actions of management.

I believed him unquestioningly and wondered whether LRH guided them through telepathy or whether he would actually appear to the executives at certain times. As they exited the stage, I filed outside into the warm dark Californian night. I sat on a low wall next to Julie and lit up a cigarette. Julie's eyes were teary. I wondered out loud if this was the end for me. With Hubbard gone, would Scientology fold up?

Julie must have had the identical thought because she just said: "We should carry on for now and see what happens."

I agreed with her.

Over the next few weeks there was a sense of

uncertainty throughout the Complex. We didn't know new management very well and we were awaiting some sort of news or direction from them.

About a month later, a special briefing to all Sea Org staff was organized at the 'Leb Hall'. This was a large auditorium in the Complex that served many functions, including that of dining room and event space. As we took our places, we found a beautiful brochure on our seats. It showed a fine white ranch house, surrounded by rolling hills with miles of neat white wooden fencing following the contours of the hills. In the dip below the house stood a horse racing track, with a neat little viewing stand at the north end. The place in the picture looked idyllic.

A dark haired woman in full officers' uniform got up on the stage and introduced herself as Jeannie Bogvad. She was one of Hubbard's personal assistants, based at Author Services Incorporated (ASI). On paper ASI was an independent company operating as Hubbard's literary agent. In truth it was then a powerful and secretive Sea Organization unit headed by Miscavige.

Jeannie told us to pick up our brochures and proceeded to describe Ron's last home on this Earth. Set on over 200 acres of prime mid-Californian land, in the acclaimed horse breeding area of San Luis Obispo California, it was the beautiful home in the picture. She described how Hubbard had lived out his last days, engaging his favorite hobby of photography. Pictures in the brochure showed huge glass cases where his full range of Nikon, Canon and Hassibald cameras and accessories were displayed. Soft focus prints of the surrounding countryside at dusk and grazing horses were shown as examples of shots taken by the Founder.

She described how he had written the huge science fiction novel, 'Battle Field Earth' here and an 'as yet to be released' ten volume work of fiction called 'Mission Earth'. LRH had spent his days writing and audited himself daily. He enjoyed steak and had been friendly and helpful with the hired help. She described how one of the workers seeing Hubbard taking pictures, had asked his advice on the ideal camera to get for his wife. After discussing some possibilities, Hubbard had driven off to the local town of San Luis Obispo, bought the man a fine camera and presented it to him as a gift.

We were left with the impression of a fine man quietly, yet purposefully, living out his twilight years in harmony, with everything around him.

Bogvad told a wonderful story of a road trip he had taken in his huge motor home just a few years previously with Pat and Annie Broeker and herself. She related one incident that happened when they had stopped for fuel. A gang of Hells Angels were parked in the same station and Hubbard's crew got nervous. But after a few moments, Hubbard was out there discussing engines and Harley motorcycles with this dangerous looking mob. He apparently made a huge and positive impression on them and within minutes they were helping to refuel and restock the motor home.

We came to understand that our dear Founder had reached the condition of 'power' on all of his eight dynamics. The dynamics were a central concept to the whole Scientology philosophy. I had first come across them within my first few weeks in Stuttgart. Each dynamic represents an 'urge to survive', through specific areas in life that start with the individual and the care of his or her body and move through survival in a family, in a group and on up to survival in infinity as a spiritual being.

Jeannie started to fold up her things and came to the end of her talk. We never really had much time to think through the scenario that had been spun to us. Before she finished, she very quickly told us to focus on the next major Scientology target. This was to make every organisation on the planet as big and booming as old Saint Hill was back in the late 1950s and early 1960s. This was a new push forward for Scientology and it was all hands-on deck. The brochure was given to us to re-enforce the image of Hubbard's pleasant, quiet final days on planet Earth. Her speech was basically a campaign by new management to get us motivated and working flat out.

Shortly after these events, I was assigned to work on a project with a Scientology front organisation called 'The Crusade Org'. Its function was to: 'rally Scientologists internationally, to protest and fight the efforts of government and self-serving individuals in their attempts to close down Scientology, mankind's only hope.'

At that time, many former Scientologists were suing the Church and an attorney called Berry had organised a class-action suit. It was an attempt to force Hubbard's operation to rectify human rights' abuses and criminal actions they had taken against perceived enemies. The class-action involved a string of court cases across the US. If one case was successful, the Scientology Corporation stood to lose millions. One of the most threatening cases was going on down at the LA Superior court. A former Scientologist and Mission Holder, Lawrence Wollersheim was suing for damages in a dramatic court case involving allegations of physical violence by Church members during takeovers of his Missions. Wollersheim had not only invested in a very large stock of books and tapes, worth in the region of $2 million, but he had also used his own properties as delivery centres. The takeover of all assets by the Church cost him over $5 million.

Wollersheim had also taken an advance course on board *The Apollo*. He claimed that he had been held captive on the ship and subjected to 18 hours a day 'thought reform'. He said that he had been refused medical treatment and had been forced to abandon his wife and family. Later when he tried to leave, the Church staff had subjected him to financial ruin through its policy of Fair Game. It was the same type of thing in the newspaper article Joachim had showed me about Paulette Cooper. We were told that Wollersheim was a Supressive Person. In Sea Org we had read specific policies written by Hubbard that described how to deal with SPs. Fair Game had been devised by Hubbard in the 1960s and was later withdrawn because it had caused a lot of bad press relations for the Church. But we were still practicing it and studying documents about how to apply it. It involves spying, harassing and suing any person and their family who speaks out against the Church.

In Wollersheim's case alone, his team was aiming to get over $30 million in damages. The Crusade Org, and Scientology in general, spared no effort in prosecuting this 'holy war' on several fronts – legal, public relations, harassment and character assassination. I was assigned to a number of duties. One of my main roles was calling public Scientologists across the United States. I had to persuade them to move down to Los Angeles and join us in protesting our right to practice 'our religion' at the court house. A lot of people I phoned seemed to be intimidated by my call but most did agree to come to the court.

On days the court was not sitting, I was based at the Scientology Celebrity Centre on Franklin Boulevard. It had become the headquarters of 'The Crusade'. There, we would phone around all public Scientologists, who had ever bought a book or attended a course, trying to get them along to our rallies. It was so important to drum up as much support as possible to make the Church look popular and under threat.

Every morning, we would head to downtown Los Angeles in a fleet of buses and people carriers. My team alone needed two buses and four people carriers but other teams from different parts of LA had to be transported there too. After assembling in the adjacent park, we were organised into teams and directed to march around the area, picketing the courthouse with pre-printed signs. The American flag was a backdrop to one sign, stating in bold script: 'Religious Freedom Now'. Thousands of Scientologists showed up every time there was a hearing or the case was up for mention. Allies were also found in a number small independent evangelical Christian churches. It was a highly organised effort. To us new recruits, the Scientology PR machine did succeed in making the prosecution seem like an anti-religious war.

As the trial progressed I was assigned to a special taskforce. We were deployed inside the corridors of the courthouse to work some Scientology magic from within. A group of Sea Org members, like myself, had to infiltrate the body of the courtroom and anywhere else the prosecution team might be, including the toilets. Our mission was to intimidate witnesses, legal teams

and the jury members. We would dress in non-descript
business suits or nice civilian clothes so we wouldn't be
instantly recognisable. Marcie from the Office of Special
Affairs would have us line the corridors. She'd give us
a series of Training Routine commands learned during
the Communications Course and through further
studies. I remember often when the jury were walking
down the hall, Marcie would shout: "TR0"! We would
all immediately stand stock still and stare at the jury as
they passed down to the courtroom. There were over
200 of us so it must have been quite unnerving.

Eventually we were assigned back to our normal
duties and told that we had successfully scared
Wollersheim off. Crusade Org was not to be disbanded.
Instead it was to continue aggressively pursuing
religious freedom.

I was glad to go back to the Scientology Celebrity
Centre. The centre, or the 'Chateau Normandie', is a
grand old building constructed during the boom days
of Hollywood. It is absolutely beautiful and its gardens
were done in the Italian style, providing a little oasis
of green in the concrete desert. It was a far cry from
the soulless, dull and institutional Complex. I loved
being down there and was happy when I wound up
working directly under a C list celebrity called Jeff
Pomerantz . He had been the Marlboro Man actor and
was in the process of moving in to a permanent suite
at the former hotel. It was to be designed exactly to his
specification. For a few weeks I was borrowed from
SMI to help unload all the new materials and begin the
work on the rooms.

The Celebrity Centre is not for the average
Scientologist. As its name suggests, it is dedicated to
the many Hollywood stars and people of influence

that the Church has, or is constantly aiming to attract to its ranks. Hubbard wrote that celebrity recruitment is a way to forward the cause of Scientology. He urged the Church to nurture well known stars so they could become the public face of his religion. We all knew that huge bonuses were in the offing for anyone who got a VIP, whether political or entertainment, into the Scientology fold. I watched an event where David Miscavige introduced Patrick Swazey, who left the cult within a very short time. He also recruited a US Senator from the Republican Party. Hubbard went so far as to produce a 'hit list' of famous personalities, demanding that the Church recruit them; included in the list was the mystic writer and pilot, Jonathan Bach.

Kirstie Alley, Tom Cruise and John Travolta, who were some of the best known members in those days, came into the centre through a special celebrity entrance. They were taken to exclusively designed suites where they would perform their auditing sessions and work on course material. I was taking a break one day and watched John Travolta drive in to the parking garage in his beautifully restored 1950s Mercedes convertible. I waved in greeting. He grinned and waved back. Paul Haggis, the director of the acclaimed film 'Crash', was there a lot at the time, as were a many people who were involved in music for the Hollywood film industry.

Once Pomerantz was ensconced, I was back at SMI where the work seemed bland. We started our day with musters at 9am and studied throughout the morning in a special staff study room in a building across the road from The Complex. I was doing various administrative courses, or 'Hatting' in Scientology language. I found the material and the study very heavy going. There were so many new concepts and terms to be learned off while my previous world views were still being taken apart. The course tackled both the minutia of our specific posts and the broader administrative world view of our founder.

I learned the recruitment process off by heart. Firstly you need to get the guy in and do the Free Personality Test. This test is a vital part of Scientology recruiting and is often referred to as the Oxford Capacity Analysis – although it has absolutely nothing to do with the University of Oxford. The list of questions was there to measure aspects of a recruit's personality, including happiness, stability and empathy. It also measures a person's ability to look at and handle life situations and communicate with others. Each answer is given a score and nowadays the results are fed into a computer which produces a graph sheet analysis of the test which indicates three states; desirable, normal or unacceptable. Most people who fill one in will find that they are mainly unacceptable.

Then it was our job to point out to the person how Scientology could save them and handle all their problems. Then you sell them a book and make an appointment, preferably for the following day. That is where you whittle out the time-wasters as it is only the hookable or the hooked that come back. After that you do not let them go. You don't let them think, you do not let them choose, you sell them courses and auditing. Most Scientology Registrars are extensively trained in hard sell techniques. It is a very clever way of focusing a person's attention on things that are wrong in their lives and convincing them that they need help no matter what the price.

A lot of the other material covered Scientology's version of business psychology and how to deal with 'wogs'. This was a derogatory term describing those who had not yet accepted the brilliance of our Founder, meaning most of humanity.

On the Human Evaluation Course we were introduced to the 'tone scale' and the 'Chart of Human Evaluation'. People were to be graded by 'tone level'. Anyone from 2.4 on up was a very good person and could be trusted; anyone from 2.0 down were factually dangerous. I learned how Hubbard wanted us to deal with lesbians and homosexuals. These people were automatically in a tone of 1.1, or 'covert hostility'. Hubbard described them as 'sexual perverts' and listed them, along with criminals, in the lowest band of 'tone scale'.

We were given a large number of indicators or 'cues' to look for in determining a person's tone level. These could be as basic as looking at the condition of their possessions or what material goods they had, up to more esoteric criteria such as skin tone and eye movement. Perpetually damp hands would indicate that the person was in a chronic tone level of fear, or 1.0 on the numerical scale. Grief was low-toned and unwanted; enthusiasm was high-toned and desirable. This scale would form an integral role in all our dealings with both fellow Scientologists and the 'wog' world. It was to be learned exactly and applied with precision.

Hubbard provided us with models of how he would like us to deal with people on the lower bands of the tone scale. In one policy he cited a story about a Venezuelan Dictator who had rounded up all the lepers from his town and tricked them. He put them on barges, telling them that they were being taken to a beautiful island, just for their use. Once the barges were far enough out from the shore, hidden explosives were detonated, killing all these 'lower humans'. Hubbard seemed to relish this tale. He also indicated that homosexuals 'should be despatched without remorse'. Learning to adapt to this strange world view was difficult.

Exchange is fundamentally good but in Scientology it was taught as a very precise form of interaction. If someone gave you a lift in his car, you had to give the driver an exchange, maybe money. To not do so was to degrade yourself, by entering into the realms of 'criminality'. Under this ideology, Scientologists do not donate to charities unless there is something specific in it for them. A donation of money has to buy something in exchange.

In addition I learned that: "A person is always utterly and totally responsible for his own condition" So, if I was not doing well in Scientology it was my fault, never Hubbard and never 'The Tech'. If Africans were being mistreated it was because they 'pulled in', the condition due to some wrong, possibly way back in previous life times. Either way, a starving African was responsible for his own condition. Such concepts were integral to the world view with which we became inoculated.

As a teenager, I had been a supporter of the anti-Apartheid movement. I had also read many books exposing human rights' abuses by US and imperial forces throughout the 20th century. In Scientology the very concepts I ascribed to were being subverted by our Founder, who had stated in his diaries that: 'China would be a great place, if it wasn't for the Chinks'. At this stage, however, I had been stripped of certain mental faculties and always gave Hubbard the benefit of the doubt. I found it impossible to criticise him.

A very typical example, from a former Scientologist

'Spork', of Hubbard's educational methods and 'being on study in the course room' goes like this:

'Communication' is a fundamental part of the formal study of Scientology. I had to demonstrate my grasp of the term to pass the course. The definition for communication was given by Hubbard to be 'the consideration and action of impelling an impulse or particle from source point across a distance to receipt point, with the intention of bringing into being at the receipt point a duplication of that which emanated from the source point.' I guess I must have been frowning or shaking my head as I read this because the Course Supervisor walked over and asked:

"What's happening?"

I said I didn't really get the definition. What was this business about an "impulse", or in other words, a "particle"? A 'particle' is the thing being communicated. It can be an object, a written message, a spoken word or an idea. In its crudest definition this is communication.

The Course Supervisor wanted to know whether there was any word there I didn't understand.

"It's not that," I naively replied, and launched straight into an objection. "Let's say the particle is an object like a button or a piece of chalk. Impelling the button or the chalk over a distance from a source point to a receipt point is an easy thing to understand. But why does that count as "communication"? That's not communicating, it's just tossing an object about."

"Okay…." said the Sup in a noncommittal tone.

"Also, how can anybody "duplicate" a piece of chalk? You can duplicate a memo or some information, but not some chalk," I continued.

"Why don't you make a clay demo?" the Sup suggested. I remember playing with the clay for a while, making two crude figures and a little ball labelled "Particle" and so on, until the Sup said "Pass". Later on the Sup walked over again and asked me what was happening.

"It's this particle thing again. Here's what I don't see. The two of us are communicating now, right?" I waited a beat.

"... Right," said the Sup, finally taking the cue.

"Okay," I acknowledged. "Now where's our particle? I don't see it anywhere, do you?"

The Sup said he couldn't answer my question as that would be "verbal tech" – a specific policy by Hubbard which says that only he can teach the subject. But perhaps I should go back and look for misunderstood words. Hubbard taught that disagreements are often founded in simple linguistic misunderstandings. I did so for a while but soon found myself thinking only of further difficulties for Hubbard's notion of communication.'

'Spork' gives a far clearer rendition of the typical scenario than I could hope to. To put it simply if you don't agree, you are not understanding and you have to go through an excruciating process of 'going through the policy'. This involves looking up each and every word in dictionaries and you even have to second guess words you 'think you understand'. Failing that you must do endless 'clay demonstrations' of the concepts as described above. If, despite extensive 'word clearing' you still have disagreements with the concepts, you are routed to 'Ethics'. There a trained Master At Arms will have you disclose any unethical behaviour, in thought or deed, and carry out corrective actions on any situation thus revealed. Most people eventually stop arguing, capitulate, and simply try to make some sense out of the weirder of the Hubbardonian concepts.

After lunch, which was still mainly the ubiquitous beans and rice, we would head back to the SMI office. There we worked until 11pm most days. I was assigned to typing up new contracts for Mission holders and it was intensely boring work. My enthusiasm was blunted due to the crap pay and food, the boring study and the monotonous job. But I was certainly not disenchanted with Scientology. I knew I had to do the work in order to forward the Sea Org but I did hope that something more exciting would come up.

I hadn't phoned home at all since I left Stuttgart. I had sent a few postcards to tell my family that I was in LA and the weather was nice. I have since learned that they were sending me letters but I never got them. All letters to Sea Org members must be first opened by the Hubbard Communication Office (HCO). This was to filter out any potentially critical comments that might upset the staff member. It also resulted in a lot of money being stolen. A poor Sea Org kid on five dollars per week pay, opening letters, often could not resist the temptation of pocketing cash sent to Sea Org staff by parents or other family members.

Like every Org in Scientology, SMI had to fund itself. Our office, which was the International Missions' headquarters, received weekly percentage payments from offices across the world. We also raised funds by selling 'Mission Starter Packages'. These were bulk materials required by anyone wishing to start their own Mission. They cost $30,000 and were a very lucrative sales item. The commission on the sale was often as high as 15%. A starter package could be sold to anyone by anyone, but due to the huge amount of money involved, it was mainly the very experienced sales people at Fort Harrison who got to bag these big sales.

At this time, I observed, but due to the Hubbard world view that I was adopting, I did not really question, bad situations that I saw around me. A family, a husband, wife and two young children, from Colorado were recruited into SMI while I was there. It was acceptable practice to recruit complete families to the Sea Org. With promises of full-time care and education for their children and pay and housing being provided while the parents dedicated themselves to the expansion of Scientology, it could sound like a very attractive proposition. That was until they got there and saw what the reality was. Typically the Colorado couple had been promised family accommodation either at The Complex or in another of two large church-owned apartment blocks on Fountain Avenue. The reality unfortunately was a far cry from what was promised by the eager recruiter, desperate to get his or her 'statistics up' with a juicy recruitment 'close'. There were simply never enough 'married rooms' at The Complex or other buildings. The result was many families were split up and placed separately in dormitories. Their children bunked in with the mother or in special kids' dorms. The children suffered terribly. The Colorado couple's marriage broke up after a year; the husband simply would not accept the conditions. He left, while she and the children stayed.

During the day, children were sent to the Cadet Org. When I was in Los Angeles, the authorities had carried out two surprise inspections and attempted to close the place down. But I knew that they were just Suppressive Persons in local government, who were

attacking our religion in any way possible. As for the
the Cadet Org I didn't really care that it was badly run
– it didn't impact on me. I was glad when Scientology
legal teams once again saved the day. Some cosmetic
changes were made and the children suffered on. It
was not that people didn't care, it was the system
Hubbard designed, and that Miscavige perpetuated,
that created the problem. There was no real valuable
'final product' from children and child care. With the
huge and ever present demand for 'up statistics' in sales
and delivery of Church products, the most valuable
people were put on key income-making posts. It was
the less able, illiterate or less intelligent who were put
on posts like child care and other 'estates' functions.
Why put valuable resources into something that gave
no direct return? With parents on post up to 16 hours
a day and often absent for months on 'missions' far
away from their children, as many as 30 kids would
be left under the poor supervision of a young teenager
or an incompetent nanny. I often saw these raggedy,
dirty-looking little children at the 'childcare' facility
either on Fountain Avenue or on Franklin, near the
Celebrity Centre.

To Hubbard, there was no such thing as a child.
These were 'adults with small bodies'. This statement
was issued as part of the policy on child rearing within
the Sea Organisation, and applied only to the Sea Org.
Hubbard, realising that most of humanity would not
only reject, but react with revulsion at this concept, had
a book written in his name for broad public issue that
gave a far more acceptable approach to child rearing,
but that was for 'public' not Sea Org. In the Sea Org
policy, called Flag Orders, he stated that 'play was
psychotic' and that a child had to have a 'post'. The

Cadet Org tended to graduate children to the EPF at the age of 12 or 13, even younger if the Sea Org could get around national legislation. These children, if they had a suitable ethics record, would then go on to the Commodore's Messenger Organisation (CMO).

The CMO was born on *the Apollo* where children were used to relay Hubbard's orders to officers and crew on board. Parents were proud to have their children working for Hubbard. These kids were eventually formed into an actual organisation with their own Commanding Officer and executive structure. Hubbard wrote a policy that stated that a Messenger relaying orders or operating in that capacity carried the same authority as Hubbard himself when dealing with 'lower' organisations, officers and crew. As the complicated structure of the many disparate kinds of Sea Org organisations developed, the Commodore's Messenger Org had assumed more power.

Eventually, as Sea Org bases spread over seven continents, each was assigned its very own Commodore's Messenger Organisation unit. They had a direct line to Hubbard when he was alive, and later, to David Miscavige who was himself a CMO child soldier. Members would, with uncompromising zeal, carry out some of the most brutal operations in the history of the Sea Org. Trained on exclusive and secret 'CMO TRs' these kids could make Sea Org veterans quake with fear. Much later I watched *The Killing Fields* and I found myself shocked and transfixed by the Khmer Rouge child soldiers depicted in the film. They displayed the exact same demeanour, attitude and cold, brutal dedication that I had seen in Hubbard's young messengers.

The CMO were aloof and looked down on people

from lower management organisations such as SMI. I was never comfortable with standing to attention and addressing children as young as 12 with 'Yes, Sir. No, Sir'. Years later, children I had taken time to care for were graduated to the CMO. Some acted like they had never met me. Even parents of Messengers were given brutal dressing downs by their very own children. I never understood how either parent or child could reconcile themselves to this.

Although it was several months since I had graduated I had not had any time off. There was no such thing as Sea Org staff availing of Bank Holidays or National holidays. Very few of us got home at Christmas and I only ever met one couple who actually got to take a full week's annual leave. If statistics were up we were allowed one full day off every second week. This 'work ethic' had been put in place by Hubbard even before the Sea Org was set up but formalised with its inauguration. A normal schedule had us working seven days a week with Saturday morning off to do our 'hygiene time', meaning laundry and cleaning of rooms. The communal laundry was always packed on Friday night. Most of us tried to get it all done so that we could get away from the Complex for a few hours on Saturday morning. I used to try to walk up to Griffith Park near 'The Greek', a famous music venue set in the pine woods near the north entrance of the park. I would climb up high above Los Angeles and look out over the vast plane below and just absorb the sense of space and the all too brief moments of freedom.

Day-to-day work continued. Drawing up the contracts meant a lot of paperwork and I had to spend a lot of time in the huge file rooms which were located in the labyrinth-like basement of the Complex. Below the ground, along with the RPF spaces, there were a number of very elderly people who had set up some kind of home there over the years. In the multitude of rooms and alcoves, hidden among the miles of piping and dimly-lit corridors that formed a kind of subterranean Complex, they organised workspaces for themselves. They appeared to have cut themselves off from the world. In my first months at the Complex and on subsequent visits, I rarely saw any of them leave their unpainted little rooms.

The old guys who looked after the boilers really struck me. They must have been in their late sixties and wore white overalls and sandals. They had come from the old ships before The Complex was purchased as a land base. Service to the Church was the only life they knew. They were incredibly pale, decrepit looking men that nobody bothered with and they did not bother with any of us. They even took their meals down there. They had no family and from what I could see, no friends.

Another old couple, possibly in their late fifties, had formed an archive in this basement of Hubbard's policy letters going as far back as 1958. They occupied a series of inter-linked rooms below the ground level of the west wing. Hundreds of old filing cabinets sat on every available piece of floor and lined every inch of wall. This couple would spend their days reprinting copies of policies or Hubbard's Technical bulletins for a small fee on an old printing press. I would often have to get some from them. They had created a life for themselves, around Scientologists who required the policies for making up training packs or for submission of plans and proposals, all of which had to be based on exact Hubbard Policies. The enclosure of the appropriate printed copy would normally fulfil this requirement.

This old couple spent their 12-hour days sorting and cataloguing this vast record of the official 'policy' of the Church of Scientology. They did not socialise. Part of me thought they were weird and I found it difficult not to grimace at them. Another part of me felt sorry for them but the overwhelming reaction I had to them was my Scientology one – which was that they were 'down stat' or Degraded Beings.

Under the east wing was another similar space, run by a lady called Marcie. She had worked with Hubbard since the 1950s. She was at least 70 and again had frighteningly pale skin. She had taken on the function of keeping an archive of the multitude of ethics issues and orders that the Hubbard Communications Office (HCO) excelled at issuing, on all and sundry. A few years later I was to spend many hours in her little domain looking for the issue that had declared my girlfriend, Julie, a Suppressive Person.

I had been looking forward to seeing Julie again after a two year separation and was astounded when I heard of her 'SP declare'. The 'HCO Ethics Order' I eventually found, that formalised her fate, was located in a file cabinet in this ugly room. This yellow sheet, devoid of emotion or reason had banished Julie from all contact with anyone in the Scientology world. It provided me little comfort and confirmed that this bright, blue-eyed, beauty was now worse than dead to her Scientologist parents, me and all of her former Scientology friends and colleagues. We could not even mourn our loss. Although it shook me, it didn't shake my devotion. I just assumed she had done something very wrong to have had this happen to her.

Our relationship wasn't the first and wouldn't be the last to crumble under the Sea Org regime. One of the first FLAG orders read to us upon entering the Estates Project Force lays out rules of sexual conduct within the Sea Org. It was another level of subtle control. Sex outside of marriage carried the penalty of an immediate assignment to the Rehabilitation Project Force. Yet getting married could be incredibly difficult. Time, money, legal documents, all had to be organised. The people who succeeded then had the problem of accommodation. There was only so much '2D' – second dynamic – berthing available. Some newly-weds that I met were able to organise 12 hours 'leave' for their honeymoon but then had to go back on post. They then had to wait six months until a '2D berthing' room became available; meanwhile they had to live separately in their 'men's and women's dormitories'. There was to be no heavy petting and absolutely no sex before marriage. If you were with a girl and felt her breast, that would be wrong. The order actually ruled out everything bar light kissing, sitting and talking or maybe watching a movie together.

Brad, who had done his EPF with me but was on a separate unit, was a brash California kid who had been brought up as a Scientologist. He was dating a very pretty Valley girl whose parents were also in the Church. His parents lived in an apartment close to The Complex. On the sly, despite orders banning it, he tried to stay there rather than in the uncomfortable and crowded dorms. As night follows day he had sex with his girlfriend over at the apartment. Everything was fine until his statistics went down. As a recruiter he had one of the most difficult jobs in the organisation so it was easy for the stats to go down, but as his stats continued to slide the Church started investigating him. The investigation is more like an interrogation.

It involved daily confessions about his 'overts and withholds', the names used for anything you shouldn't be doing or thinking. Hooked up to an E-Meter, the Master At Arms brought him through any misdeeds he may have committed, in thought or action. When they got to sex, his meter reading showed up an area of disturbance, or 'missed withhold'. They had him and got his confession fairly rapidly.

His confession was used against his girlfriend too. She was working on complicated legal documents when two Ethics Officers and the Master At Arms strode in. She had to go through the same interrogation as a matter of course. I have no doubt that she must have been terrified. Neither of them was given a chance to pick up their belongings; they were both marched straight to the Rehabilitation Project Force Office in the dark basement of the Complex. I walked past them one evening as they were sweeping a roadway with a group of six other 'prisoners'. They turned their faces away in shame and looked down at the ground. I actually treated them with disdain. The sight of their black overalls was enough to make the rest of us cast any thoughts of sex from our minds.

For the first few months I didn't miss home but, come July 1986 I was really feeling that I didn't want to be in Sea Org anymore. Of course, I never voiced my opinion or my doubts. Even my closest friends would have been obliged to report my words to Ethics in the form of either a 'Knowledge Report' or a 'Things That Should Not Be' report. Failure to do so would be actionable by Ethics, no matter what the circumstances. Even married couples had to report to the Hubbard Communications Office on each other's 'out ethics'.

Luckily for me my visa was running out. While

the SMI legal people were desperately trying to get me an extension, I was secretly hoping the application would be turned down. On top of my own misgivings, INCOMM, the 'in house' computer organisation, was trying to recruit me. If they succeeded I would have to work at the Church's secret Gold Base. It was in Hemmet, California and was the Church's international headquarters. I didn't want to go there because I was feeling the need to get back to the UK and closer to home. I knew that if I was at Hemmet I would never make enough money to buy a ticket home. Based in the UK, I was far more likely to be able to save enough for the ferry from Fishguard. While I had no say regarding which post I was ordered to, my boss didn't want to lose me so she refused to transfer me. Although I had a B1 Multiple Indefinite visa, it only allowed me a 12-month stay at a single stretch. I had used it for a year while working with the Covenant Players and had only been allowed to extend it for a year when I agreed to join Sea Org. Their application to extend it again failed.

I was thrilled, although I couldn't show it. When I was then offered a choice to go to SMI Copenhagen or SMI Saint Hill, East Grinstead, I jumped at the chance to get to England. I knew that Saint Hill was Hubbard's former home, a beautiful stately manor on 59 acres set in the Sussex countryside. It served as the UK headquarters of the Church of Scientology. I reckoned that I would give it a try and if it didn't work out I would be nearer home.

Before I left the US, as one of the few SMI members with a valid driving licence, I was put on transport duty. I was charged with borrowing or hiring a car, for the lowest possible amount, to ferry our Finance Directors on Mission licence inspections.

My mechanics training back in Cork came in handy for the first time when I did a deal with another Sea Org member who had a car but needed it fixed for free. I agreed that I would fix it if I could have the use of it a few times a week. This deal fitted perfectly with the Scientology concept of exchange where you don't do something for nothing. Hubbard's philosophy was that giving without exchange would encourage a person to become criminal.

The car gave me a little bit of freedom. Sometimes if I got finished with work early, at around 10pm, I would take the car up along Mulholland Drive and put on my John Williams classic guitar tape. I would let the calm music and the rare sense of being alone wash over me. I couldn't do it every night but I relished that little bit of solitude and sacrificed sleep for it.

One of the Mission inspections was up at Monterey, in California, the setting for some of author John Steinbeck's most celebrated works. I had borrowed his books from Raphaela and Michael while babysitting for them back in Cork. I had always wanted to see this lovely coastal town. I dropped the finance directors off and grabbed an hour to myself. I made my way down past Cannery Row to the bay and watched the sardine boats coming in with their catch. It was a brief and special moment of peace.

I left SMI Int and the Complex with little regret. Clair Gaiman, the second-in-command at SMI, gave me some materials to deliver to the Commanding Officer SMI UK, Rolf Glatt. She had grown up near Saint Hill, in the lovely village of Forest Row. I could see that she wanted so much to be going back there with me. I was glad to be getting away from sun-baked Los Angeles, and the ugly blue building.

Myself and my cousin, Coleman, off the coast of Cork.

Me and my family around.1979. I'm the one sporting the hat in the middle.

An E-Meter.
© *Roy Berman*

Pacific Base, The Sea Organisation's Headquarters, on Fountain Avenue in Los Angeles. This building is colloquially known as The Complex.
© *Chuck Beatty*

L Ron Hubbard.
© *Michael Ochs Archives/Getty Images*

The flagship 'Apollo', Hubbard's home and the world
headquarters of Scientology between 1967 and 1975.
© *Simplon Postcards*

David Miscavige, Chairman of The Board of the Church of Scientology International.
© *Photographer: Robin Donina Serne. Courtesy of* St Petersburg Times. *Reprinted with permission.*

Sea Organisation crew members on the road, tending the verge in front of the International Scientology Management Base and the Golden Era Studios near Hemet, San Jacinto, County, California.
© *Chuck Beatty*

The Scientology Celebrity Centre, Los Angeles.
© *G Wiedemuth*

Lisa MacPhearson. Her highly publicised and mysterious death became a focus of the popular movement to expose the crimes of the Scientology cult.

Flag Building, Florida – 'The Mecca' of Scientology.
© *Lyssa Oberkreser*

Vancouver Scientology Centre, c.1994.
Taken while I was installing finance
and database computer systems.

Scientologist Volunteer Ministers of London.
© *Andrew West*

Journalist Paulette Cooper.

Tom Cruise, at the opening of the new Church of Scientology, in Madrid, Spain.
© *Pierre-Philippe Marcou/AFP/ Getty Images*

John Travolta and Kelly Preston at the grand opening of the Church of Scientology, Mission of SoMa in San Francisco, September 2001.
© *Randi Lynn Beach/Getty Images*

I was brought to the airport and watched as I made my way through the departure gates. My thoughts were confused as I buckled in for the long flight to the UK. I had been heavily indoctrinated to believe that life outside the Sea Org was bad. I knew that if you left the Sea Org you were classed as a 'Degraded Being'. You were a person lower than the 'wog' and lower even than an RPFer. My mind had been invaded and was under the foreign occupation of Hubbard. The little bit of me that was fighting back was weak and demoralised, yet it fought on bravely.

Alone for the first time, I tried to examine my conscience. I tried to get some clear thoughts and plans in place, but it was painful. I felt like I was swimming in molasses and the only clarity of my mind dealt with getting to Saint Hill. I felt as if I were torn. I shut down the noise in my head and stared out at the vastness of America below me.

For the time being the Scientology mental conditioning had won another round.

At Heathrow, I was picked up by a Scot called John. It was the height of summer and as we drove through the lush green countryside, I began to relax again. It was lovely to see old houses, bridges, horses and open fields. I'd had my fill of that desert landscape I'd left behind in California.

Saint Hill Manor was every bit as stunning as the photographs I had seen. The grand old mansion was built by the Crawford family in the 1700s and overlooked a meadow with tall oaks, which swept down to a boating lake bordered by beech woods. The local villages of Forest Row, West Hoathly and East Grinstead were full of ancient buildings, rich in history; I could almost see knights on horseback heading off to do battle in Hastings.

John dropped me at the Continental Liaison Office (CLO) building at Saint Hill. I was met by a tall German who introduced himself as Rolf. He brought me into an office where I met Ernst. Ernst was Rolf's deputy and the idea was that I would replace him so that he could be promoted to SMI International. Ernst took me over to Brook House which was to be my berthing for the foreseeable future. I was assigned to my bunk and went for a bit of a sleep.

The following day I was put to work on statistical graphing with the two Germans. The work was boring but I was glad to be in England. I felt closer to home and a desire to leave Sea Org and head home was getting stronger as the days slipped by.

One day, not long after my arrival, instead of heading to the office I went for a really big long walk. I walked to Forest Row and back to East Grinstead, stopping outside an employment agency to check what work was available. I went in and told the receptionist that I was looking for work as a van driver, and that I would be back from time to time to see if any jobs came up. I then kept walking, but eventually made my way back to Brook House and lay down, exhausted.

I woke up startled to find Ernst shaking me a few hours later. He asked where I had been and what was going on. I looked at him, took a deep breath and told him I didn't want to be there anymore, that I wanted to leave the Church. He was taken aback but made me get up and come to Saint Hill with him.

When I announced my change of heart to Rolf he immediately routed me to the Hubbard Communications Office where I was to begin the long drawn out process of 'Routing Out'. I was assigned to the 'Decks', a cross between the EPF and RPF. People are assigned to this workforce if they have been removed from post pending further Ethics action, such as routing out of the Sea Org. The Decks Project Force (DPF) carries out physical work as assigned by HCO. I joined three other people, John, Martin and Alison, who were all aiming to leave.

We were given a work and study schedule. The study would involve the subject of personal ethics only and would be carried out 'twinned'. This meant that we had to get each other through the programme before we would finally be allowed to leave the organisation. My twin was John.

I knew it was an option to just walk out but I didn't do that because I was very frightened of the outside world. Although I was only in it a year, it seemed as if I was very disconnected from my family and from the rest of society around me. Mentally I know now that I was still very fragile then, as it wasn't long since my nervous breakdown the previous summer. Scientology owned me and I didn't seem to have the capacity to just get up and leave.

Hubbard states that the only reason a person would 'blow' or decide to leave is because of undisclosed contra-survival actions against the group. He must have undisclosed 'overts' and 'withholds'. The Sea Org was not going to invest the time of a trained Auditor to help us find our evil hidden acts with the E-Meter. We would have to do it ourselves and were given a huge list of items to study, check sheet style.

It was during this time that I read what Hubbard wrote about what lies in place for the Sea Org member who leaves. He is a 'degraded being' or DB looked on by former colleagues as a lower and weaker form of humanity. 'Let them go and smoke pot,' he wrote. 'They couldn't make it in the Sea Org because they just aren't up to making it in life.'

So it was either find the 'ethical' situation that was making me want to leave or join the gutter ranks of society. I found Hubbard's statements deeply troubling; I began to really question my motives and to worry a lot about doing badly and failing in life outside Scientology.

I had plenty of time to contemplate these things as we carried out many different kinds of tasks around Saint Hill Castle. These ranged from painting an old boat shed at Stonelands, to barrowing out huge piles of rubbish from the half constructed west wing. I liked the work. It was mentally taxing in a completely different way to the office work and I loved being out in the fresh air.

A week later Charlene, who was the Executive over all Hubbard Communications Offices in the UK, walked up to me and looked me purposefully in the eye. "You still want to leave?" she said.

I told her I did.

Then she said in an almost nonchalant tone: "I don't think you will". And she smiled.

To this day I do not know what it was about her response, whether she used a very clever psychological trick, or maybe it was purely an emotional response, but I felt something change in me. In that instant, I agreed.

I heard myself say it: "OK, I don't want to leave."

That was it; the desire was gone, just like that.

A near defector like me is often taken off administration and put onto physical work where a person can see the results of what they are doing. I was left with the Estates team and I loved the job. I was able to do work and see what was happening in front of me, I was in total control of what I did, whether it was picking up a pile of horse manure with the tractor and trailer, chain-sawing fallen trees or being trained to install banks of strip-lighting in the castle.

For the first time I felt in control of what I was doing in the Scientology world. I was more dedicated than ever to the Church and its leaders.

Six

TIME TRAVEL

"What do you see?" Peter asks and I scramble around in a state of semi-awareness to try to find anything at all in my mind.

My eyes are closed and I am sitting in a mild trance hooked up to the E-Meter. "All I can see is green," I say, trying to find something in the darkness.

I have spent hours in auditing sessions like this and so far I haven't been able to break through into any of my past lives. I desperately want to find this elusive world that is at the core of practicing Scientology.

"Keep looking. What do you see?" he asks again.

This time there is something there and as I concentrate I realise that a bizarre scene is now playing out in my mind.

"Desert," I suddenly tell him.

"Good. What else?" he says.

"Sandblasted rock formations are falling rapidly behind me. Everything is tinted green."

"Look again, what is happening?" Peter urges me.

"It is bright. The midday sun is beating down on me. There is a weight on my back," I say.

"What is the weight?" asks Peter.

"It is the carry strap of a heavy sub-machine gun and it is cutting into my shoulder," I say. "My desert goggles are protecting my eyes and that is what is giving a green tint to the terrain."

I tell Peter about the canvass like webbing I can feel on the seat underneath me. I tell him I am in a big, stripped down, open jeep. I'm not driving but it jolts and bashes as we speed over a rudimentary track in a dry North African desert. I somehow know it is 8000 years ago and I'm in what is now Tunisia.

Eventually he stops me. "That's it, your needle is floating," he says in a congratulatory tone.

I shake my head and open my eyes. I am a bit confused as to why there was modern military equipment in an ancient land but yet I am elated because the E-Meter needle has floated and that means I have finally got there – I have broken through the veil that separates this life from our previous incarnations.

That first past life memory was a defining moment for me in my Scientology career. It cemented my commitment to what I had signed up to. Since that first time I had read Hubbard's book 'Have You Lived Before This Life' in Stuttgart, I had been utterly fascinated by the concept of past lives and the promise the Church gives of a way to journey back to them. Now it had finally worked, I was exhilarated by the experience.

It was at Saint Hill that I was truly exposed to this 'religious counselling', used in Scientology to free a convert from traumatic past experiences and put them on the road to Clear. My subsequent auditing sessions took me on similar tours of Ancient Earth and outer space. I could see and even smell all elements of the fantastic pictures playing out in my head. Each session became a huge adventure which was encouraged and confirmed by the E-Meter.

"Remember a time you couldn't communicate?"

Suddenly, I am cold and very frightened.

Peter is asking me: "What is it that you see?"

I tell him: "I'm sitting on an asteroid in outer space and I see the form of a huge white spaceship not far below me, up against a larger piece of rock."

The meter registers something significant and Peter asks: "What has happened?" "Something very bad has happened and I am dead," I reply

"Tell me more?" he says.

"There is something horrific in the spaceship that has killed everyone. I have left my body and I'm sitting here on an asteroid, feeling sad, confused and frightened," I say.

I can see and sense everything from the absolute blackness of deep space to the brilliant, harsh, cold light from the sun. It bounces off the skin of the ship and outlines the group of asteroids. It is like an incredibly vivid dream and yet I am awake and conscious. We deal with my sense of horror, and once more, with the needle floating, we end session.

Another time Peter asks me to think of a loss. I find myself looking down on an oriental pagoda-like structure, nestling among green hills. I have a sense of deep calm and peacefulness. I have just died and I know that I am a Tibetan or Taoist monk. I am taking a last look at my monastic home before I move on to assume a new identity, beginning a life cycle anew.

This is a strangely life affirming memory.

During those auditing sessions the memories were as real, if not more so, than the memory I have of taking the helm of our boat, back in the summer of 1977 and struggling to keep her on course when Frank went below to make a mug of tea.

What were these memories? I know only that they were, for me, a glimpse of places that I had never been to, and a person that I am not now, and until then, had not encountered. It was spooky. It was exciting but most of all it was confirmation that the promises of Scientology were true.

When I made this breakthrough into past lives for the first time it was my first major step on the Bridge which promised salvation from this eternal cycle of life. I fully and totally believed Hubbard's 'tech' and never once questioned how he had come up with this therapy.

Early auditing sessions, in most cases, stop at childhood. It can take quite some time to break through that boundary into the 'Alice in Wonderland' place where reality and illusion are blurred. My early auditing was very useful for me. My auditor, an ex-British Army corporal and former Hell's Angel, had started by asking me to remember a time I had a pain in my foot. I'd talked about the last time I had something wrong with my foot and we'd torn the incident apart. The E-Meter needle reaction had alerted the auditor that there was something there to look into.

Again, he'd asked me to go back further, to another time that I had pain in my foot. I'd recalled what I could from my memory and found another time that I had fallen, or dropped something or stood on glass or whatever. We'd analysed that incident until it had been fully stripped down. But still the E-Meter had indicated that there was more.

Over those two and a half hour sessions I'd slowly brought myself back to my childhood and Scotland and the real trauma that sat buried within me. I recalled one time when I jumped on a nail while my parents were arguing and it went up through my foot. Through this process of deeply analysing an incident, we'd deciphered that I had done it on purpose, to stop my parents fighting and it had worked.

Another time, while 'remembering a time' I had fainted, I was brought back to a similar incident, which I had forgotten. I had fainted during a row at home, causing my parents to break up their shouting match and tend to me.

I had long thought I was quite a stupid child who suffered from bad reading and poor communication skills. Through the therapy, I was seeing that child in a completely different light. From the sessions, an intelligent and deep-thinking being emerged. One who could work out how to manipulate a situation but simply couldn't articulate himself. It empowered me. I'd gained a deeper understanding of myself and how I had evolved from that damaged home in Scotland.

I found a series of processes called The Objectives to be very helpful too. Through a series of auditing sessions and very controlled exercises, I seemed to gain more of an understanding of my physical self. These exercises involved moving around a room and undertaking very specific actions directed by my auditor. "Pick up the bottle," he would say. I would lift an empty wine bottle, replace it on the table and then carry out the same command for a book lying next to it.

I would run these commands for hours, often with little happening. Then all of a sudden I would feel different. No doubt the repetition, combined with indoctrination, was making its mark on my mind.

I felt like I had gained better spatial awareness from the process. For someone who had spent long periods feeling disassociated, this was a fantastic 'gain' or realisation. I thought I was more capable of controlling the objects in my world. It appeared to me that my driving improved greatly. After grasping the concept, I had the feeling that I could see further ahead on a road than I ever had before. My judgement about where I was and what I needed to do to get to the next place, felt like it improved dramatically too.

Shortly after these auditing sessions I was in a car driving to Plymouth, speeding down country roads. I felt I had a fantastic sense of clarity and thought that I was operating the vehicle utterly focused in the here and now. It was one of those early spring days where the weather can change in an instant, with dark, heavy clouds moving in and out of the sunlight. While the conditions should have been difficult, I thought that I was automatically adjusting my driving and the vehicle for each change in conditions. As I came down a hill I saw a huge line of traffic backed behind a tractor and trailer. My spatial awareness appeared to be so good that I was able to look, measure and work out exactly when I needed to overtake to get past. All the other drivers were honking their horns and looking at me incredulously as I flew by them. But I never had any doubt that I was going to make it. I just know how I felt behind the wheel of that Ford Estate hire car that day. It was wonderful. The new awareness also seemed to help me read maps better, something that I had difficulty with in the past.

These experiences made me feel really good about myself. I got the sense that the capacity a human has for doing things is really very large but we just don't know how to tap into it. Scientology instilled the belief that it had given me the tools I needed to improve and to operate on a higher level – just as Hubbard had promised.

It was the same for celebrity members. Over the years I heard Tom Cruise saying how Scientology helped him with a learning difficulty. Kirstie Alley was converted to Scientology while on the Purification Rundown Course, which she stated, helped her quit cocaine. When John Travolta joined in 1974 his career was on a downer and he credited the Scientology system with getting it back on track. These celebrities often spoke about the effectiveness of Hubbard's techniques – or 'tech' for short. We'd all avidly read the Scientology in-house Celebrity magazine which told their success stories. I remember finding a book at one stage in the Saint Hill library which contained the testament of a British golfer in the 1970s. He had been a big star but his game was suffering. He did a lot of the same lower level auditing I was doing. He described how during his auditing he was told to look at the golf course and to turn the grass blue and the trees yellow and the holes red and all of a sudden everything became very clear to him. It meant that he could do anything he wanted with that golf course. It did not control him; he controlled it. He explained that he used the technique while competing and it seemed to heighten his control of the ball to such an extent that he credited the process with giving him his form back.

That day when I found myself in the desert of

Tunisia, 8,000 years ago, I moved to a different level with Scientology. From then on in auditing sessions, I travelled back in time on a regular basis as I headed towards that dream ticket – the 'State of Clear'.

My feelings of disillusion when I had told Rolf I wanted to leave were now totally forgotten. My arrival at Saint Hill had marked my most lucid time since my recruitment to Scientology in Stuttgart. Ironically, within a few months the intensive auditing I was undergoing had made me more dedicated than ever to the Hubbard 'Tech' that ruled my life. All thoughts of leaving were firmly abandoned as I became more and more immersed in the strange counselling that promised me superhuman powers.

I accepted that Hubbard had built thought control into the whole complex pattern of Scientology. I knew that attaining levels also involved confessing sins, which were any bad thoughts about the organisation, its senior managers or its founder. Sexual thoughts were banned and deeds, including masturbation, were stringently over-analysed during mentally exhausting sessions. E-Meter checks were done weekly. Every Friday we queued up to be 'put on the meter' and were asked a series of leading questions. Any digressions showed up as the needle reacted and all confessions were fully written up and added to each Scientologist's ethics file. It was a pain having to queue up every Friday but we accepted it in the same way we accepted everything else in our strange world.

Following my attempt to leave Saint Hill, I'd been left with the Estates Organisation and I was still working there. It was a job I really liked. We were charged with looking after the grounds and off-base buildings where staff were housed. For our 98 hour working week, we were paid between Stg£15 and Stg£55.

The organisation owned three properties, all within a five mile radius of Saint Hill. This was where the bulk of the Sea Org crew lived. I lived for a while in Brook House but moved to Stonelands, when a berth became available. It was the largest of the three and was located about a mile from the tiny hamlet of West Hoathly. It was once a beautiful, big 16th Century mansion. Under the Church of Scientology it had become an overcrowded slum. At least 100 people were living there, in big ballrooms that had been crudely converted into dormitories. Two showers served the men and two served the women and the place was absolutely grotty. One guy, an old Indian fellow called Joe was obviously suffering from dementia. He often used to just get into the shower fully dressed when he wanted to wash his clothes.

Transportation fell under the responsibility of Estates and we had assembled a fleet of old vans and buses. There were still a lot of young kids around and they had to be bussed up to school in the morning and then back to the Stonelands' nursery in the afternoons. This was a grim converted shed, surrounded by chicken wire, where the little ones spent their afternoons and evenings before being sent off to bed, well before their parents came home. Once they could walk, all Sea Org children joined the Cadet Org at Saint Hill which had its own Commanding Officer, executive structure and uniforms. They had to earn money to fund their Org so the children would be hired to wash cars, help with filing projects and clean buildings. Money would go to each child's weekly Financial Planning and 'set asides' would be made to pay for rare school trips, treats and often uniforms. Once they turned 12, they were

not called children. Instead they were referred to as
'Cadets'. At Saint Hill they normally had to wait until
they were 15 to start their EPF. I would often see these
young teenagers drilling and working around the base.
They were then fully exposed to all the Scientology
administrative and ethics 'tech' that we were living
under. It made me think back to LA and how tough
I'd found the gruelling regime in the Complex. Most
of the mothers tried to do as much as they could for
the children but the long days, often from 8am until
midnight, seven days a week, didn't leave much time
for their nurture and care

If Stonelands was bad, Brook House was even
worse. Located close to East Grinstead, this rotting
pile housed at least 70 Sea Org staff and also for a time
took in trainees from the Class V organisations (these
mission offices can offer courses and auditing up to
a certain level) dotted around the United Kingdom.
Then there was Bullards, a fine and graceful country
residence on almost ten acres of neglected land. The
four bathrooms and small kitchen were completely
inadequate for the 60 people who squeezed into its five
bedrooms and converted dining and living rooms each
night. The most senior executives lived in a converted
stable block on the Saint Hill grounds.

On Estates we were responsible for the maintenance
of these properties but it was always just a patch-up job.
The Church never seemed to have the money to pump
into facilities for its workers. We looked after the roofs,
the plumbing and the electrical wiring, but each of the
properties needed to be gutted. A few years later the
Church ended up being prosecuted for failing to ensure
Stonelands was safe for human habitation. An article
in 'The Independent', claimed that the newspaper was

'leaked documents from the Church headquarters that showed it may have misled safety inspectors over the number of adults and children living in the commune'. It went on to report that environmental health officers had been led to believe only 50 people were living at the house but the real total numbered 130. Money was supplied by International Management as a loan the following year, to buy up a former boarding school complex in Crowborough. This was fitted out to house 300 Sea Org members and about 20 Cadets. That same year the Church pulled the children out of mainstream education and set up their own in-house school at the new property.

To supplement my income on Estates I started working even longer hours. I helped out at the public canteen where Scientologists from Germany and the US, studying OT levels, were fed. The canteen paid me up to Stg£50 but must have violated every health and safety rule ever written. We would often go down to the staff dining facility, take their leftovers and then re-serve the food to the public scientologists.

The Estates Commanding Officer was a lovely, old, Chinese-Australian called Mick. He got my purchase order approved, so that I could do my British driving test as I couldn't get insured on my American licence. Unknown to him at the time, it gave me the extra tools I needed to get myself out of Estates. I wanted to move on to a much more attractive Organisation, one that I had been closely monitoring since my decision to stay in the Church.

Tours Organisation was by far the best place to be. Tours sold big auditing packages, worth tens of thousands of pounds; everything from The Objectives to Clear and all of the OT levels. They targeted any public person they could and were charged with encouraging business in the Orgs and Missions throughout the UK. They also sold an awful lot of books and Mission Starter packages. This was a very attractive and lucrative job due to the 15% commission given on all books and materials sold. A good Tours Registrar could potentially, and often did, make Stg£3000 a week.

The Commanding Officer, a Scotsman called Craig Mathieson, was the epitome of cool, and I knew I wanted to work with him. He was a charismatic ex-70s rock musician. He owned a Mercedes, had a swanky office and would not accept the conditions the majority of Sea Org members lived in at that time. As he had show business connections and was pulling in a fortune for the Church, something like 90 per cent of the income for Saint Hill, he was largely left to his own devices. He had managed to refurbish part of the stables at Bullards berthing house for himself, his wife Karen and their kids. He treated his staff quite well and was known to throw them a few bob extra to buy decent clothes and maybe even go out once in a while.

His wife, Karen, was a senior executive holding the position of Deputy Commanding Officer Internal in the Commodore's Messenger Organisation – one of the highest management structures on each Scientology base. She worked directly for Ginger Smith, the Commanding Office Commodore's Messenger Organisation UK. Ginger had been a dancer in the musical 'Hair' before she got into Scientology and rose up the ranks fairly quickly. As she and her husband Greg lived in a spacious apartment at the stables, they were the focus of a bit of jealousy. They were some of the very tiny percent of people in the Church who were smart enough to work the system.

I was no salesman and Craig had the best working for him. But still I was determined. I went to his office one day and told him that I wanted to work for him, firstly as an assistant and then eventually as a sales registrar. Craig took a liking to me because of my Scottish childhood and as a Scot himself, he wanted an all-Scottish team in his office. He agreed to my proposal and got me transferred.

The Tours Organisation opened up a whole new world for me. Craig was a fantastic musician and had once recorded with Paul McCartney. His contacts in the music and show business industry were of huge importance to the Church, which has always nurtured celebrity. He was an attractive guy and the women seemed to fall for him. On one occasion I watched him deal with the antics of a wealthy Lebanese divorcee, Lana, who was the daughter of a rich sheik. She drove a gold-painted Porsche and was madly in love with him. She would often pop into the Tours, with her even wealthier brother, buy hundreds of thousands of pounds worth of packages and shower Craig with gifts. Sometimes he would go on a sales trip to London with her and it inevitably emerged that they were having an affair. Craig was not RPFed as most people would have been because he was just too valuable. The income statistics would have crashed to disastrous levels if he was not on post. He got a slap on the wrist and Lana was persuaded to take the rest of her courses at the Fort Harrison in Florida.

I wasn't long working for him when we all got invited down to Stringfellows nightclub in London. The Church were delighted to be seen to have Stringfellows on board. We were sent with high hopes for the PR that might ensue. Peter Stringfellow's wife at the time was the organiser and I had to drive Craig's car down to London because he was drinking. We parked the Merc next to the place and went in. My eyes must have been out on stalks staring at the girls serving cocktails in their bikinis with their long legs and gorgeous figures. Craig performed on stage that night and I always remember Stringfellow's wife gazing up at him. She was wearing a flimsy, see-through dress. Unfortunately, nothing came from the connection with Stringfellows.

Craig looked after me and I fitted in. With my bleached hair and cool clothes, thanks to the money he threw me, I managed to match the image he wanted. Although I was still in dorms, I was better dressed than the other guys. I had also inherited Craig's old Mercedes after he upgraded to a newer model and there was a distinct undercurrent of jealousy towards me. I was not overly concerned about it though.

Craig was planning to set up a 'Music Org' and had taken over an old barn by the stables. He set it up as a rehearsal room for the band he had formed called 'Spirit of Play'. He was grooming me to eventually take over his job. It is a fact that if you want someone to sell Scientology, that person needs to have a personal reality on what they are selling. Without this, Craig believed the salesman would not be sufficiently convinced of the value of the product to get people to part with the very large sums of money involved. It was primarily this that motivated him to pull strings to get me audited to Clear.

Although staff members are supposed to get auditing as recompense for long hours and hard work with very little pay, the reality is that delivering auditing is a time intensive and expensive job. Every session has to be reviewed by a Case Supervisor who guides and corrects the auditor. If the auditor messes up, he has to go to 'cramming' where he is interviewed by a technical training expert and given a series of policies to study. Time is money and proper auditor training takes time and costs money. As a result I had realised that Sea Org and staff members got very little true auditing. After spending a few months in Saint Hill I'd resigned myself to the fact that most of my Bridge Progress would be done while I was used as a guinea pig for the trainee auditors to learn their skills. Craig changed that.

I could never have afforded to pay for proper auditing myself so Craig's gift was a fantastic bonus to me and I was thrilled to get started. I quickly started to move up the grades, as I became quite expert and addicted to finding my past life experiences deep within my mind. Unfortunately for Craig, his interest and investment in me would never pay off. Instead it would result in my being poached from under his nose by Central Marketing International back in LA.

It was still not a year since I had stood in the Hollywood Palladium and watched David Miscavige deliver the news of Hubbard's demise. A lot had been going on behind the scenes at the secret Sea Org compound in Hemet, California since then. It was a Monday and an otherwise regular working day, when a very unusual bulletin arrived at Saint Hill for the eyes of Sea Org staff only. Craig looked very disturbed when he read it. He was OT III and had been in the Sea Org since 1979. He had seen some pretty heavy stuff in his time but he said that this was something else all together.

The memo stated that Pat Broeker had lied about his appointment as 'Successor to the Founder'. It told us that he and his wife, Annie, were now off post and 'being handled'. Broeker, we were informed, was not a high level Lieutenant of Hubbard's as he had claimed. He had merely been an Estates man carrying out menial tasks like driving, house repairs and provisioning. Miscavige had discovered the extent of his deceit and moved swiftly to correct this astounding perversion of the Founder's actual wishes and intentions. Miscavige had since assumed the post of COB RTC or Chairman of the Board of the Religious Technology Centre the highest ecclesiastical authority in the Church of Scientology.

The title 'Loyal Officer', which Broeker had given to Miscavige on the Palladium stage, was an invention, according to Miscavige. The bulletin went on to say that this title and any position or power that Broeker had assumed was hereby cancelled.

In other words Miscavige had stepped into L Ron Hubbard's boots.

This limited distribution Flag Order sent shock waves through the Scientology world. I looked to Craig to measure my own reaction to it and found he was deeply perturbed. He immediately sat down and penned a personal letter to Miscavige demanding that he explain himself further.

The reply he got essentially told him to shut up and not rock the boat.

As David Miscavige began to consolidate his powerbase within the Scientology Corporation, we realised he was going to run an even tighter ship to achieve his goals. One of the first directives he issued as Chairman of the Board was a decree that Sea Org members could no longer have children. While Sea Org could still actively recruit existing family units, those who were in the paramilitary ranks had to forget about becoming parents themselves. It was seen as a distraction to the work that had to be done to 'Clear the Planet'. From this point on it was considered an ethics offence for a woman to get pregnant. The 'handling' for this offence would be devastating. The choice given to the expectant mother was either abortion or banishment to a struggling Class V Org – the non-Sea Org Scientology centres found in major cities.

With low Sea Org pay, couples often did not have the money for contraceptives. Many were teenagers when they got married and simply were not educated in the realities of life. In the space of a year eight couples, totally unequipped for the job, ended up being moved out of Saint Hill to run 'outer orgs'.

When my friend Susan became pregnant with her first child, herself and her husband were moved from top posts on the base and placed in a remote Scientology Centre. They were not allowed to work in a 'wog' job as they were Sea Org members. Nor were they allowed to take social welfare, as that was 'criminal exchange'. They had to make the little centre make money so that they could rent a flat and feed themselves and the child. They lived well below the poverty line.

I was sent down to them on a brief project and was disgusted at how degraded they looked, how dirty they appeared and how badly their little Church was doing. It served as a lesson for all of us to keep our noses clean.

For people whose self-esteem was inextricably linked to their standing as a senior Sea Organisation Executive, being sent out to these little organisations to produce more money and deliver new Scientologists for good 'stats' was crushing. The natural urge to give birth and nurture a baby was now treated as an ethics offence, on par with embezzlement or theft. Many took the option to undergo forced abortions. One woman had two abortions in a year. Later I witnessed women weeping on the grounds of Saint Hill and in the management HQ in Los Angeles. They were on senior Sea Org posts and were not being given the option to go to a Class V org. They were being forced by the ethics section to have an abortion. I also heard how a senior auditor at Saint Hill divorced his wife when she fell pregnant.

In March 1987, I was promoted to Petty Officer 3rd Class, beginning the long road to Officer Status. It meant little in terms of privileges and conditions, but it was important for a Sea Org Member's self-esteem. Central Marketing Unit International (CMU) had been formed in late 1986 in LA. It was tasked with creating a whole new image for Scientology and enticing an influx of public Scientologists onto Church services. A confidential brief that I read at the time gave an unusually honest picture of the state of Scientology internationally. Staff morale was very low, the average income per organisation had crashed to below 1979 levels, few people were being recruited and when they did join, they were not staying around very long. David Miscavaige had ordered a huge push for Scientology to really get it out there. Every Sea Org continent had to provide a certain amount of recruits to get back to the Complex and drive the ship.

My statistics were good, I was doing well on the auditing and deemed to be progressing well in Scientology. With my new promotion it meant that I was one of the few people who were considered for the transfer to America. As application of Scientology auditing, training and ethics was supposed to create observable improvements in IQ, personality and behaviour, our progress was monitored by testing. The full battery of tests was required whenever we were considered for promotion, a new posting or a transfer. I was given a new series of tests, including the Personality Test and I scored quite highly, including around 130 in the IQ range.

At the time, I was also facing recruitment to a job I loathed. They wanted to post me in local management, which as far as I could see would be a horrible administrative job. I had been sent on a lot of missions to UK Scientology Organisations and was spending less and less time working in the Tours Office. Sea Org missions are normally short-term, special projects ordered by management to accomplish specific tasks. They can include teams being sent out for anything from the purchase of new properties to infiltration of enemy organisations. Personnel can be taken from any unit and when I was ordered to go, I had no choice but to comply. I had carried out five such missions, back to back, and I felt there was a danger of my being transferred out of Tours Org into the much less desirable Continental Liaison Management Office. Being transferred to Central Marketing International would not only avoid that, but it was also a good career move. Despite Craig's unhappiness that I was leaving him, I felt I had to take my opportunities when they came up. I was delighted when I was offered a post in marketing in LA. I would only be given specific details about it when I got there.

I packed up and left Saint Hill a few weeks later, on a flight paid for by Central Marketing International. As the aeroplane took off I was filled with a sense of

excitement and anticipation about a new phase of my
Sea Org career.

Back at the Complex life was completely different
to my earlier experience. International Marketing Org
was on a different level altogether to most of the other
Orgs there. Central Marketing Unit was an 'Int' level
org. This meant that it would normally function from
the secret base in Hemet. But that was too far away from
the real world and we had to interact with the 'wog'
world in a big way. We had to poll everybody, from
printers and designers to students at UCLA, to find
out what made them tick. We were not subjected to the
heavy ethics of the lower level organisations and had
modern offices, with modern furniture and glass doors.
We also had better dorms. To mark our importance we
got the best uniforms. I had brand new everything and
wore full US naval-styled dress and working whites.
We were recognised everywhere we went and were
the envy of the place, dressed as we were like Richard
Gere in 'An Officer and a Gentleman'. As an added
bonus, we received a full pay allowance of $35 a week, a
luxury that staff in many of the other organisations that
peopled the vast Complex could only dream about.

I was posted in the Research Branch. Ries and Ries,
a major marketing company in the US, had carried
out a review of the 'Scientology brand' and they had
recommended bottom up overhaul. Their brief was
to make it more appealing to the general public. A
report they carried out on public awareness of what
Scientology had to offer made for grim reading. It
showed that it was way below 1 per cent and those few
people who did know about it had a bad impression.
It advised that the idea of 'Church' was driving people
away in droves and that the only way to attract new

business was to drop the religious thing.

Chairman of the Board, David Miscavige, didn't like the findings. Our status as a Church was vital. It protected our assets from being taxed and allowed us to import staff from abroad to work in the USA under 'The Religious Worker' visa system. It also allowed us to plead 'religious discrimination' in the many ongoing court cases still being prosecuted against our religious community. We would also be seen as a business and staff would have to be paid at least the minimum wage. The religious cloaking made good business sense to Church management so not long after they were hired, Ries and Ries were dropped. However, CMU continued to work on aspects of the re-branding recommendations that did not affect the organisation's standing as a 'Church'.

In the research branch of CMU, our first major remit was to corner 5 per cent of the world book market, a Hubbard strategy that had failed during his lifetime. The paperback book 'Dianetics: The Modern Science of Mental Health' was to be the spearhead of the new marketing campaign. The cover and dowdy 1970s layout was vamped up, with bright colours and big embossed lettering. The artwork had to feature the volcano but everything else was changed. Inside it was newly typeset, with a clear layout, new fonts and lots more explanations and an easy to use index. This new version was launched at the Indianapolis 500 car race during the spring of 1988. We sponsored a car and used it and the driver, Roberto Garriro, in a morale boosting campaign for staff and public, on posters, in TV adverts and for an ad placement in 'Publishers Weekly'.

On the day of the race all the top Scientology executives were at the track. The car was a fire engine red, emblazoned with the Dianetics logo. Sky and NBC did a segment on us, as it was the first time a car had been used to promote a book. Garriro set off with millions across America watching. It was a breakthrough moment for all of us – we were out there, we were proud and we were winning.

The car crashed after the second circuit.

After that, we bought slots at big baseball games to advertise Hubbard's 'Dianetics: The Modern Science of Mental Health'. We backed Scientologist Charles Lake, a gymnast and the Olympic gold medallist, and featured him in full-page adverts in sports, computer and health magazines.

We took all the rest of Hubbard's books and repackaged them with bright and exciting new covers. The cover design for 'The Fundamentals of Thought' was a picture of a tree with the reflection as a nuclear bomb. It was quite a striking cover and carefully researched. 'The Dynamics of Life' was redesigned, with a chain breaking over the cover.

Our research into our target audience indicated that 18-35 year old college students or graduates were our main market. They were people interested in self-help and we used that phrase extensively. We dubbed 'Dianetics: The Modern Science of Mental Health' 'the number one self-help best seller'. We targeted high income bracket earners, pulling in over $80,000 a year. We advertised in New Age magazines, sports and computer publications, plugging Dianetics as the new up and coming thing. Our work brought a huge amount of new interest and Church statistics began to respond.

We were also charged with promoting Scientology front organisations like Narconon, our rehabilitation programme for drug addicts and alcoholics. Its most avid supporter was Kirstie Alley who said she had a cocaine addition problem until 1979, when she joined Scientology. It is not the only front organisation operating under the umbrella group, the Association for better Living and Education. Others include Criminon, which was involved in reforming prisoner reform through Scientology. All of them try to hide their Scientology connection until they have hooked the recruit. We were aware of this and knew we had to be careful about revealing the Church's involvement.

We did some work for WISE, Hubbard's brain child. It was designed to tap into the many Scientologists who ran businesses. They were allowed to use Hubbard's ground-breaking administrative technology, but had to pay a license fee of 10% of their earnings. If you were a Scientologist running a business using any other system, then you were quite obviously 'out ethics'. Incredible pressure would be put on you to 'see the light' and get 'on source' with L Ron Hubbard's breakthrough administrative technology.

We also worked with celebrities as much as possible. The film 'Look Who's Talking' was riding on a wave of late 1980s fame and had given huge career boosts to both John Travolta and Kirstie Alley. They were bolstering one another's careers and were, then, our most high profile stars so they were signed up for as much as they would do. John Travolta had certainly given the go ahead to use his image on some Dianetics adverts and Kirstie Alley was weighing in behind Narcanon in a big way. Charles Lake was used again in a series of TV adverts, as he was then on the Purification Rundown at Celebrity Centre Los Angeles. Paul Haggis, of 'Crash' fame, directed the ads, along with Jeff Hawkins, the brains behind Central Marketing International and our head of production.

I enjoyed the work despite the long hours. I had two very close friends in the job, Tom and Chuck. Tom was a Canadian but his mother was German so he spoke the language fluently. We had fun with that and it became our own code. That winter we were all provided with a complete kit of winter dress blue uniforms with dark Burberry-styled over coats and warm 'Bridge Coats' for less formal wear. Tom and I had a laugh with this one night when we dressed up in full Class A Blues, caps, leather gloves, overcoats and shiny shoes. We looked quite imposing and when it got dark we goose-stepped across the big parking lot bordering Sunset Boulevard, fingers over our upper lips and singing 'Deutschland, Deutschland uber Alles'. We cracked ourselves up. Then we went to the local Denny's for a late night coffee, barging in the doors and scaring the waitress. We pretended to speak only rudimentary English the whole time and really wound up the poor staff on duty that night. Had we been found out, we would have been in severe ethics trouble for 'joking and degrading'. Scientology does not do humour very well.

Toward the end of 1988, David Miscavige was anxious to develop full control over the marketing operation. He wanted to consolidate Marketing with the in-house film and recording organisation, called Gold, at the secret church HQ, the sprawling, former golf club. It was situated near the town of Hemet in San Jacinto County, about two hours drive beyond Pasadena. The reaction in the office was mixed; many didn't want to move to the high-security base, while others saw it as an opportunity to mix with the big wigs. I had heard that everyone spied on everyone else there and that the perimeter was surrounded by a razor-wire fence and armed security. For me, a fast expiring visa meant there was no decision. As my colleagues underwent excruciating security checks to get a pass for the Gold base, I was set to return to the UK.

The extensive vetting and preparation could involve four or five months of ethics handlings and security checks. It was a thorough examination of their entire lives, covering every sexual contact, any drugs taken and an examination of all friends, family members, schools and colleges attended and religious affiliations. I was actually grateful that my visa was running out. While my friends spent hours attached to E-Meters, painstakingly analysing their every action, I helped pack up and transport the office to Hemet. I of course was not 'cleared' for Gold, so I would often take a lorry load of documents to a pre-arranged location, swap trucks with a driver from Hemet and head back to the Complex. It was very James Bond and typical of the paranoia that sections of the organisation seemed to thrive on.

I was loading up a truck one day when I encountered Miscavige for the first time. It was an unnerving experience. I had parked my truck in 'the horseshoe', close to the front door of the Complex and run up to get some stuff. When I came back down a security guard, a Cherokee Indian, told me: "COB was here. You blocked his parking space."

Not too worried I got into the truck and started to reverse. I pulled back out onto Catalina, aiming to park up in the big lot on Sunset. Suddenly, Miscavige was standing in the middle of the road, in front of the truck. He stared at me with the most piercing eyes I have ever seen. I sat there looking at him and realising that it was the Chairman of the Board. I felt a bit nervous and wondered if he wanted to talk. He just kept standing on the road, staring through the windscreen, with a cold, malevolent look. He stood motionless like that, without blinking, for more than seven minutes. Then he turned on his heel and walked away. Although he is small in stature and I was way up above him in a big truck, it was very obvious which one of us was in charge that day. I was relieved that I was flying back to the UK instead of moving in with him in Hemet.

It was a full year since I had seen Saint Hill and I was happy to be headed back there. I was looking forward to seeing green trees and grass again, but I really hoped that accommodation had improved in my absence.

I was posted to the Central Marketing UK branch office and began getting stuck into local marketing research work. Within a few short months the Marketing/Gold consolidation was completed. The continental branch offices were considered redundant and were shut down. I was made jobless over night. I ended up being swallowed by the Continental Liaison Management Office. I lost my 'Int level' status and became 'just another crew member'. In between uninspiring filing and administrative tasks, I was sent on various missions all over the UK.

It was on one mission to Scotland that I uncovered information about the power struggle that had blown up at the top level of the Church, just as I was signing up. Scotland always had an uncomfortable relationship with Scientology and had not allowed it to operate as a Church. In Edinburgh, we had a separate corporation, The Hubbard's Academy of Personal Independence. It was run in exactly the same way as our churches elsewhere in the UK and across the globe, although it was ostensibly not a Church of Scientology. As a result of this it was used as a storage space for highly sensitive documents. That way the Church could distance itself from the files if they were ever found.

Over my few years as a Scientologist I had heard of the Guardians Office and of course had read about it when Joachim showed me the newspaper article in Stuttgart. I knew about the huge FBI investigation that had almost destroyed the Church but I had never paid close attention to what really went on as a result of that. The aftermath of Operation Snow White and the subsequent incarceration of 11 Guardians Office officials, including Mary Sue Hubbard, had been written out of the Church's history. All we had ever been told was that the Guardians Office was disbanded by David Miscavige. This was after it went power mad and a group of 'Guardians' decided to take the law into their own hands. In 1982 Miscavige, we were told, had wiped out the old order and set up the new Scientology Corporate Structure. As all Scientologists knew, the Office of Special Affairs had taken on the functions that the GO had previously been responsible for.

Miscavige had used old policies of Hubbards to rid himself of these enemies. He 'Declared' countless top level Scientologists around the world 'Suppressive Persons'. As I had discovered when my friend Julie was 'Declared' SP, it is the ultimate condemnation by the Church. The top level Scientologists could no longer practice Scientology or have any contact whatsoever with Church members, including their immediate families.

Among the hundreds of officials 'Declared' during the purge, which ran from 1979 until late 1983, was a man called David Mayo. I had heard his name before but was under the impression that he was a low level Scientologist who had tried to break away from the Church and set up his own organisation using the 'tech'. What utterly stunned me was to discover that Mayo was far from low level. Instead I found out that he had been Hubbard's personal auditor and case supervisor. Mayo had long been seen as the natural heir to the Scientology throne.

The bombshell was dropped by Brian Henderson, a public Scientologist who had done some of his OT levels. I'd been sent to locate old Guardians Office documents and we got talking one day. He told me that the Scottish Church was still reeling from the corporate schism that had literally split it in half. Although he had remained on the Miscavige side, he'd watched as lifelong friends joined Mayo's English Independent Scientology Movement. They were all 'Declared' SPs. It split families and ruined friendships. There was not a man or woman in the Scientology community in Scotland who hadn't suffered enforced disconnection from a close personal friend or family member. About 15 years later I met a young woman who had been a three year old child when her mother was 'Declared' in 1982. She'd had no contact with the mother since that time.

In the boxes of old files I found more information about how Miscavige had handled the seat of the Guardians empire at Saint Hill. The files included the official Church of Scientology account and detailed how a mission, under Norman Starkey, had been sent to England to remove all GO officials. It recounted the story I had heard about how the GO had taken power into their own hands and acted alone, without Church authorisation. But the files also included witness accounts from missionaries and people who had been in the Guardian's Office. They conveyed the far more brutal scenario that had played out at East Grinstead. The accounts suggested that Miscavige had sent a team of heavies to Saint Hill. Their mission had been to clear out the GO, who were vehemently resisting 'new management'. Jane Kember had been in charge and, according to the statements, she still believed that she was one of Hubbard's 'Guardians'. She was adamant that she wouldn't be taken out without a fight. Kember and her staff barricaded themselves into Saint Hill and locked the doors. Miscavige's crew of 20 arrived and physically broke down the old doors. They then 'Declared' everyone in sight. Kember, who was later jailed, and her team, had to leave everything and flee.

I left Scotland feeling a bit rattled. I realised that there was more than met the eye about what had gone on in my Church while I was training in the Complex. I had got my first grasp of the corporate nature of the Church and a tiny insight into the intense power struggle that had taken place. It would take me a long time to fully understand Miscavige's palace coup and the scheming, lies and deceit that had gone on behind the scenes, as he consolidated his power base. It was not until I left Scientology that I truly understood how cutting out top people, such as Kember and Broeker, was the final act in a brutal takeover reminiscent of Stalin's rise to power in the 1930s.

As I left Edinburgh I couldn't understand why brilliant and effective marketing projects, drawn up by the Guardian's Office and filed away, all had to be dumped. It seemed that Miscavige was willing to throw the baby out with the bath water.

It was the first critical thinking I had ever applied

to the Church but I was still utterly convinced by Hubbard's teachings and the path I had chosen in life. As always, when I got back to Saint Hill, there were more new projects, long hours of intense work, auditing and group indoctrination to keep my mind fully occupied. It would take many more years before the seed of doubt really germinated.

SEVEN

An African adventure

By 1990, I was five years in the fold and since my recruitment I had only been on Irish soil once. This was for a fleeting sales visit to the Scientology centre in Dublin with Mick Wenlock. Mick was and is a big, gregarious, burley ex-biker, long since out of Scientology. He has a great sense of the ridiculous. I will never forget arriving off our flight from Luton to a dark, rainy Dublin. Mick insisted on making a pilgrimage to honour an ancient tradition before getting down to any work. We took the bus to the city centre and found a small pub, somewhere off O'Connell Street where I ordered us two pints of Guinness and a cheese and ham sandwich for Mick. In true Irish style we got two sandwiches, one cheese and one ham.

I had spent the previous two years working around the UK for the Continental Liaison Management Office doing market research and campaigns. I was also sent on special assignments to sort out problems in various

Scientology Churches, trying to drive up statistics and keep the money flooding in. During the summer of '89, I was posted to a line management post at Saint Hill. My main function was to analyse sales and promotional statistics from the seven Scientology Churches dotted around the UK. I had to send orders to each, based on the conclusions I came to from looking at the various trends. It was a mind-numbingly boring and pointless task. Despite the Founder's insistence that an accurate statistical analysis would solve all the organisational problems and cause a huge boom in income and delivery, the real reason these little churches remained impoverished was simply that the general public did not, never had and never would like Scientology. I came to this conclusion quite quickly but had enough sense to keep it to myself. I was frustrated, sitting at a cramped desk in front of piles of binders in a crowded office from nine in the morning until eleven thirty every night. It was a 14-hour day, broken only with 'team drilling', marching and reciting quotes from the Founder. It was not my idea of fun.

As the New Year rang in I resolved to get out of that posting in 1990 and on to a more challenging area. One night in the early hours when I sneaked outside for a cigarette with one of my colleagues, Tony, that chance came up. We often had to work late on Wednesday and into Thursday morning to get off big reports to LA. They had to be there for the Friday morning meeting of senior management, so they could access the health of the global operation. That night Tony mentioned that a mission was being put together to go to Zimbabwe. He advised me to throw my name in the hat. It sounded wonderful and like the break from the mundane I needed. The following day I put my name down on Tony's list. I then proceeded to badger and beg our new Commanding Officer, Jeannie Bogvad, the self-same former ASI Executive who had briefed us on Hubbard's last few years on this earth back in 1986. Africa was one of those places I had always wanted to get to. I was also aware that if I wanted to move my Sea Org career forward, I had better get some challenging field experience under my belt.

After much pleading, I was eventually told that the job was mine. My Mission In Charge was Edward Mallinson, a suave, 50-something, former Etonian and all round English gentleman. A well-invested, and carefully guarded, inheritance meant that he was able to keep a nice Jaguar, his pipe full of aromatic tobacco and himself clothed in tweeds, cardigans and quality brogues. As part of his normal duties he was in charge of the upkeep of the Manor, a job that suited him down to the ground. But he had an adventurous streak and a real love for Africa where he had spent much of his colourful youth.

We spent two weeks in an intensive briefing for the trip. We were told that it would be an observation mission to examine the state of the two Zimbabwean centres, Harare and Bulawayo. In the normal course of events any Church activities in Africa would have been run from the Sea Organisation Management base in Johannesburg, South Africa. The increasing tensions with De Klerk's government, however, had resulted in the communication traffic between the two countries being heavily monitored by Mugabe's secret police. The militaristic language Hubbard had evolved as part of the Church management style had drawn unwanted attention to Scientology in Zimbabwe. When messages were intercepted by Mugabe's police, phrases like 'for blood', 'over dead bodies' and 'take no prisoners' were not taken in the spirit in which they were intended. The result was that in 1984 several Sea Organisation executives had been imprisoned and eventually deported. This had led to a virtual information blackout for Scientology's International Management. Now, as a new decade dawned, the Church needed to go in there and assess the situation itself, regarding the possibility of expansion.

Usually a Sea Org Missionary visiting any Scientology operation would be dressed in full 'Class A' dress uniform, including our officer's cap and lanyards. I have to admit that I found this tradition acutely embarrassing whenever I was on assignment to the UK-based organisations. I often had to go for lunch or to a shop dressed up as if I had just come off the bridge of a naval vessel. So I was relieved to learn that we were not allowed to wear anything even vaguely nautical or military in Africa. We would be 'going native'. The two weeks 'mission briefing' was not very informative. We were shown the skimpy reports that had arrived every three months or so but they were practically illegible. We were given a laptop and codes to use and had to learn them off by heart. Our reports were to be written as if they were letters home to a friend in England. It was quite complicated and I was glad that Edward, as Mission In Charge, would be writing them.

We were ill-prepared for the scene on the ground out there. Our flight stopped in Addis Ababa giving us about a day to acclimatise ourselves to the strange and wonderful world that is Africa. I was taken aback to see so many very young looking Ethiopian soldiers patrolling the airport with lethal machine guns. Out on the runway our Air Zimbabwe 727 sat surrounded by a bunch of engineers. The plane had broken down because of some problem with a rear engine unit, and it looked like we were going nowhere fast. The engine was open and, as I watched, I saw one engineer get up on it bang it with a hammer and then shut down the cowling. Shortly afterwards we were directed to board. We both remained very tense until the flight was well underway and it was fairly clear that nothing was going to fall off.

Since the end of hostilities in 1979, Zimbabwe had been trapped in a time warp. The war had left the country practically bankrupt and unable to buy foreign goods. Most of the cars, buses and trucks on the roads were from the 1970s and looked really odd. The terminal building was like something from the set of Casablanca. We were picked up by George, an old friend of Edward's, and brought to his spacious bungalow in the suburb of Eastleigh. We were treated to a fine meal and, afterwards, as we sipped drinks and smoked cigars on the huge veranda, I realised I was going to like being in Africa.

Edward was pretty eccentric. He had completed OT Level V some years before and since then he had busied himself pottering about the Manor. He really didn't seem to care much for the church authorities. He never got terribly excited about Hubbard and his only family connection to Scientology was his wife. There seemed to be little love lost between them and as it happened, they divorced not long after we got back to England.

Scientology Zimbabwe was made up, in the main, of white Rhodesians, all of whom had been involved since the 1970's. They were, like the country itself, existing in a bit of a time warp. Most of them were living out the colonial dream in big spacious houses run by cheap labour and servants. We moved up to Bulawayo for a couple of months, staying with Tracy and Tom, who owned a fine restaurant on the dusty main street. We were treated like royalty. Servants looked after all our needs and we would dine at the restaurant for both lunch and dinner, making the odd foray out into the bush to view elephants and giraffes in the wild. Edward loved it. The pace suited him and he simply relished being back in Africa.

Driving to the office each day we would pass a white couple begging on the street. He had one leg. Tracy told me that they used to run a safari holiday camp up near Lake Kariba but that he had been attacked by a crocodile. On regaining consciousness he had found the croc biting into his leg; pulled out a knife and cut what was left of it off. After medical expenses the couple had nothing left. There was no such thing as social security in the country.

Unlike the beggars, Scientologists were fairly well off by Zimbabwean standards. While they, and we, could live very comfortably on their dollars, the money had no value in the outside world. That is where the problem lay for the Church. Scientology is all about moving people up 'The Bridge to Total Freedom'. It costs money and once a person has attested to the 'State of Clear' in his local Scientology Organisation they must then move onto an Advanced Organisation, like Saint Hill or The Flag Service Organisation in Fort Harrison in Florida. All of the long-term Scientologists had reached the 'State of Clear' years earlier but were stuck due to currency restrictions. They couldn't buy expensive services outside the country. Our task was to present an accurate picture of the problems Scientology faced in Zimbabwe and see if there was any way to help these old-timers get their money out and into the Church's coffers.

Edward's mission was cut short when he was required for an urgent posting at Saint Hill. He had to depart within days, leaving me to continue the job. I had to spend some time shuttling between Bulawayo and Harare. Sometimes I could afford to get a train but other times I hitch-hiked. Travelling was always an adventure but the last time that I boarded a train in Zimbabwe was an experience of a different kind. Unable to find a place in first class, I was consigned to the bedlam of third. I got talking to a charming and well-spoken African woman on the platform. She told me that a nice white man should not be in third class and that she would sort me out, once the train got moving. In the meantime, I squeezed myself down on the wooden bench seats, among the hundreds of poor people heading to the big city. I was sitting with a group of young men who were drinking from a huge carton of 'Ndlovue' beer, a kind of home brew, surrounded by some women and children. One of the men kept trying to sell me his 'sister', a young and heavily pregnant teenage girl. I politely declined and hoped for an up-grade. Then a ruckus started further down the carriage. A fellow in his late teens was causing a huge scene. He was apparently high on a concoction of street drugs and alcohol. My new friends told me he was AWOL from the army. He had become quite violent when three burly Military Policemen suddenly came up the carriage and began laying into him with clubs and boots. I watched as they dragged him, bleeding from head wounds, further up the train. The woman I had met on the platform eventually found me and motioned that she had secured me a place in the first class coach. On my way up the train I passed a dark alcove, and saw the corpse of the young AWOL soldier lying on the floor.

I was pulled out of Zimbabwe a few weeks later because the mission couldn't be completed without Edward. I didn't really want to leave but at least I now had some field experience under my belt and would be selected quicker when other similar missions came up. I returned to the normality of Saint Hill and was taken on by the Commanding Officer CLO as her Programs' Operator. This meant that I took note of, and followed up on, any orders she issued to staff.

A few weeks into the posting, all of Scientology's top management came to the base to launch a new phase of Church growth and expansion. I was updating some logs in the CLO office when a Commodore's Messenger told me to report to the Saint Hill Castle main entrance. When I got there I was surrounded by the visiting top brass; Marc Jeager, Norman Starkey, Guillaume Lesevre, Lyman Spurlock, David Miscavige and a bunch of lesser known management types. I was told that I was now the new Estates Project Force In Charge and would be training up new Sea Org recruits. Sea Org recruits had always trained at Saint Hill but I hadn't done my own training there because I was recruited by the US body. I was asked what I felt about the post and under the gaze of the Church's top men I saluted and replied: "I am looking forward to doing well in the post."

I was surprised by the appointment because normally there would have been a lot more deliberation about a post like that, and it is extremely rare to get appointed by such senior executives. As far as they were concerned I was easy to transfer and I had the actual qualifications required for the job.

Taking his cues from Miscavige, Jeager decided to personally oversee my initial on-the-job training. It was quite a surreal experience. We were all standing on the flagstone steps in front of the castle, me in my Petty Officer 3rd Class uniform, and all these big American senior officers with gold stripes, lanyards, campaign ribbons and caps. Jeager ordered one of the Commodore's Messenger Organisation UK staff members, a Scottish girl called Christine, to step up to the front. Then he told me to 'bawl her out'. Lower level Sea Org members do not order Commodore's Messengers so I was pretty nervous. I mumbled something like "get that fucking job done now".

The executives laughed. "Don't swear. Try again," said Jeager.

I did equally as badly the second time.

Jeager ordered Christine to take me off for the day to learn my Training Routines again and after the drilling I did manage to 'bawl her out', passed and took up my new post as the EPF In Charge.

Running the EPF was normally quite enjoyable, except when the overall Saint Hill Base recruitment statistics went down. Usually the Hubbard Communications Office (HCO) was fully responsible for recruitment. Their senior body, called Senior HCO, from where I worked, got its statistics from the total number of Sea Org recruits for all Saint Hill Base organisations that week. If stats were down for one week, each of the lower HCO operations would be investigated. If the statistics were down for two weeks then all production executives would be investigated. If statistics were down for three weeks, all of Senior HCO, including my area would be investigated for crimes, withholds and undisclosed critical thoughts of L. Ron Hubbard or senior management.

It was during one such purge that Africa came on the cards again. I had only been back a few months and this time I didn't have to beg or cajole. I was instantly selected to return to Zimbabwe. I was delighted to get the chance to explore that part of Africa again but I had begun a serious relationship with a Hungarian Sea Org woman called Gabriella. It was a whirlwind romance and we had gotten engaged to be married in an effort to make a real go of our relationship, taking account of the restrictions imposed on the single Sea Org member, namely no sex. She came in the taxi with us to the airport and, as I left her at the departures gate, I kissed her and said: "We will definitely get married when I get back."

She looked at me tearfully and said: "John, I don't think I'll be there."

I brushed it off thinking she was upset that I was going away.

A guy I had trained up on the EPF, Derek, was sent with me on his first mission as a newly graduated Sea Org member. He was a Dubliner and had owned several businesses and worked in sales for many years. He had met his wife, Gráinne, in England and they had married just before joining the Sea Org. What I did not know was that they had met in rehab and both were recovering alcoholics.

Zimbabwe had not changed much in the few months since I had left, although politically things were a lot tenser. The Movement for Democratic Change, led by Morgan Tsvangirai and at that time supported by Ian Smith, had been holding rallies; Mugabe had initiated a campaign of harassment against the party. A few days after we had set up shop in our new offices in Harare, in the State Lottery Building, I came face-to-face with the violence that was rapidly overwhelming the city. What had started out as a peaceful protest degenerated into a blood fest after Mugabe sent the police in. I had to run back to the office to escape the violence. I climbed out onto the roof, with the sharp tang of dispersing tear gas making my eyes water. I watched riot police beating people senseless while the streets were blocked with overturned cars. This was the 'wog' world at its worst.

The initial stage of our mission was to pull the main national organisation in Harare out of the near-bankrupt state it was in. We had to get it geared up for high levels of sales and delivery of Scientology's very own brand of psychological counselling. We went out and visited Church members and looked for ways to get them active again. Unlike England or Ireland, where you are usually offered a cup of tea or coffee when visiting, in Zimbabwe the drink of choice is a strong alcoholic beverage known as Cutty Sark. I never really liked alcohol but I began to notice that Derek did. He liked it too much and his behaviour became increasingly unpredictable with each passing day. It reached a head when, after spending an evening with a wealthy couple, we got into our pick-up truck and Derek shoved me over to the passenger side and insisted on driving. He was all over the road, swerving and barely missing the telegraph poles and the deep ditches. When we came to a junction, I leaned over and grabbed the keys from the ignition and rolled out through the passenger door onto the ground. Derek went mad. He jumped out and we tussled in the scrub. I was able to get a couple of solid punches in before he got the keys off me again. He began sobbing and rambling drunkenly about what a fantastic person I was, how much he missed home and how sorry he was that he was a useless drunk. I drove us home and went to bed while Derek slipped out again.

As the weeks turned to months, Derek evidently became as fond of the women as he was of the drink. I studiously ignored his behaviour and particularly the fact that one young woman, the daughter of a public Scientologist, was now sporting a swelling belly. He was very aware that his behaviour was going to get him in deep trouble back in England and my fate too hung in the balance. I knew from my time with Craig in Tours that we had one way that would keep us both out of trouble and that was to make the Org so successful that everything else would be overlooked.

We sat down and worked out our strategy. We needed something big and decided that we would have to take this little Org to the top of the Birthday Game Table for 1991. Devised by Hubbard during the 1970s, the Birthday Game was an exercise to keep staff members focused on producing money and expansion. Pitting various Orgs and Missions against one another, the one with the highest cumulative statistics for the year ending on March 13, Hubbard's birthday, would be declared the winner. They would be awarded international recognition at a gala event at The Flag Service Organisation in Florida. In a setting replete with red carpets, winners get to dress in beautiful evening wear and make a speech, which was televised in every Scientology Organisation on the planet. Photos would appear in international Scientology publications. For me this would kill two birds with the one stone – keep me away from any harsh discipline and boost my career.

Scientology Zimbabwe had not produced anything for years, so it wasn't hard for us, with a little effort, to get it moving again. High points were awarded for statistical graphs that showed 'affluence' or 'power' trends. Thankfully a graph that had been creeping along at 0 for several years could be made to leap up into affluence quite easily. It was soon all over Scientology newsletters that Harare was top of the league. That also meant that the UK Continental Management started to win The Birthday Game. Our affluence created their affluence.

We employed all sorts of tricks to get our stats up. Routing people in was absolutely no problem because unemployment was so high; the streets were teaming with the destitute and desperate. We were able to exploit them without mercy. To get recruitment stats up we would hire a bunch of them and then let them go again the next week. We would then recruit a new batch to take the statistic up again. Crime was high, so there was a boom industry in security work. We ran a little course called 'The Investigations Check Sheet', and issued certificates to people who completed it. In Africa a certificate is worth money and the barely literate young men from the 'bush' were desperate to do our course. This counted as a course completion and was worth a lot on our graph.

The African guys didn't really care much for true Scientology. While they would sign up to the basic courses in order to better themselves, they weren't going to be big players or spend money on auditing. We had been sent with specific instructions not to try to sign any of them up to the Sea Org. When they had been brought to East Grinstead in the past, they were far too quick to smell a rat. They tended to go AWOL or 'blow' in Scientology speak. In East Grinstead they had gone to the authorities, which had resulted in a police investigation into Scientology potentially being involved in people trafficking.

We couldn't transfer money out of the country, as Zimbabwean dollars were still not recognised by the international banking community. So the long-range plan was to accumulate as much as possible within Zimbabwe and purchase assets there. We did try to get some out and I ran a test with some people. I bought some nice leather goods and carvings and shipped them out to England in the hope of selling them. It wasn't a runner and the prospect of doing it in any volume posed huge logistical problems.

Ashley Belbin came and hunted us out. He was one of those rugged, immensely capable and very intelligent wild men you meet in these former colonies. He was third generation English-Rhodesian and his family had been gold prospectors before settling into manufacturing during the 1940s. Ashley, among other things, was an accomplished stunt pilot. I remember the picture of his plane coming out of a hangar at full throttle, and taking off just as it cleared the big doors. The man was quite mad. Ash had been on Scientology Org staff in Johannesburg for a while but got fed up with it and moved back to Zimbabwe. By rights, he should have been declared Suppressive, but we found him far too valuable to allow rigid application of policy to get in the way. We needed his boundless energy, access to the countries movers and shakers and his logistical support to further our drive.

Ash was pretty wealthy and was running a hardware

company. He knew everyone and had identified a guy called The General who he felt we absolutely had to recruit. The General was in fact a full general in the army and a man of huge influence. He had fought along with Mugabe in the struggle to liberate the country and remained a very high level military man. He was well over 6 foot and incredibly fit. He must have been in his 40s and drove a luxury Mercedes. Ash had told us that he had 50 grand in cash in the back of his car at all times and that nobody messed with him. He would have been a fantastic recruit due to his influence but he wouldn't bite. I did meet him for a beer and I used all my hard sell training but it seemed as if he had no problems in his life that I could tap into.

Ash's business partner, however, was a different story. He was in a very bad way. He was a heavy drinker and smoker and already had serious heart problems. It had resulted in him having a leg amputated. His clogged arteries meant that he was on a mix of blood thinners and I would imagine he was a diabetic. But we wanted him because he had money. He wasn't interested in the basic training or the Communications Course or the Free Personality Test and all the rest of the stuff we hard sold. But Ashley and Derek managed to sell him the Purification Rundown.

The Purification Rundown is like Scientology's own cult diet. It involves massive doses of vitamins and minerals, coupled with five hours of sweating in a sauna and running exercises. It was developed by Hubbard, as one of his many introductory services to Scientology. Many health experts believe that the huge handfuls of Niacin and Vitamin B3 tablets can cause hallucination and have similar effects to taking drugs. They also criticise it for the damage it can do to the liver. The Purification Rundown forms the basis of the rehabilitation offered by the Scientology front group, Narconon. It purports to cure drug addicts while removing all toxins from their systems. The Church says the rundown can improve personality and increase IQ by up to 30 points and has an 80 percent success rate. The theory behind the programme is that it 'dislodges drug residues and other toxins from the fatty tissues so that these substances can be eliminated from the body.' In Hubbardise, that means drug use in this life or in previous lives, the toxins from which have clung on and still contaminate the body. In other words, it is a diet for the soul.

The program takes two or three weeks and during it participants are urged to drink lots of water, avoid alcohol and maintain a healthy diet. I had been on the Programme myself numerous times and to give Ash's partner the support he needed, went on it with him. I had been given the use of Ashley's Land Rover by this time and would drive over to Borrowdale and pick my charge up, then drive across town to the Harare Sheraton. We would have a light lunch and then I would, like a personal trainer, take him through a gentle weight-lifting regime. After this he would down his huge doses of vitamins. Niacin is taken in such huge doses that it actually causes skin irritation, which Scientologist say is past life radiation or sunburn leaving the body. In truth it's just a reaction to the 10 times over the normal limit of the Vitamin.

We then went and sat in the sauna, being careful not to dehydrate, while taking a balance of salt and potassium tablets. I stayed with him in the sauna for five hours a day with breaks in between. I had enough sense to know we didn't want to kill the guy. We wanted him to see some improvements so I made sure he came out for air when he seemed to be flagging. On a sensible diet for the first time in years, off the drink and cutting down on cigarettes, the man made obvious improvements. He felt mentally better too because he felt physically better. I had done other rundowns with some people who got a bit drugged and hyper on it and I had often felt that way myself over the years. Ash's pal simply felt better than he had in years and at the end gratefully handed over about $6000 to add to our growing pot. I shudder now to think about what could have gone wrong if he had suffered a severe adverse reaction. It was only by sheer luck that the poor fellow didn't keel over and die.

Mugabe's spies were monitoring us carefully all the time. I eventually realised that we had employed two of them on staff. I went in one morning and told them to get the hell out. I didn't even bother declaring them as Suppressive Persons, I just told them to pack up and close the door behind them. Unfortunately, shortly after that my 6-month visa ran out.

In the passport office a very nice woman served me. I told her my name and my problem and handed my passport through the steel grill. She smiled and told me to hang on for a minute. I should have known there was going to be trouble. Within a few minutes two burly security police asked me to follow them. They led me out the back where they put me under arrest. They confiscated all my personal belongings and locked me up in the caged back of a police pick-up, with two other unfortunates. We drove across town and through the arches of the Central Police Station.

My first interrogator must have watched a lot of

Hollywood movies because he was very theatrical. I was taken in handcuffs to a bare room and sat in front of an old table. The detective entered shortly after, pulled out a pistol, checked the barrel and laid it on the other side of the table. He had a file that seemed to cover much of my activities over the past few months.

After the initial 'place and date of birth' questions, he accused me of spying for a South African political movement. I told him that was rubbish and explained what I was doing for Scientology. The police had a very big file on the Church and treated it with some suspicion. After about three hours, I was informed I was being prosecuted by the police for violation of the terms of my visa. I was taken over to finger-printing and then left in an office, under the eyes of a regular police officer.

My problem now was that I was on my way to prison and none of my people had a clue as to what was going on. The Zimbabwean prison system is not fun. We'd had a case a few weeks before where a couple, who had been doing some peripheral Scientology activities, had run into trouble with the law. The wife was working as a secretary for a very wealthy but incredibly tight-fisted businessman. She had embezzled about $3000 because they were having serious trouble paying the rent and feeding the children. The poor woman had to be rescued from the prison. Being a white woman, she would have faced a very harsh time indeed from the guards. While rape is commonplace in the system, some of the authorities overlook other even more abusive practices. Ashley bribed and cajoled his various contacts and eventually secured her release, but it served as a stark warning for me. I knew I had to think quickly.

I started trying to make friends with the police officer guarding me. After a bit of small talk and the handover of $10, he allowed me to use the phone. I called Ash and told him I was incarcerated in the Central Police Station and needed to get the hell out. As only he could, he told me not to worry and within minutes had a top Harare lawyer, David Barclade, on my case. Barclade came in fighting soon afterwards. There was a lot of noise and he eventually got legal custody of me on the basis that I would not be allowed near the Scientology Centre. I was moved over to Ashley's ranch and a court date was set for the following week.

On the morning of the case, Derek and the former Guardian's Office representative, Bulaweyo, came down to the court house. It was a huge circular structure, with the symbols for each of the star signs decorating the upper tiers. My own, Scorpio, did not look all that convincing or positive. David handed me over to the khaki-clad police officer at the defendant's entrance and I was led down to cells at the base of the building. These cells were a frightening affair. They were packed with prisoners in transit, to and from the main state prison. A truck was loading as I got down there and about 30 men were crouched on the ground, under the watchful eye of a machine-gun-wielding policeman. On command they jumped up and filed onto the back of a truck. I gave the one white man there a nod.

My case was called. The judge, a large woman in formal robes, announced that she would be adjourning the case for a further week as she was off shopping in Botswana. There seemed to be, in this strange land, a far more lax attitude toward jurisprudence than would be considered acceptable in the world's wealthier nations.

David was furious but there was little he could do.

I saw Derek for the first time in a week. He seemed troubled, and so he should have been as his carelessness was the reason I was there in the first place. He had refused to get the visa renewed at the time and it was two months over when I was arrested.

The judge released me into the custody of David. He brought me back to Ash's ranch where I waited out the week.

Seven days later we arrived back in court and the case was heard by a different judge. David argued that the mitigating circumstances of my case be taken into account, after all I was here to help the country. The judge did not think so, but fined me $5,000 and gave me a week to leave the country. It was the best we could hope for. I was to remain in David's custody until I boarded the plane for England.

From the court, I was led back down to the cells and holding area below the courts. I signed a receipt for return of my possessions and was then handed over to a big moustachioed sergeant. He grinned and led me to a cell with about 20 others in prison garb. A number of big guards seemed to take great pleasure in smiling at me as I got more and more uneasy. I had been released, but here I was being held in a cell. I shared out my last cigarettes with my cellmates, most of whom were in for petty theft. Hours later I heard the welcome ruckus of David shouting at the police sergeant that they were 'messing with him'. Before I knew what was happening I was led from the cell and passed over to David. The fine was paid from organisation reserves and Ashley bought me my ticket back to the UK. I spent a quiet week on the ranch, going for walks, watching the local wild life and catching up on some reading. When the time came, I took a taxi to the airport and felt a sense of sadness as my flight was called. My visa was stamped 'Persona non grata' and I knew I would need to wait for a regime change before I would be allowed back into Zimbabwe.

On the approach into London Heathrow, I looked down on rows of Council houses and envisioned people packed like sardines. As usual, these long flights afforded lots of time for contemplation, and I was wondering if I had had enough of the Sea Org. It was hard work and the conditions weren't ideal but at least I knew the boundaries and the rules. Anyway, here I was travelling the world, getting to see places I could have only dreamed of. I was having such wonderful experiences when I could have been living a constrained existence in those little houses below. I could see little outside my career with the Church, except a grinding 'wog' world.

Back at Saint Hill I was shocked to discover that Gabriella had left the Sea Org and gone back to Hungary. There was little sympathy or empathy for anything emotional like this in the Sea Org. It was considered 'Down Tone' so instead of getting upset, I brushed myself off and got on with it. Anyway, there was plenty of drama awaiting me. Within days of my return I was taken aside by Derek's wife Gráinne.

"John, did Derek go out 2D?" she demanded, obviously suspecting that he had cheated on her.

"I honestly don't know for sure," I told her.

But Gráinne grabbed my arm and walked me up to the auditing folder storage area and demanded his Pre Clear folder, which I had brought back from Africa with me. Only technical people were allowed to look in these folders but she was an executive in the CLO at the time. She demanded it from the guy in charge who gave it to her because he didn't have her seniority. I watched her as she ripped into the folder and read several pages.

"Was he on the whiskey," she asked me.

"Yeah, he was drinking a lot," I admitted.

"He's fucked!" she said in shock. It was only then that it really hit home to me that he was a chronic alcoholic.

Within a week of my return he was ordered back and went straight to the RPF. Gráinne initiated divorce proceedings and later disappeared or 'blew' from the Sea Org.

Meanwhile I assumed that I would be due some leave to go home. I was wrong. Instead I was told that if I just covered a post for Tony Phipps, the man in charge of the Saint Hill event hall stage and sound systems, I would be allowed a week to go home after he got back from his mission. I accepted.

As thoughts of Gabriella were suppressed, I soon started a relationship with a German girl called Nicole. We had met when I was the EPF In Charge and she was a new arrival. She had been on staff in Germany for about a year before joining up with the Sea Org. We had got talking one day and she told me she was delighted to see me back. We began meeting every single day and one day I took her hand and that was it. We were an item. Although we couldn't go out or do the things normal couples did, we could spend time together, go for walks and on Saturdays, during laundry time, we might even borrow a car and go shopping. It was nice.

I was still pushing hard to be given at least a week's leave. At the same time my uncle Frank began to notice something was not quite right. It seemed that every time they received a letter from me stating my intention to pop home for Christmas or for a short summer break to Carrigaline, another posting or promotion would come up that would scupper my plans. He became convinced that the Church were reading my post and sending me on the move whenever I considered going to see my family. He was not wrong. All our mail was sent directly to the Hubbard Communications Office, who opened it and read it before it was forwarded to us. Legal mail was sent on to OSA. Just as Frank had started to suspect, any yearning for Ireland meant a plane trip as far away as they could get me. This time I was told I had been selected for a training program in Marketing Research in Los Angeles.

My week's leave was sidelined, I said goodbye to Nicole and I was booked on a flight to LA before I knew it.

EIGHT

THE WAR IS OVER

I was excited about going back to America. I was street-wise enough to know that I did not want to stay in the dormitories in the Complex but didn't know how to avoid it. Fortunately just after I landed, I bumped into an acquaintance called Ed, who worked in middle management. Ed spent a lot of time on missions in different parts of the world. I got on well with him. He had been divorced for about two years; his ex-wife was declared a Suppressive Person and was no longer around. He had gained full legal custody of their child, Jason. Ed was about to be sent off to Austria and knew that he would be gone for a long time. He had a small one-roomed apartment that he shared with Jason in the Anthony Building on Fountain Avenue. He wanted both Jason and the apartment looked after. These apartments could be taken over on a whim by senior management, but that would be far more difficult if a 'family' was living there. So I became Jason's stand-in

Dad for the next 12 months.

At this time, in 1992, there was a huge effort to train up new management teams for all Class V and Sea Org delivery centres across the planet. Management training was carried out in Los Angeles in The Hollywood Guarantee Building, on the corner of Hollywood and Ivar Avenue. So far they had teams from about 20 organisations there wearing green smocks to designate them as administrative trainees. Scientologists doing technical training were more often than not based out in Clearwater and wore red smocks.

I got into the routine fairly quickly. In the morning I would get Jason dressed and onto the bus that would take him to the child care facility at the Complex. I would then either grab a ride or jump on the bus going the other way, heading for Hollywood. On Saturday mornings I would take Jason for a treat of some form, normally getting him some toys or a trip to McDonalds while we washed our clothes at the local Laundromat. I was able to get Christmas day off and took him down to Santa Monica beach and tried to make a bit of a fuss of him. He seemed cheery enough, but part of him missed his mother and he definitely missed his dad. We had a nice day all the same and later on a bunch of the kids got to watch videos back at our apartment at the Anthony Building.

I was being retrained for a major new marketing launch back in the UK and I had to first take the Key To Life study course. It is a major part of Scientology study, which essentially regresses a person's education back to childhood. It is a three-pronged in its approach, first convincing you that you don't know the meaning of words, then that you have no concept of grammar and finally that the education system you went through was a failure. Afterwards a participant is re-educated in the Scientology thought process. The effect can be quite significant.

It is a long course and it took me the better part of four months to complete. But I came out realising that Hubbard had discovered how to really teach people basic English, something that even the greatest educators of the past had failed in doing. This was followed by an intense study of Hubbard's writings on the subject of marketing.

Hubbard had stated as far back as 1967 that a Sea Org member should be proficient in the use of martial arts and weapons handling, as well as being a top-level administrator and Scientology counsellor. Few Sea Org members had had such training, probably because it didn't sit well with our status as a Church. Towards the end of my studies' period a group of us were called on late one Sunday morning. We were ordered down to the Hollywood Guarantee Building. We were told we would be meeting the Security Chief for the whole LA area, a guy called Geoff. Sure enough he greeted us on arrival and told us we were going to get initial weapons training and that some of us would have to go further with the training, others would not.

The training involved an introduction to a selection of pistols, handguns and machine guns that were displayed on a large table in a room down at the building that day. We were introduced to a number of different kinds of weapons; we got to handle a couple of different hand-guns, some had rotating barrels and others used magazines clips. We were shown how to arm pump-action shotguns with a flick of the wrist and how to hold guns. The importance of checking

the chambers carefully to ensure that no stray rounds
were lodged there was emphasised. We were urged to
handle the guns to get a feel for them and learn how
to balance them. We were given some idea of what
they could do and the ranges of each of the weapons.
Interestingly, the weapons' training was the first course
I had ever done in Scientology that was not completed
with a check sheet.

By October 1993, I was finishing up my studies.
A huge event was then announced by International
Management. Traditionally the last week in October
is reserved for the International Association of
Scientologists annual Gala event and Ball. It takes place
over three days at my own home base, Saint Hill in
Sussex. It is a huge fundraiser for the Church; donations
are coaxed out of the wealthiest Scientologists and go
to a mysterious fund called 'The War Chest'. Each year,
this event alone raises in the region of Stg£10 million
over the course of the weekend. We were told 1993 was
different and a momentous announcement was going
to be made. They rented the Dodgers Stadium in LA
for the occasion.

There was a big buzz in the air and a lot of tension
at the Complex and the Hollywood Guarantee Building.
While event preparations were ongoing, I often saw
the Chairman of the Board (COB), David Miscavige,
swishing in from Ivar Avenue with his usual entourage
of about twenty people. I was struck again by his very
short stature; he could not have been over five feet tall.
I was captivated by his youthful but always scowling
intense face and his beautiful clothes. He had a new
office on the top floor of the Hollywood Guarantee
Building where we studied. As students and in order
to 'keep our exchange in' (a student is not 'producing'

anything, thus can be 'out exchange' with the group.) we had to do renovations work all day every Sunday, from eight in the morning until six in the evening, when we would go back on study for four hours. I had been on the work crew that had helped renovate the space that eventually became COB's Los Angeles office. It was absolutely gorgeous and no expense was spared in making it the perfect working environment. The Hollywood Guarantee Building is 13 stories tall, so Miscavige, on the top floor, had a wonderful panoramic view of the city and the Hollywood Hills that formed its backdrop.

One day I was just crossing over to the Ivar parking lot as several cars arrived. Miscavige pulled in first, in a new Accura. Just behind him was the de-facto second-in-command and former Captain of Hubbard's Flagship, *The Apollo*, during the 1970s, Norman Starkey, in a similar car. Starkey was a founding Sea Org member and one of the most powerful executives in Scientology. He was now trustee of L Ron Hubbard's estate and Commanding Officer of Author Services Incorporated, the company that looked after all of Hubbard's published works. Starkey was also the man running the 'Preservation of The Technology' project. This was a huge task that involved putting all of Hubbard's writings onto titanium plates, and all of his recorded lectures on to solid gold discs. They were then sealed in atomic-proof containers in shock-proof rooms, built into a huge disused goldmine in New Mexico. The project was completed ten years later and the site is marked by a symbol carved into the landscape that can only be seen from the air. Four security guards escorted Miscavige to the lifts but Starkey didn't join him. I stood by the parking lot holding the pedestrian gate open for him but he just sat in his car. His head was in his hands and he had a look on his face as if he was facing death. When he did look up, his eyes were red. He waved me away. Within a few years he, along with Commander Mark Jaeger, had disappeared. They have since been reported to have been seen in a special Sea Org camp at the secret compound near Hemet California.

Orders went out to every continent to send as many of their public and staff as possible to the event in Hollywood. The quota for attendance was to be 50,000. Eventually 10,000 attended and that included every Sea Org Member on the West Coast and students studying at the International Training Organisation in the Hollywood Guarantee Building from all over the world.

My girlfriend Nicole was brought over from the UK, as she worked for the IAS fund-raising effort. On the day of the event, we got to sit together, near the front of the hall. The staging was quite awesome, with a huge backdrop over 100 feet tall, painted in gold and greens, dramatic lighting and ear-splitting music heralding a new dawn for Scientology. Then, in a scene that could have rivalled a Nuremburg Rally, Miscavige took to the stage following a grand flag and marching display, to announce to those gathered there and the 10,000 watching via satellite, that he had won the 'war of wars'. He described to us a US government plot that took in the FBI, the IRS, the CIA and the American Medical Association. It was a plot run by a group of powerful psychiatrists, aimed at destroying the last and final bastion of man's freedom – The Church of Scientology and its founder, L Ron Hubbard. Dressed in full dress black-tie Miscavige was not just announcing a huge 'win', but the subtext to this grandiose display was that he himself had become elevated to a position of absolute power within this Church.

Miscavige went on to tell us that in the early 1950s, just as Dianetics was born, the 'psychs' had planned to infiltrate all levels of society, so that they, and they alone, would rule.

"I'm not joking. This is all a matter of public record," he told us as he revealed the full story behind the Church's decades-long battle to get tax-free status. I knew that Miscavige and his highly paid legal teams had been working for years, trying to attain tax free status from the US Internal Revenue Service (IRS). It looked like they had finally won their battle.

Miscavige continued: "Their (the psychiatrists and psychologists) plan for the US was simple. They would purchase a million acres of land in Alaska, which they would use as a huge mental health colony. Then they would change the commitment laws so they could arbitrarily commit any citizen to this facility. One didn't need to violate a law or do anything wrong. All that it would take was a 'psych' deciding that you weren't desirable and off you would go without recourse to judicial review."

The Chairman of the Board went on with the story, explaining how the House of Representatives had already passed the bill for Alaska and it was due to fly through the Senate. The press and the public were asleep, he told us. But then 'a force out of nowhere' named the plan for what it was. That force was Hubbard and Scientology.

He received a full 15 minutes standing ovation. He grinned as he savoured every second of adoration and we got caught up in the frenzied excitement of it all.

Above his head was a huge eight-pronged gold cross.

His story continued that the 'psychs' were furious with Scientology and used the United States government and its intelligence and tax agencies to smear the Church internationally. He cited document after document that claimed that IRS officials had done everything in their power to destroy Hubbard and Scientology. The war had taken a new twist when IRS agents apparently broke into his car and stole documents. In late 1992, he'd had enough. He and four top executives walked into the IRS Headquarters in Washington DC. What was said, we were not told, but when the Scientology delegation left Washington later that day, the stage had been set for the great win. Scientology and its affiliated corporations and entities in the United States of America had been granted full tax free status and Religious recognition!

"The war is over," he boomed.

The audience screamed and cried. The applause rolled on and on for another 15 minutes. From my position at the front, I could see Cruise and Travolta cheering as loudly as everyone else. Miscavige stood there and drank in the adoration. It was a very powerful moment for him and you could feel the worship in the air. It was an experience I have not come anywhere near to encountering since. This man had somehow assumed a godlike role and we, the audience, knew it.

To this day the facts of how the Church attained tax free status in the US are unknown. What is known is that Scientology paid $12 million to settle with the IRS. More importantly for Miscavige, it meant that when Scientology services were purchased, they were classified as religious donations and thus written off against income tax.

Almost overnight, the language of sales was changed in the Church from that of 'buying' services to 'donations' for services, even though the cost did not go down. In fact the opposite occurred. All that really changed was how these services were classified in the corporate audits submitted to the IRS each year. In the US, the picture of Uncle Sam was immediately used in a marketing drive to get the message across under our slogan: "Uncle Sam wants to help you move up The Bridge."

Not long after the rally, I flew back to the UK with Nicole. Just before the event Jason's Dad, Ed, had returned from Austria so I wasn't worried about his welfare but I was sad to say goodbye to him. Things had gone well in the US. I had received a Certificate as Marketing Research Specialist and was excited about taking up my new posting in England. I was still Petty Officer 3rd Class but was rapidly moving towards the rank of Petty Officer 2nd Class.

Nicole had changed and was not as loving as before. We broke up shortly after I returned. Although I was upset, I was not allowed 'to have case on post'. In other words, I was not allowed to express my own troubles while working the 13 to 16 hour days required of us. My troubles would have to wait until I could 'go in session' or get auditing.

My new job was to launch a big market research programme all over London, Manchester and Birmingham. Just as I felt I was getting places with the material I was gathering, Miscavige issued a new directive. He decided to put the heat on the Continental Orgs and Missions to make more money. An evaluation of the Scientology business worldwide showed that direct income for services was raising only $5 million a year. That included the UK, Australia, Germany and France and meant an average 'Class V Org' or Church was making less than $4,000 a week. Miscavige decided that since he had won the war with the IRS, then the reason that the Church was not expanding, the reason Class V Organisations were not reaching Saint Hill size, with thousands of new Scientologists buying courses and getting auditing, was because Scientology Management was out-ethics.

Never one to use subtlety when a battering ram would serve, he had new management teams trained up in Los Angeles. These were to be the ruthless Stormtroopers of Scientology management. As we soon discovered, they were unreasonable, uncompromising, unquestioning zealots who would carry out Miscavige's plans, no matter what blocks might appear in the road.

Any thoughts of my getting a chance to go to Ireland on leave were put on hold again as the new UK management team landed. It included Ron Norton, a New Yorker and his wife Jan, the technical expert. With them came a new system of management. Ron arrived with three handpicked young officers, Bruce Perry, Thomas Sproule and Bart Van Lock. All three had been UK-based staff and were called to Los Angeles under mysterious circumstances a year before. I had seen them there but they had not been allowed to divulge what specialised training they were engaged in. The team also included two other senior executives, Debbie Koval and Angie Kelly. They landed in the UK covered in brass and lanyards and replaced the existing Continental Liaison Management Org teams overnight. It was an extremely aggressive takeover and they were trained to take no excuses whatsoever.

The new management style was one that instilled fear, with a barely contained and consistent threat of violence and dire consequences for any non-compliance to orders, no matter how ridiculous. It became a matter of course that I was dragged to either of the Commanding Officers offices. I would be screamed at and have my personal inadequacies rubbed in my face. Jan Norton had a look that could make you feel an utterly contemptible creature. They had all been briefed that the UK people were dirty and did not bathe enough. The fact that we only had two showers between 50 men was not taken into consideration and their comments on personal hygiene were common and hurtful.

I was promoted, without joy or fanfare, to the post of 'Dissemination Aide'. This job is equivalent to that of a Marketing Director in a regular business and essentially I was responsible for all sales and promotional activities in the UK area. The pressure was incredible. I was expected to study each Mission and Org, identify why their statistics were down and then send a stream of orders to the sales or promotional people to remedy them. That was at the same time as responding to daily demands to get tens of thousands of promotional pieces out across the continent. In the heady atmosphere everyone began to play off everyone else while looking out for number one. As far as I was concerned, it was an absolutely no win posting. Every time something would go wrong I was dragged into some of the most intrusive and aggressive interrogations I had encountered to date in Scientology. The toilet became my only refuge. I could hide out there for up to an hour before Bruce or Thomas went on the hunt for staff missing from post.

One day I had enough. I cracked and told them I wasn't going to do it anymore.

I was surprised when I wasn't immediately assigned to the RPF. Instead, I was sent to London to work under Deputy Commanding Officer for Ethics and Image, Bruce Perry. His brief was to clean up London Org, which was an utter mess. While London should have been the flagship for Scientology in the UK, it was barely scraping by. I was assigned to help sort out the disastrous state of the organisation's filing system. It needed to be prepared for computerisation and the task was immense. London Org had an entire basement room full of hundreds of thousands of folders. They contained the records of correspondence, sales of materials and services to former and present clients, dating back to 1952.

Anybody who buys anything in Scientology, even a single book, has a file opened on them in the organisation where the sale was made. If you buy a paperback Dianetics book while on holiday in America, your name and address is entered into both the local and international Scientology data-base. It may never be removed. Even when an individual requests that their name be removed, it is not. Their file is merely marked 'No Mail'. The system is clumsy, largely due to a firm Hubbardian rule, enforced with threats of dire consequences, that a file may never be deleted. That means that if someone moves house, divorces or marries, the old file has to be kept and a new one created. If someone buys a book or service in another organisation, a file is opened there too. Statistically both organisations count the person as one of their own parishioners.

Most of the files in London Org contained the names

of people long dead or lost to Scientology. Piles of them had been loaded into filing cabinets at the back of the basement area 20 years previously. Then a wall had been built effectively sealing them away from view. I happened on them by accident one day. I was looking at how to extend the useable floor space in the basement and banged a hammer on the back wall. I was amazed when it knocked a hole into this long forgotten room.

Going through the files was quite an experience. Many famous people had at some time flirted with Hubbard. Amid the countless documents, I found Beatle George Harrison's file from the late 1960s, which indicated that he had bought one book and given up. Singer Van Morrison's file had quite a lot of invoices in it. The file showed that he had got a lot of auditing back in the 1970s but evidently Scientology wasn't for him. Although he had not got as far as 'Clear', he appeared to have been on the 'bridge'. Writer William Burroughs had a file as well. He had been audited to 'Clear' but rejected Scientology quickly afterwards and wrote about it. I placed all three to one side for special attention.

Despite the mess, I did quite well on the project. Once I got started I actually enjoyed it. I liked living in London too and being my own boss. Norton and Perry were sufficiently impressed that they decided I wasn't such an 'out ethics' scumbag after all.

Shortly afterwards I was assigned to a very high level mission. It was run directly under The Commodore's Messenger Organisation International. We had to prepare all UK records for eventual entry into a computer database currently under development at the Sea Organisation's in-house computer and software research and development centre in LA.

Since the early 1980s the Scientology Corporation
had been attempting to set up an advanced computerised
administrative system of their own. Hubbard had
claimed to recall that entire planetary systems had
been run and administered by dedicated computerised
networks. He demanded that the Church management
develop such a system for Scientology. Hubbard's
scathing opinion on the 'wog' world's barbaric state
of science and the humanities' meant that everything
had to be developed 'in-house'. Instead of buying
and installing a known database and administrative
software package, they had tried to develop their very
own using 'whole-track' recall. It was hoped that if a
person could be audited to recall systems used in the
Galactic Confederacy, then this would beat any of the
primitive systems in use here on planet Earth.

The initial stage of the project saw Sea Org members
going to Taiwan and buying up components and
microchips from several manufacturers. They were
all shipped to Los Angeles. A large group of Sea
Org members were then taken off normal duties and
assigned to assembly lines, to build our very own
computer servers and PCs. The initial batches were
shipped off as a beta test to Orgs in the US but they
didn't work. The software package was a mess as well.
Eventually all those involved in that stage of the project
were either sent to the RPF or in some cases, declared
Suppressive Persons. The Church conceded that Earth
civilisation might have something to offer in the field
and did a deal with Cisco, Novell and Microsoft for the
software and IBM for the needed hardware. The goal
was to computerise, and thus centralise, everything
and in particular the finances, as the IRS deal brokered
by Miscavige required that the Church file electronic

accounts with them every quarter.

By the end of May 1994, I was back in Los Angeles and the Complex. I was shown to my dormitory on the seventh floor and I had mixed feelings about being back. I had flown out via JFK, New York, with Tony and Richard. We had a couple of hours before our connecting flight to Los Angeles and I wanted to take a taxi to Manhattan. Tony could be a real laugh or a complete grump, that day he was in between. As the oldest member of the team and the one with the longest and most distinguished Sea Org career, he was the de-facto 'In Charge'. He vetoed the plan but did want to get photos of us with a New York feel. So we went out to the taxi rank where he took a load of pictures with Richard and me pretending to get into the New York yellow cabs.

While we had come over to Los Angeles to train on the new IBM system, we were ultimately to work with an elite team. We were charged with both installing and implementing this new way of dealing with finances in every single Missions, Class V delivery Organisation, Sea Organisation Advanced delivery Organisation and at all levels of Sea Organisation management across the world. The training lasted two months and we were working around the clock, and back in dorms at the Complex. The only upside was that because we were in Finance the dorms were better and the food was served in the exclusive Int Level Dining room which meant some decent meals. When we were told that a tour had been arranged to install these systems in the San Francisco Bay Area, Australia, Canada and back in the UK, I was thrilled.

The tour took me through some of the world's gay capitals. We were appalled by the countless, emotionally 'low toned' people we had to brush shoulders with every day. Hubbard's hatred of homosexuals had been instilled in us from our initial training at the Complex and was firmly cemented as we continued up the Bridge. During my training I had been drilled in the dangers posed by gays and lesbians, who were no different to paedophiles in Hubbard's view. Hubbard's solution for these 'sexual perverts' was to quarantine or institutionalise them or to put them under Church processing to cure them. In 'Dianetics' he wrote that homosexuals and sadists are 'actually quite ill physically.' In his 1952 book 'Science of Survival' he had developed his tone scale, which I had learned about while doing my 'Hatting' studies back at SMI. It ranges from -3 to +4 and, homosexuals or 'perverts', as he referred to them, fall in at 1.1. "Here we have promiscuity, perversion, sadism and irregular practices," he wrote. He went on to describe them as 'intensely dangerous' and a 'flaming danger signal, which must be heeded if the human race is to go forward.' I had never had an opinion on homosexuals before I joined the Church of Scientology but as a Sea Org member I had learned to despise them.

In San Francisco, I was actually freaked out by its gay reputation. I treated most non-Scientology people I encountered with suspicion and disdain. In Sydney the walk to the office meant a stroll down Prince's Street where we saw the outrageously gay individuals that hang out there, on every street corner. I couldn't believe what was happening to society and realised that we would need to work twice as hard to influence politics and weed this germ out. One day we encountered the city's colourful gay parade and were appalled to see that the Australians were allowing gay men into the army. I remember one of my group remarking that Australian civilisation had reached its end and if there were gays in the army that meant they were in politics too. We all soberly agreed.

A few months later in Toronto, we made our way down Yonge Street, clad in our uniforms. We looked in disgust at the gay bars and outrageously camp men hanging out on the streets that led off it. We spoke among ourselves about how, when we took over, we would have to go down those roads and clean the place up.

I used the final leg of the trip, in Vancouver, as an opportunity to catch up with an old Sea Org friend, Tom. I had worked with him in Central Marketing back in 1988. I knew he had left the Sea Org and I wanted to know why. When I finally tracked him down on the phone, it was the day I was due to fly back to Toronto so we couldn't arrange to meet up. We did spend hours talking though and he told me what had happened to him over those six years. After his Central Marketing post he was moved to Hemet and, because he had worked in the music industry, was posted as a sound engineer. He married a really lovely woman who was posted in a very senior position on the Hemet base. Life went along fine until she got pregnant. She was immediately removed from her post and ordered to have an abortion. She initially refused but then agreed to do it. Afterwards she was assigned to the RPF. Tom had lost it when she was being pressured into having the abortion. He began drinking, was dragged through ethics and eventually off-loaded from the Sea Org. He was also forced to divorce his wife. He had been doing odd jobs in Vancouver ever since.

I felt sorry for how he had been treated but never

thought to criticise the Church. His story simply served to harden my resolve to ensure that I never would accept a posting to the International Base at Hemet.

After finishing up my project in Canada, I was back in Los Angeles for about two days. While I was over at the Celebrity Centre Los Angeles, I was given a report that had just come in from the UK. It was a follow up to the Van Morrison report I had submitted when I found his file in London two years earlier. A jive and swing band had been recruited to Scientology in 1990, called the Jive Aces. They had been further recruited to the Sea Organisation in the UK, as a working professional band. They were placed in the Public Relations division. As well as playing all major Scientology events, they toured, and still do, jazz and swing clubs, doing festivals across Europe and the USA. They had even played *The Apollo* in New York. They are a top-notch band and are allowed to do what they do because they promote Scientology to celebrities at gigs. They also recruit people into Scientology while on the road. They are a major recruitment pool for the Sea Org. People will join, thinking that they are joining a travelling jazz band, only to find themselves posted in offices, PR jobs or even as auditors.

Ian Clarkson, the group's leader, had submitted the follow-up report to management. It covered a meeting with Van Morrison at the Cork Jazz festival in October 1995. The report detailed several conversations they'd had with him over the weekend.

The band had done a live set for RTÉ, the Irish national broadcaster, at the Metropole Hotel where Van was staying. Ian was interviewed by RTÉ and as usual mentioned Dianetics and how it was responsible for the Jive Aces success as a jazz and swing band. Ian had then left a message with the hotel reception to tell Van that he had a letter for him from the Scientology Celebrity Centre in London. After the set, Van's manager came over to Ian and asked about it. The report indicated that Ian told the manager that he did not have it with him, but could get it the following day, as he wanted to give Van the letter personally.

At a gig at the Silver Springs Hotel Van's manager told Ian that Van had invited the band to his own gig at the Cork Opera House. Backstage after the gig, Ian sat down with Van and his sax player Leo Green, who used to jam with them before the 'Aces' got into Scientology. They did not talk much that night, but Van bumped into them at the hotel lift a few days later. According to the report, Van asked how long they had been Scientologists and told them he had got a lot from it initially. He said he had liked his early Scientology auditing, which he described as very high quality, but that as time went on he met an impasse. His then girlfriend, Michelle Rocca, a former Miss Ireland, came down the lift and they left together.

Ian wanted to follow up his meeting with Van, so after a gig the next day he went and hung out near his room. He saw Van and Michelle and they invited him in for a drink and a chat. They talked about Scientology and Van's messed up auditing until six the next morning. In his report Ian states that Michelle was constantly at Van's side and interjected a number of times as he attempted to draw Van back into Scientology. Van told Ian that he thought that Hubbard was right and that the Scientology process does work, but it had not been able to deal with his individual and specific problems.

In Ian's report, he said that Van went on to tell him that he did not like all the hassle of fame and that it was very difficult to cope with. Ian explained that the Scientology Celebrity Centres were designed to help protect the famous from negative effects of being famous. Later on they went out and watched the Drifters show. Ian reported that Van caused a stir when he entered the hall but clearly wasn't comfortable with the attention at all.

After that show, Ian and the Aces sat and talked with Van and his entourage. Later on, Ian and Van's manager went over to Van's room. Michelle Rocca was in bed. Ian explained to Van about Hubbard's theory of communication. They also discussed the Affinity, Reality and Communication Break theory. They talked about music and Van commented that he liked what the Jive Aces did, especially the Louis Prima numbers. He wanted to do a jamming session with the Jives sometime. As it was 6.30 in the morning at that stage, Ian had said goodbye. He'd given Van one of his Jive Ace business cards and he reported that Van might be in touch in the future.

I read Ian's report with delight and was glad that I was the one who had discovered the original report. A high profile celebrity like Van Morrison was exactly the type of guy the Church would like to get on side. Even though nothing came from the contract with Van, and I wasn't going to get any credit, it was a job well done on my behalf. I was thrilled for the sake of the Church.

A re-organisation of the Finance Office marked the end of the three-year computerisation mission. I turned over the bug handling and technical support functions I had been doing for Canada to Cindy, then packed up to head back to the UK. I was still a UK staff member and was going to be re-posted at Saint Hill.

I arrived back from Canada, shortly before

Christmas 1996, to find the Saint Hill Base quiet and security unusually tight. I soon discovered that Tom Cruise and Nicole Kidman were staying in L Ron Hubbard's old home for Christmas. They had a metallic blue Range Rover, with blacked out windows, parked outside the grand old house. I heard they spent the week walking, watching videos and being entertained by Miscavige and a special set of Religious Technology Centre people brought in for the occasion. I bumped into them one morning as I walked down the drive. There was a light dusting of snow on the ground and very few people were around. A couple walked out from the chapel area where there was a gorgeous, self-contained entertainment lounge and video room, done out in wood, with leather sofas and lounge chairs. The man was about my height, he was sporting a thick and obviously fake beard, but the million-dollar smile was unmistakable. Nothing could disguise the statuesque beauty of Nicole. They both smiled at my stunned expression and seemed very relaxed at that time. I didn't talk to them, as that would not have been allowed. In fact, we were all under strict instruction never to address them if we came across them on the grounds.

I worked for a couple of months with Richard on technical support and inspections but was then transferred back into the Continental Liaison Management Office. In typical Scientology style, my new job carried an elaborate title, Dissemination Chief, and brought with it long hours and new challenges. My position meant that I was the Editor of all magazines and promotional publications for COSRECI, or the Church of Scientology Religious Education College Incorporated, registered in Southern Australia. This is the corporation, or legal entity that houses all Scientology activities in the UK. This Australian-based company operates in this fashion to avoid certain UK tax and legal responsibilities. I was drafted into this editorial and design area due to my background in art, which I'd studied in Cork as a teenager, and my training in computers.

The guy who was running this area, Adam, was a brilliant artist, but he was completely useless both administratively and technically. He was creating some real problems due to his incompetence. In Scientology you are supposed to be able to just do any job assigned to you with no practical training whatsoever. You are supposed to remember, from your previous lifetimes, how to do the tasks. Adam must have had a bad memory. Within a week of taking up the job I received a baptism of fire, as a crucifying project was about to hit my lines.

As fate would have it, a special magazine design, with very specific articles, came down from International Management just as the Easter Bank Holiday was about to hit. The main body and the artwork of the magazine were identical for all Scientology Churches across the globe, translations excepted. Each Continental Liaison Office was sent these parts on disc. My job was to edit them for each of the eight UK delivery organisations and add an accompanying sales brochure in time for the Easter break. A number of new releases were coming out and that always meant a big sales boost for the Church. The deadline was impossible but, with little or no sleep, I managed to put together all of the copy, photography and other UK-specific items, using a couple of very slow Macintosh computers. At the last minute, just when we thought we had it done, we were told that we had to insert an additional series of graphics. We were also informed that we had to do the print and mailing along with the Continental Liaison Office Europe. This way we would save money by doing a single bulk print and consolidated mailing in Spain. I knew this one was going to be tricky and I wasn't going to get much sleep.

To prepare everything in time I needed some professional help and lots of modern up-to-date computer processing power. In the end we got clearance to hire a graphic studio in London. We got set up in the studio and the new files were sent down the ISDN line to us. Some of the files from the US were corrupt and we had to spend three days without sleep repairing them.

Once the files were ready, it was off to Madrid to the print and mailing works. I remember getting on the plane, closing my eyes and being woken up by an airhostess in Spain. I had absolutely no memory of the take off, flight or the landing. Another week working around the clock and the job was eventually completed and dispatched.

I got a tiny bit of free time during the mailing part of the job. We were near a lovely little village about 40 kilometres north of Madrid. I spent a few days there and the mail house owner was a wonderful host. We would start the job in the morning, and then break for 'cafe con leche' in a lovely little coffee bar in the old village square. He provided lunch as well, in his own restaurant, and the food was exquisite. I decided that I could handle living in Spain. This rare break, in a gruelling work schedule, felt like a holiday. I hadn't had time off in years, as I still couldn't get permission to go back to Ireland.

If I thought the Madrid project was tough, what landed on my desk coming up to Christmas 1997 would really show me just what the Sea Org expected of me. With the New Year fast approaching, international management wanted a huge spike in sales. Like the diet firms, quit smoking forums and health studios, Scientology wanted to cash in on people's New Year resolutions. They wanted to encourage people to continue on the road of Scientology, buy more services, spend more time on courses and involve themselves more in Church PR activities.

As usual within the Church management, there was a flurry of last-minute activity. People like us on the production end of things always tended to bear the brunt of poor management planning. In early November, I received an urgent telex that demanded that I drop everything. I was told to start preparing a very complex mailing package and to schedule print runs and graphics work so that every Scientologist on the UK mailing list received a full promotional pack by Christmas. That meant that I had to have all the items printed, packaged and addressed for mailing by the Royal Mail's shut off posting date of December 19.

I was furious as it gave me about a month to carry out something that most 'wog' companies would allow a minimum of six months to do. As usual the expectancy from management was always 'make it go right'. I opened up the raw files from the disk that I had received and saw that it contained 20 separate items. These included two 30-page colour magazines, a large fold-out wall-chart and about six two-colour American-sized briefing sheets.

We had a crisis meeting with Continental Liaison Management and I tried to point out the difficulties but to no avail. The job just had to be done and there were no excuses.

My deputy Suzy and I got our heads down and spent a full week, of 18-hour days preparing the UK artwork alone. Meanwhile it was decided that we cost share the print and mailing job with our European counterparts in Denmark. I flew out to Copenhagen where our Danish counterparts were running a 'Condition 1 All Hands'. They were under even more serious pressure than us.

After a week there, working round the clock, we boarded a flight to Rome. A group of us were then transported across the mountain range, to a little village. A print company, owned by a high level Scientologist and staffed by Scientologists of various levels, had been contracted to do the print work. Unfortunately for me, they had never before handled anything like the one million, four-colour magazines, pamphlets, wall charts and briefing sheets I needed printed up in eight languages. From the minute I arrived I had a foreboding feeling that this was the project where I would discover what it was like to fall from grace.

Delay stacked on delay and the problems became almost crippling. Several senior executives were flown in from both England and Copenhagen to report back. They had to find out if we were sabotaging the job ourselves. Luckily, Beryl, the senior executive sent to inspect my end of things, was quite a good friend of mine. She was also a graphic designer by trade. Despite the fact that Beryl had reported back that I was not the problem, I began receiving more than ten phone calls every morning from executives in England. They were loud, screaming demands for situation reports and I got veiled threats about what would happen to me if I didn't sort out the problems. The most daunting of the calls was from Craig Wilson, the CO of the Commodore's Messenger Organisation UK, the second most powerful Scientologist within the UK at that time. Wilson was someone capable of wrecking a career in Sea Org with the stroke of a pen.

I was terrified and could see all my hard work over the years going to waste.

Somehow, amidst the confusion, we managed to pull off the print job. But just as I thought I was out of the woods, I discovered that our box of 8,000 UK mailing labels had disappeared. I felt a sinking feeling in the pit of my stomach. I didn't want to report it to Craig but I had no choice.

The phone call was a one-hour, one-way stream of invective, put downs and disparaging comments on my character, moral fibre, breeding and upbringing. The various Italian executives, and British and Danish management personnel, decided they would use my situation as a way to protect themselves. They dug up 'ethics out-points', on me and the Scientology print firm. All the time, Craig threatened me with a ten-year tenure in the RPF.

As if it my situation wasn't bad enough, Beryl then decided to stop being my friend. Instead she became a colluding party in plotting my downfall. It seemed that the view on home base was that I had caused all the problems. I was the bad apple in the box.

I eventually found the labels and we sent everything off to Tirano to be posted but the damage had been done. Over the next couple of days, as I wrapped up the project before I returned to England, I would take early morning walks on the beach. The churning in my gut told me all I needed to know about what was

happening at Saint Hill. I assumed the Committee of
Evidence had already been drawn up. Renane, who
was the Executive In Charge of Internal Security, CLO
UK, called me a couple of days later and told me to get
a flight to Gatwick immediately.

I told him I had no money but his reply was the
usual Scientology mantra "make it go right". I had just
enough money to get to the airport and in true Sea Org
'make it go right' style, walked up to the BA desk and
wrote a cheque for Stg£200 pounds from my overdrawn
bank account.

I made no attempt not to go back as I didn't
have anywhere to run to. Throughout my career in
Scientology, I had rarely strayed from the rule book.
Although I was only a young man in my early 20s
when I joined up, I had managed to resist the urge
to consummate any of the few relationships I had
experienced inside the Sea Org. My statistics had
largely remained high since I was first put on post and
my ethics were nothing to get too excited about. Along
the way, I suppose I was simply interested in furthering
myself and my Sea Organisation career. While there
were small misdemeanours nothing had ever seen me
face the harsh discipline that had driven so many to the
edge of suicide and psychosis.

Back from Italy all that was about to change.

To this day I do not know why the chaotic print
job evoked such severe reaction, straight from the top
of the Church. It is likely that Miscavige had bigger
fish to fry than me. I believe he used the botched job
as an opportunity to purge people he wanted out. But
whatever the reasoning was, when I got back it was as
if I had walked into the fictional world of 'The Lord
of the Rings' and the Eye of Sauron was firmly fixed

on me.

Renane picked me up at Gatwick with two burly security guards. We drove back to Saint Hill in silence. The mood in the car told me all I needed to know about what awaited me.

I looked out at the familiar fields and played out the last week in my head. We had been set up for a loss when we had received the orders to print and mail this job in November. There was no way it could have been pulled off. We had done everything we could to salvage it and had, eventually, managed to get it done and to a mailing house in less than seven weeks. There was no way it was going to make the target date, however, because the job and the time frame were just unrealistic. Then again I thought, this was not the Sea Org attitude. I had sworn upon my EPF graduation to 'Make things go right and persist until they do'. So – no excuses. I had made it go wrong and now I would have plenty of time to contemplate why I had allowed the job to fail.

We drove through the gates and straight up to the mock castle of Saint Hill. My thoughts were all over the place when the car stopped. I was thinking that building had been started as far back as 1967 and only completed, mainly with Sea Org RPF labour over the past 10 years. The security guards walked me up to the east wing and towards what was known as The Tower.

I had been Deputy Security Chief of the UK base for a few months back in late 1989. The job involved ensuring that staff were staying in line and that there were no external spies or internal leaking of documents to the outside or the 'enemy'. The Tower had, at that time, been used to store watch equipment, such as spare walkie-talkies, chargers, torches and uniforms. It was now a holding cell for security risks and 'ethics particles' like my good self.

I knew I was going to be kept under 24 hour watch here while writing reams of confessions, sins, bad thoughts and searching my soul for those moments where I failed in the upkeep of 'Sea Org Standards'.

I groaned as I was marched straight past the reception area and up the stairs to the turret room where I would be confined until my fate had been decided. I sat down on an uncomfortable chair facing an empty desk and sighed as I realised it was just days to Christmas and the New Year. I would more than likely spend the festive days here in this grim room.

And so it began, my first true dose of ethics handling, Scientology style. For hours on end I was ordered to write knowledge reports and scribble down all the 'overts and witholds' I could think of that may have contributed to my failings in Italy. I was given piles of Hubbard policy to study. I started with writing up a huge report about how insane the job was from start to finish. I wrote it to Ronnie Miscavige, David's brother, who was at that time Marketing Executive International. I had known him quite well back in 1988 when he was my boss while I was at Central Marketing International. He was always a fair-minded and intelligent man but I didn't know that he and his team were undergoing an even harsher 'correction' program in the Sea Org compound in Hemet California.

Naively I did my best to explain my position and I hoped that someone would understand. Nothing came back and slowly, over the four weeks, I realised that I would have to start taking the blame if I was ever going to get out of The Tower.

Every morning, I was picked up at 8am in my dorm and brought to the tower for the endless confessions. I wrote painstaking reports on cigarette and coffee breaks I took when I should have been concentrating on the job in hand. I pilloried myself for the few hours' sleep I had grabbed during the 16 and 18-hour days I had worked. I criticised, condemned and censured every breath I had taken during the job. At 1am I would eventually be removed from the room and brought back to the dorm. I would sleep under watch until the following morning, when it would all start again.

I was succeeding in destroying my own self-esteem and undermining any sense of self-respect and pride I had maintained.

It was what the Church wanted.

As days passed, I felt worse and worse and worse about myself. The only relief came when I would be put on an E-Meter. A floating needle would mean I could leave each criticism behind and move on to a next one. Christmas 1997 and New Year's Day 1998 passed, while senior executives including my erstwhile friend Beryl discussed my fate. What was obvious was that someone up-lines wanted a head on a pike. For a time it looked like it would be mine. At night, during fitful sleeps, I knew that I was facing the RPF.

Then as suddenly as it had started, it stopped. The week after New Year, the mailing hit everyone's doorsteps. Income for Scientology rose to unprecedented levels. I was later told that the job made Stg£2 million for the UK Corporation alone. All of a sudden, I was the good guy again. I was released from The Tower and told to go back on my post. Although I was hugely relieved that I wasn't going to be RPFed, I was angry. I felt demeaned that my character had been disparaged in front of my comrades and peers. I was sure that this had been unjustified and unwarranted discipline.

I demanded from Jenny, a Senior Commodore's Messenger, that a published retraction be distributed to all staff exonerating me. Otherwise I said I would not go back on post.

This caused severe consternation, as management 'could not be wrong', only individuals could be wrong. However, there was another major print and mailing project coming up and I was desperately needed back at my desk. So, what was agreed was a limited distribution 'ethics order'. It didn't quite exonerate me but it did acknowledge the extreme effort and conditions that I had gone through to pull off the job in Italy. Management hoped that I would be sufficiently placated with this small gesture but I was still very annoyed. While I took what I could get, I went back to work with a heavy heart.

I was utterly bent out of shape about the harshness and lack of sympathy from management within the Church but I separated that from my feelings about Scientology and from Hubbard.

Over the few weeks I had been on ethics watch, the Church had replaced me with a young Sea Org member called Suzy. She was a clever girl and wanted to be the Dissemination Chief but she didn't really have the experience to handle the huge print job coming our way. Suzy was initially upset by my return but we soon sparked a very close friendship. We ended up working fantastically well together.

After a few weeks back on post I was given the olive branch I needed to forgive and forget – I was told that I was going to be allowed back to Ireland for a holiday. To make matters even better I was given leave of three weeks.

Just months before, I had received a small inheritance

from an investment Granny Cotter had made for us after our mother died. The cheques had cleared while I was being held in The Tower. The money was about IR£4,000 (€5,000) and to me it was a small fortune. I'd gone out and bought my own Volkswagen Sirocco and I knew I had enough left to really enjoy the holiday at home. I planned to head straight to Kilmony and I was aching to re-visit the remote islands off West Cork and Galway.

As my departure day drew nearer I had to undergo a thorough security check and be audited for clearance. As a result of the incredible workload expected from Sea Org, I could only convince someone to 'sec check' me on the actual day I was booked to travel. I wasn't too bothered because it promised to be a very easy check due to the amount of 'overts and witholds' and the reams of knowledge reports I had spewed out just a month earlier in The Tower.

But, as is often the case, the more rush the less hurry. Hours before my ferry was due to leave I was sitting in Saint Hill, hooked up to the E-Meter, willing the damn needle to float. But because of my excitement about the trip and my worries about missing the boat, the E-Meter needle kept refusing to sway. What I'd hoped would be a simple quick question and answer session, had turned into a lengthy process.

My anxiety about getting on the road was threatening to be my undoing and my trip hung in the balance, as the E-Meter repeatedly found problems. Eventually the needle did float and I was let go.

I had a race against time ahead of me to the ferry at Fishguard. I drove like a maniac for almost five hours and just made it to the port in time to see the big ferry depart the pier. While I was upset, I was also exhausted and I slept in the car for the seven hours until the next ferry.

It was 14 years since I had been home to Kilmony. Lots had changed since I had been there last. Frankie and John Paul, who were only tots when I left, had grown up to be fine strapping men. Clare had graduated and was living in Berlin and Dan was completing a degree at UCC. Aunt Cath and Uncle Frank had aged too and no doubt they were struck by my own appearance but little was said. Granny Cotter had passed away and although there had been a large family funeral, I had been absent. Auntie Julia's eldest son, Eoin, had also died shortly before my visit. He was an electrician and was working in London when his bike had hit a tree on the way home from the nightshift. My commitment to my Church had meant that I hadn't attended his funeral either.

My arrival home was very congenial and nothing at all was made of my long absence. Cath and Frank were wonderful as usual. They tried to make my stay as relaxing as possible and steered clear of any unpleasantness about Scientology. I had a few nice evenings out in the local pub with Claire, Dervla, Dan and Frankie. They did ask me about the Church and I tried to describe it to some degree although it is very difficult to do so. But they were willing to listen and there was no pressure put on me at all to change my view or my opinions. I had a few nights out with Maurice too and was glad to see him. Declan was in England and I resolved to try to spend the odd day with him when I got back. Unfortunately, I didn't get to see Jeremy as he was living in the US at the time.

I stayed for five days in Kilmony and then travelled up to my sister Kate in Galway where I met her children, my niece, Realte, and nephew, Shaun, for the first time. Then I headed over to the Aran Islands. I found a charming B&B and walked the islands during the day. The remoteness of it helped me recharge my batteries and I thought a lot about life in the Sea Org. While I had just come through some hard times, I was very accepting that it was my job and my life and what I did. Although I had started to become slightly critical of the Church, I wasn't able to really think about all that was wrong with it. While it wasn't all rosy and while there were problems, I examined my conscience but felt I couldn't find an argument to make me change. Looking outside at the rest of world, there didn't seem to be a place for me there, just like Hubbard had warned. 'Those who don't make it in the Sea Org, won't make it in life,' he wrote and that really rang true for me in the so-called 'Wog' World.

I thought about Saint Hill and it seemed like there was a normalcy back there. There was the job and there was Suzy who I had started hanging out with quite a lot. Although I had enjoyed spending time with my family, I felt I couldn't really connect with people outside Scientology. Our whole experience of life was so different that there didn't seem to be any middle ground. I struggled with people, even my family members, to find something we could talk about. Small talk was hard and functioning in a world without Scientology seemed near impossible.

After my three weeks, I went back to Saint Hill rested. The break had done me some good and yet another promotion awaited me. I was moved up the ranks to the status of Midshipman which meant I had jumped from Petty Officer 3rd Class through three ranks.

My graduation ceremony was very grand and in full military style. I stood up on stage in my new uniform and lanyards and was handed my certificate and stripes. It was a great feeling but brought with it greater responsibility to uphold the ideals of Sea Org. Now, the onus was really on me to present the impervious image of an elite, dedicated officer willing to push through all barriers, to the attainment of the goals and purposes of Sea Org and The Church of Scientology.

NINE

AN OFFICER AND A GENTLEMAN

Back in LA by late 1999 things had changed drastically. I had just been promoted to a new job as Commanding Officer of Scientology Missions International (SMI) in the UK and I had flown over for an intensive study course. It meant heavy training at the Hollywood Guarantee Building and a gruelling daily schedule that left little time for sleep, let alone any other dalliances. Gone were the days that we could just step out the door and spend a few stolen hours sipping coffee or walking under the hot sun. Instead an atmosphere of tension and paranoia gripped the place and nobody was allowed to leave without an escort. I was flabbergasted by how strict the system had become and very quickly learned that even tiny misdemeanours meant being dragged away and put on very heavy ethics checks. Everyone was on edge and you could feel the stress in the air.

Within days I discovered that my regular cigarette breaks weren't even going to be tolerated, as it meant that I had to step outside the building onto Hollywood Boulevard and would need to be accompanied by a staff member. My boss, the Commanding Officer of SMI International, would get annoyed with me every time I suggested that I needed a cigarette. He made a huge deal of organising someone to go with me. Although we were working with computers, there was no Internet and the only people allowed access to it were those that worked for the Office of Special Affairs (OSA).

Three months later, I was back in the UK and quickly realised that my so-called promotion was a poisoned chalice. Huge problems had been brewing at SMI UK for quite some time and it had lost five Commanding Officers over a four-year period. There had been no one on the post for a year when Bruce Perry 'promoted' me. Bruce, as Commanding Officer of the Continental Liaison Office (CLO) and ultimately responsible for all UK operations, had been put under incredible pressure to get the UK Mission Network sorted out. The once affluent and powerful network had collapsed about ten years earlier and had never really recovered. With a Stg£30,000 price tag on the mandatory Mission Starter package it was never going to be an easy sales job. Running a mission was essentially authorising the Sea Organisation to bully you for sales and statistics, morning to night, seven days a week, while earning less than the minimum wage.

My remit, as Commanding Officer SMI, was to get the Mission stats up and to go in and force them to make more money. I shared an office with an interesting bunch of Sea Org folks. Susan, a Canadian in her 60s who had been shipped over to the UK after getting involved in the Canadian Guardian's Office problem. She was one of the people who had actually broken into Government Offices there. Susan had stolen files for the Church and had to get out of Canada before she was jailed. She had lived at Saint Hill ever since and was suffering badly with MS. Trisha, a really close friend of mine, and Commanding Office WISE UK, was a highly-strung Irish woman. She had never been healthy and the stress of her job was beginning to tell. Trisha was plagued by back trouble, kidney stones and other ailments but never really had the time to stop and take care of herself – the demands of the job were too great. Then there was Gerald, my own deputy, who had just come off the RPF. This was the same Gerald who had recruited me all those years ago in Stuttgart for the Sea Org. An ex-British Navy man, he had been put on the RPF because of his addiction to pornography and had spent the last 10 years being re-educated. He complained incessantly, bemoaning the 'old days', pre-Miscavige, when, he said, Sea Org life was better. Now it had become a corporate nightmare, he groaned. I paid little heed to him.

I knew that I had to expand our Mission Network in the UK, Pakistan and India. I began recruiting 'upper Bridge' OT Scientologists to help me achieve just that. I started working with an OT Level VIII called Malcolm, a public Scientologist, who owned a chain of hairdressers. To be granted eligibility to start and continue on the OT levels, part of the process involved 'contribution to the expansion and the power of the Church'. When a Scientologist is on OT Level VII they are expected to be doing work with Scientology operations and donating time and energy to a given field of endeavour. Malcolm realised the problem I was going to have encouraging people to open up new Missions. He reckoned if he could raise the funds to open one in Soho, it could just manage to give SMI UK the boost it needed.

The LA-based celebrity musician, Mark Isham, was playing at the famous Ronnie Scotts nightclub at the time. He is very well-known in the US as a jazz trumpeter who has penned a lot of movie soundtracks. As a Scientologist he had got as far as OT Level VI. In order to get eligibility for OT Level VII he needed to make a major contribution to forward Scientology. When Malcolm asked him to help out with funding Soho he was only too happy to come on board. Mark provided the Stg£30,000 to set it up. Malcolm then located a building and purchased the licence and starter package, which included E-Meters and books. The premises opened to great fanfare. There was a lot of stress and trepidation involved in getting it open because it was not a done deal until it was running for a month, so I was quite tense about it. I was worried it wouldn't succeed. Unfortunately I was right and it closed within a few months. Malcolm had quickly realised that he hadn't a hope of making enough money to even cover his rent. It was a real sign of the difficulties I was going to face trying to pull the UK missions out of the mire.

Scientology is always on the lookout to recruit actual and potential celebrities. We had established a contact point with Guy Richie, who had just released the film 'Lock, Stock and Two Smoking Barrels'. One of our OT people working in the industry managed to get a meeting with him about movie production. Richie didn't know he was going to be talking to Scientologists. There was excitement at the time but nothing seemed to come of their efforts. The singer Peter Gabriel was also very much on the radar, as he was doing a lot of work with OT Level V Scientologist and musician Hossam Ramsey.

Another person I recruited was a music producer and OT Level VII, Horst, to my team of potential Mission executives. Horst eventually decided he wanted to try his hand in Calcutta, a city he had travelled to a lot in his day job. He was a public Scientologist and a very clever guy. Looking back I think he had realised the truth about Scientology but had no way out as his wife, children and business were all tied up in it. To leave would have meant being 'Declared' and losing everything overnight. Out in India he could live pretty cheaply, stay out of the way of everyone and even make some money. He gambled right and his Mission started doing great in Calcutta. It upped my statistics no end and opened new doors for us as a Church. Gerald soon piped up that he wouldn't mind going there too so I sent him with my blessing. Between them they opened a second mission in Delhi and then a third, making my life slightly easier in the process.

I was only months on post when I was sent on a special project to Poole in Dorset where a major problem had evolved for the Bournemouth Mission. Ironically the mission would mark the first steps on my journey to discovering the truth about this cult I was immersed in. A woman called Andrea Catt, who had been a recruiter at Bournemouth throughout the 1990s, had threatened a major legal action against the Church. Rather than allow the case to become public, our legal team had settled the suit for Stg£600,000. We had six months to pay her off. If we failed the Scientology Corporation, COSRECI, would be sued in the courts and the whole story of the fraud that had gone on in Bournemouth, with management's blessing, would be exposed.

Catt had been involved in some serious financial irregularities at the Mission. They had been overlooked and encouraged, due to the ever-present pressure to constantly raise statistics. The Mission seemed to be doing incredibly well under the stewardship of the Mission Holder, Roger and his team of dedicated staff. They were making between Stg£30,000 and Stg£80,000 a week. All of the management was benefiting, particularly SMI UK and SMI International. Loads of money and up statistics had meant days off, no heavy ethics investigations and generally far better conditions all round. When a series of court cases, from former Bournemouth clients, suddenly hit the Church the whole story had come to light and everything changed overnight.

It had emerged that recruits were being persuaded to borrow money to help pay for courses and auditing. This was common practice, but in Bournemouth, instead of being sent off to the banks, the Mission actually had their own handy stash of application forms from all the regular banks and building societies. They would help the new recruits to fill in their loan forms in the office. Not only were recruits helped with this but they were also urged to lie to the financial institutions about what they wanted the money for. In many cases they were encouraged to say they were making requests for car loans rather than Scientology courses. In 1993, a loan application, purporting to be for a computer, was discovered to be fraudulent by a bank. When it was later established that the money had been spent on Scientology instead, a major problem exploded for the Mission. Other recruits then sued because the amounts they had signed for on the loan forms had been increased by Mission staff and as a result one man lost his house.

Catt has since said that she was forced to sign a confession exonerating everyone else at the Bournemouth Mission and laying all the blame in her own lap. She was suspended for six months but the mission income collapsed to nothing and heads began to roll all the way up the lines. She was ordered to go back on post. Ron Norton and Bruce Perry were dealing with her and the mission holder, Roger. Members of staff were forced to endure some of the harshest and extreme conditions experienced in the Mission Network since Miscavige set the dogs loose in the early 1980s. For Andrea, this meant a daily ordeal of being screamed at, pushed around physically, taunted and being called a criminal. She was forced to solve some of the looming legal suits and even the running costs of the organisation by cashing in her husband's inheritance. She was then declared a Suppressive Person. Andrea was shattered by the whole experience and, after two years spent recovering, she had decided to sue.

The Church's legal heavyweights had been sent to Bournemouth to hammer out a deal to minimise the bad publicity that would likely ensue. Once the Stg£600,000 pay-off was agreed, we had six months to make up the sum. That is where the problem started for me as the Church left the bill with the Bournemouth Mission. At that stage they were pulling in no more than about Stg£1,500 to Stg£4,000 a week. To make up the legal bill the income was going to have to increase tenfold and I was the one that had to make it happen.

As a Sea Org member, I was under strict orders not to make friends with Mission staff but to approach them in a cold and clinical fashion to get my own mission done. I did it for a while and started putting the 15 or so staff under enormous pressure to up their game and work longer hours. But they were devastated by everything that had gone on and gutted that this massive legal bill was being left at their door. They had already been working 16 hour days, trying to keep the place running and were very dedicated to moving people up the Bridge. Now they had to achieve the impossible and one-by-one they broke down in front of my eyes. I soon realised that there was no way I could stand back and just expect that they would deal with it.

In the Scientology world, according to a Hubbard policy letter called 'The Magic of Good Management' people are described as 'particles' being run through a manufacturing line. Specific actions are done by each to result in 'the end product'. But it didn't ring true for me as the Scientologists in Bournemouth were not 'particles'. They were real, intelligent and dedicated people. I thought back to all the good people that I had known who had been declared over the years – declared for standing up for what they saw as right – and I realised that there was something fundamentally wrong with the Sea Org approach to management. I just didn't want to face up to what it was. I decided on my own that we had to all be in it together if we had any hope of succeeding in this challenge.

Pulling out all the stops to try to bring the money in had left very little spare money in the pot. For months we all earned no more than a few pounds a week, often eating nothing more than bread. The job was a nightmare and we had to beg, steal and borrow to try to meet this huge demand. We got some money back that had been paid to the Advanced Organisation at

Saint Hill four years earlier for undelivered services. We ran campaigns for donations, boosted sales and did everything we could to up the stats. In the midst of all this, I was stopped on the motorway by the police on my way home to East Grinstead at 3am one morning. One of the rear lamps on the ancient Ford Escort I had borrowed was not working. I had to report to the station the next day. When I realised that the car had an expired car test certificate, I knew I was in bad trouble. As well as having to find Stg£20 for the fine, public relations wrote a cutting knowledge report on me. I received a full ethics hearing for 'dropping my hat as a Sea Org Commanding Officer and executive. These actions were devastating to my already hard-tested self-esteem.

During those six months, I often had to go online at night to try to sell things people had donated on E-bay. The computer I was using was not fitted with the net-nanny software that had been on all other computers I had ever used. At this stage I knew that the Church had installed net-nanny filtering software on all its personal computers to block out critical information about Scientology and Hubbard. A CD had also been sent out to every Scientologist in the world, for setting up their very own Scientology Internet site at home. The alleged idea was to make it easy to find other Scientologists and receive special offers on books and tapes. A massive majority ended up installing the system that had also contained net-nanny software to block out countless Internet pages about OT levels, Miscavige and Scientology.

I logged onto e-Bay one night and started browsing around to see what was for sale before I loaded the auction details of our collection of early twentieth century books. I was stunned to see that there were

E-Meters for sale and loads of them. I found it very bizarre. Why would anyone sell their E-Meter? One blurb mentioned that the E-Meter was almost identical to the lie detector, used by law enforcement authorities around the world and that Freud and Jung had worked extensively with another almost identical tool called the psychogalvometer. I had always been told that the E-Meter was a unique invention of L Ron Hubbard's. As I logged off that night, I felt stunned by what I had discovered. Surely there couldn't be that many people declared as Suppressive Persons?

A few days later I got a letter my Aunt Cath had sent on from my former Covenant Players' girlfriend, Greta Jo. She had got in touch through my old address at Kilmony to tell me she was running a theatre school. There was an e-mail address on it and I contacted her. She e-mailed me back and we had quite a deep online discussion about how amazing it was to have found one another after 20 years. She told me she was still in love with me and I told her I had never forgiven myself for leaving her. I actually thought about starting a life with her but then as quickly as it started, our new friendship ended – after I mentioned that I was involved with Scientology. I was puzzled by the communications breakdown.

One night, alone in the office at 4am, I happened to do a Google search on the name L Ron Hubbard and up came a picture that I had never seen before. In it, the Founder had long hair and a drugged look on his face. Another showed him at a roulette table, wearing glasses, with long hair and rotting teeth. The image of Hubbard within the church was a tightly controlled item. One was not even allowed to make jokes that might be seen as disparaging of the great man. All the images of Hubbard that were either printed or put on display had to be approved by both the LRH Communicator and the LRH Personal Public Relations Officer. These senior people had huge ethics powers and could wipe out a Sea Org or staff member's career if they were thought to have created a poor image of Hubbard. A person I knew was sent to the RPF for allowing a fuzzy picture of Hubbard to be printed in a magazine. Every office in a Scientology Organisation has to have a very carefully air-brushed picture of Hubbard on the wall. At our weekly 'Source Briefings', where the whole staff had to gather to listen to a taped Hubbard Lecture, there was always a huge picture of the Founder. He was dressed either in nautical fashion or in a suit with a silk cravat. In all the images we ever saw of Hubbard he looked impeccable, perfect and of course he did not wear glasses. His writings told us that he had cured his damaged eyesight in 1947, using the techniques that eventually became Scientology auditing.

The picture on the screen in front of me was shocking. I was intrigued and clicked on another site set up by Kristi Wachter, a former Scientologist who claimed to have lived and worked with him. In her site she told a bitter story of living with Hubbard and painted a picture of an aggressive alcoholic and a drugged-out maniac. LRH was believed to have been addicted to amphetamines at the time and was increasingly both physically and mentally ill. He began auditing himself and in his unbalanced, delusional state wrote up new Scientology levels that pertained to teach a Scientologist how to operate outside their bodies, talk to the spirit world and travel through space, visiting different planets and universes. He called these 'The

OT Levels' and had them packaged for consumption by the many devout Scientologists around the world. They, of course, offered a fresh cash boost to both him and the Scientology Corporation.

Kristi Wachter had worked directly for him, as one of his messengers on board *The Apollo*. She described how he had set up the Sea Org while on the run from the law and said he was strung out on drugs in Tunis and Algiers. She described a letter he wrote to his wife Mary Sue telling her that he was popping 'greens and reds.' The historical time frame all appeared to be correct and tied in accurately with those lectures where Hubbard described this period of 'intensive research'.

She also told a different story about Rhodesia, now Zimbabwe, describing how he had tried to infiltrate the government there, before being thrown out. The tale made sense as I thought back to my time in Zimbabwe and the deep-seated suspicion that existed there about the Church. She explained that the Sea Org had been formed after Hubbard returned to Saint Hill, having been ejected from Rhodesia where he'd spent three months in 1966. The hasty departure was a direct result of his efforts to buy political influence with Ian Smith's government, through both bribery and the 'drafting of a new constitution for that country'. His visa had been revoked. She described how his political meddling in African affairs had the knock on effect of alerting the British authorities to look into Hubbard's financial affairs. Not long after his final departure, an in-depth Parliamentary enquiry began that eventually resulted in the banning of Scientology in the United Kingdom. The ban on the Church of Scientology meant that they could not bring Scientologists into the UK to study upper levels in the teachings. However, the Church personally lobbied Margaret Thatcher who had the ban lifted when she was elected. Meanwhile, the FBI was investigating his affairs in the US, while Australia had pretty much succeeded in banning the movement. LRH had correctly estimated that he could not be investigated at sea and set up the Sea Org.

In late 1966, he'd resigned as Executive Director of the Church to distance himself from the mounting controversy. He began his plans to create a navy style military out of a group of hardcore Church members so he could disappear for a while until the heat wore off. He appointed himself Commodore and called his crew of several hundred the Sea Org, his very own Praetorian Guard and Scientology's paramilitary wing.

I was glued to the screen as I read on. Wachter wrote about Hubbard coming off his motorbike and hurting his arm and rib in 1967. The timeline fitted in exactly with a taped lecture – Ron's Journal '67 – where he claimed he had broken his back while researching OT III because it was so powerful. I had to admit that the motorbike accident did seem more plausible.

That year the highest OT level available was the newly released OT III. This level is both a product of, and a mix of, science fiction, myth and Aleister Crowley's black magic. Hubbard talked at great length about conspiracies against his efforts to 'free man from the trap'. In one lecture he described having written a manuscript for a book called 'Excalibur', just after the war. He claimed that the material in it was so powerful that people had gone insane reading it. The KGB allegedly broke into his house and stole much of the manuscript; the remainder has never seen the light of day. There are many parallels between this story and OT III. Those that make it to that level are sworn to a vow of absolute secrecy about what they encounter. Hubbard warned that exposure to this level without the mental and spiritual preparation of OT levels I and II, will result in insanity or death from a mysterious illness.

Kristi described how on *The Apollo* he roared and raged at his staff. He had to be strapped to his chair to be restrained. As he penned his master documents, the new Sea Org members were forced to work long hours, dress in naval uniform and adopt ranks. They also signed the billion-year contract to serve Scientology. She explained how discipline was harsh and members were often locked up or thrown overboard into the icy seas for small misdemeanours. By the mid-1970s the world had moved on. Hubbard was no longer being pursued by his enemies in government and was able to return to land. Under an assumed identity he arrived in Florida. Controversy continued to follow him and his Church became embroiled in an investigation by the IRS in the US. The IRS believed Hubbard had millions of dollars hidden away in off-shore bank accounts. They were probably correct, but could not get definitive proof.

Her words were a revelation and I thought, 'Oh My God'.

I clicked on one more site. It was a feature on Jon Atack's book 'A Piece of Blue Sky'. It was a highly critical book about the Church written by the former public Scientologist. It was a revelation and it actually really made sense. It had been written in East Grinstead and I personally knew quite a lot of the characters he mentioned in the book.

There was also a mention of a booklet he had written, 'The Total Freedom Trap'. He described the

Communications Course as the first indoctrination into Scientology and talked about the exercises I had done all those years before in Stuttgart. I read that they are actually known as Training Routines or TRs. Atack said they have been described by one expert as 'the most overt form of hypnosis used by any destructive cult'. The trances in the first two stages of the Training Routines are supposed to teach you to approach a situation with no baggage and just confront what is happening at that moment in time. What you actually do is subvert your natural, intuitive protective reactions to what is going on around you. By dropping all the psychological defences that you need to take care of yourself, a person is left wide open and mentally exposed to commands. Like stage show volunteers, you end up completely hypnotised and open to anything.

He explained that one TR is actually called 'Bull-Baiting'. Anyone who subsequently watched footage of the BBC reporter John Sweeney losing his temper with the Florida-based Scientology spokesman, Tommy Davis, in 2007 was seeing this training used to its purpose. Sweeney shouts at Davis, who simply repeats himself over and over again. He totally ignores what the Panorama journalist has to say and what is going on around him until he eventually succeeds in causing Sweeney to lose his temper.

Although I wasn't sure what to believe after reading Atack's views, I did know that bull-baiting was a tactic widely used by the Church to intimidate opponents. We had used it on the Wollersheim case in LA when we were protesting inside and outside the courthouse. While I personally hadn't felt groggy after bull-baiting, I had gone practically unconscious whenever I used another TR – OT TR0. It involved hours of sitting and

staring unblinkingly at someone else. Any flinch, blink
or reaction meant a 'flunk'. During and afterwards I had
always felt almost comatose so Attack's explanation
rang true to me.

Something else that had always niggled at me also
came to light in Bournemouth. It was something that
Hubbard had said on the Student Hat Tapes – a series
of lectures used in re-education courses, which I had
taken a number of times over the years. In a 1964 lecture
Hubbard claimed that he was bored one day and so he
sat down and read the full original Gibbons six-volume
set of the 17th Century epic 'The Decline and Fall of the
Roman Empire'. I had always found that an astounding
achievement, as I had only managed to read sections of
it myself over the years. It was something that would
probably take an academic several months to get
through. During my stay, I happened to be sleeping in
a house out at the other end of Poole. In my room was
a little line of books and one night as I looked through
them I found a condensed 1963 Laurel/Dell published
version of Gibbon's seminal work. It was in a handy
one-volume format by Frank C Bourne. It dawned on
me that Hubbard had fibbed.

Another realisation about my Church was waiting
around the corner when my former girlfriend
Nicole came down to Bournemouth. She was under
instructions to raise Stg£50,000 for the International
Association of Scientologists (IAS). The IAS could
go anywhere they wanted to raise money but there
was no way I was allowing them to fundraise on our
patch. I ordered Nicole out and had a huge row with
her superior, former Commanding Officer CMO UK,
Ginger Smith, now in charge of the IAS office in the UK.
In a move that surprised me, Ginger eventually backed

down. The incident left me with a sour feeling. It was clear that one of the most senior levels of the Church didn't care about our plight and were just interested in making money.

My world view was beginning to shift. I was deeply troubled by what I had learned online but I couldn't bring myself to make any decisions based on it. It was too huge a reality to fully accept, let alone to act upon.

When I got a call to return to Ireland I didn't even seek security clearance. I merely told the guys in Bournemouth that I would be gone for a few days. The reason for my return was a large family get-together, surrounding a point in my grandmother's will. Our huge extended family gathered in the lovely Maryborough Hotel in Cork for a full day. I had long since swallowed Hubbard's rant that the 'wog' world was full of somehow lesser people and that the non-Scientologist was in some way lacking an essential spiritual quality. But here for the first time in years, I was surrounded by my own and my extended family.

I spent two days with them. I relaxed and felt quite good, safe and unthreatened for the first time in quite a while. It was wonderful to see Maurice and his then wife, Abi, and my little nephew, Mossie, who was just a baby. My sister Kate and the huge brood of foster brothers and sisters were all present. I loved seeing them all again. These so-called 'wogs' were wonderful and intelligent people and I started to question why my religion was so negative and disparaging of them.

It was a great trip and it was with reluctance that I boarded the plane back to Stanstead Airport where I had left my car. Back in Bournemouth the pressure had not abated and throughout the summer it increased.

In August 2000, we finally made our target, at least half of which had been secured as donations. I returned to Saint Hill but before I could even settle back into my desk, there was another major problem for me to deal with. This time it was in the Dublin Mission. A big court case was looming and funding had to be secured for the Church's battle. Already the Church legal team were trooping into my office on a daily basis. They were making overwhelming demands for tens of thousands of Euro from the Dublin Mission to prepare for the case, secure senior counsel and get the wheels into motion for the fight. I was in despair, angry and exhausted. The mission normally made around €300 a week, now I had to get them producing something like €8,000.

A former Scientologist, Mary Johnston, was bringing the Church to the Dublin High Courts. She was claiming that she had been brainwashed, had suffered psychological and psychiatric injuries and post-traumatic stress disorder. Johnston had filed a suit against three members of the Church: John Keane, Tom Cunningham and Gerard Ryan. Cunningham knew her and had introduced her to the Dublin Mission in the early 1990s where she had signed up for a Purification Rundown Course at a cost of IR£1,200 (€1,524). After that, she paid up for some auditing and wound up visiting Saint Hill where she was heavily pressured to work for the Sea Org but did not join. In 1994, she left the Church and was going to claim in court that she had been harassed and intimidated since.

Back at Saint Hill, on post as Commanding Officer SMI, I was infuriated by the bullying and outrageous demands that hit me daily. I just knew that Dublin couldn't possibly deal with the legal costs but I was being put under huge pressure to say where the next Stg£10,000 was going to come from. Thomas Sproule, Bruce Perry's Deputy, was sent in to my office daily to badger me into making the money.

One day I just blew up. I ripped off my Commanding Officer stripes and told him to go and stuff the stupid post. Of course they didn't need that, nobody needed that and nobody wanted to have to fill the SMI job again, so they got me calmed down and I agreed to stay on post.

I eventually decided that to solve Dublin's problem, I would have to do the same job that I did in Bournemouth. I headed off to Ireland like a bulldog determined to get the languishing mission back into shape. It had to earn enough to fight the case. I wanted another success under my belt but I immediately came up against the Mission Holder, John Keane, a feisty and stubborn Limerick man. Everything I tried to do, he appeared to try to stop. Keane simply would not carry out the necessary actions to make the place earn the money. After a few weeks of flying over and back, I decided I would remove him from post and replace him with a much more dynamic person.

There is a specific procedure normally required in the removal of a person from a post he has held for more than two years. But I didn't have the time to follow protocol, as I needed to get Dublin moving immediately. I just went in one morning and fired him.

My rebellious new spirit in relation to Scientology had worked for me so far and I had no reason to think this independent decision-making was going to be any different. Unfortunately for me, what I didn't know at the time was that Keane had nurtured a close friendship with David Miscavige.

After he was busted, Keane penned a long and rambling letter to the Chairman of the Board. He detailed how I was right to put him off post but should have done so in the correct fashion, according to Hubbard's tech. Next thing I knew, I returned from Ireland one day to be met by Bruce. He told me that I was urgently required for a meeting with two officials from the Religious Technology Centre (RTC) who had just flown in from LA.

I knew what was coming. Sure enough I was back on 24/7 watch and under the most vicious investigation I had experienced to date. This was coming straight from Miscavige and it was rough. Luckily, what I was being accused of was completely ludicrous. For three weeks solid, under guard in a special interrogation room in Saint Hill Castle, I was grilled about my involvement with organised anti-Scientology groups and an Internet conspiracy against Miscavige. I was accused of working with infiltrators and told to cough up their names. The questioning was aggressive and intrusive and I suddenly realised that my interrogators were quite mad.

One of the RTC girls was an icy, young brunette with cold eyes. I was sure I had babysat her when she was just a young child at the Complex. She did her utmost, and never flinched, as she asked me her prepared questions over and over and over again. But she got frustrated as she couldn't even get an E-Meter reaction. She sent me down to the Ethics department who were to run a programme on me. It was aimed at softening me up, unbalancing and weakening my mental state so I would be more likely to reveal my so-called crimes.

I spent another four weeks under this constant

attack. I reached a point where I began to feel my mind cave in; I actually felt that I was going to go nuts. So I said no more. I told Thomas and Lee that I had had enough. I had built a wall in my mind and they could go up to that wall, but not past it. I felt myself come back, I felt sanity return and my tormenters realised that they could do no more.

I took the unthinkable step of resigning as Commanding Officer SMI UK in October 2000, an offence that I could have been 'Declared' for. I told them I was going to leave and I requested the appropriate forms.

It was agreed that they would route me out. They sent me down to work on Transport while the lengthy process began. I was prepared to go through the routing out because that was the way it was done. During my extensive ethics investigation, I had thought long and hard about my position and taken a realistic view of the world. I knew I was totally institutionalised and hadn't very good job prospects as a result. I had seen staff down in Bournemouth, who were working night-shifts in the 'local supermarket to try to pay off their loans and rent. I knew that, despite the work I had done over the years, sorting supermarket trolleys was pretty much all I was actually qualified for. I figured that the best thing I could do was route out. At least then I could get work with a company run by Scientologists such as Horst's ARC Music or the international company, Executive Software, with its branches in East Grinstead and Manchester. Many of my former Sea Org colleges were doing just that. Then, of course, there was the ever-present niggling question, what was on OT Level III? Despite those Internet revelations I still firmly believed there was something there – I just didn't know what it

was. What if it really was the true revelation and the
only path back to some immortal state? I kept asking
myself: 'What if?'

I didn't want to close the door.

The days turned to weeks and I settled into
Transport like an old pair of slippers. I really liked it and
started driving executives from the upper echelons of
Saint Hill. I initially badgered the Deputy Commanding
Officer Internal and the Hubbard Communications
Secretary CLO to start my routing out process, but there
never seemed to be anyone available for the lengthy
auditing and study sessions I was due to go through. I
suppose I settled down again and life went on. I have
always enjoyed working with my hands and I love
engines and mechanical things. I was also good at it
and I found in it a confidence I hadn't felt in a while.
I actually knew what I was doing. Transport was in a
bad state and the In Charge had really gotten himself
in trouble by trying to be everything for everybody.
As a result he was running a diminishing service with
more than half of his 13 mini-bus fleet out of service on a
daily basis. That meant that staff were being left waiting
until the early hours to get back to their berthing and
nothing was running smoothly at all. Complaints were
high and the stats were down.

I set up a workshop and base of operations at our
berthing in Walsh Manor, Crowborough. It is located on
the border of Kent and Sussex, about 14 miles from Saint
Hill. I was able to buy time and was not too worried
about Ethics' officers. After all, what more could they
do that they had not already done to me? Kill me? I
doubted that. So I began sneaking off to the Orchid
Riding Stables next door. I bought some lessons and
found that I still really loved horses. Later I transferred
my riding to an excellent centre, right in the forest. I

could gallop over the hills and really let the horses go. It allowed me to clear my mind of the mad goings-on at the base and the confusion in my head.

With the help of a brilliant South African engineer, we managed to get the fleet of dilapidated Transits back on the road. I began to enjoy the work and being off base. I didn't miss its daily routines of musters, events, briefings and drilling. Everyone seemed to be giving me some slack, even OSA. Looking back, I think they were uncomfortable with my leaving because of all I knew and in particular what I had been involved with in the Catt case.

My own troubled childhood had left me highly sensitised to the needs of children and I have always had a lot of time for them. As in the Complex, I thought the Sea Org kids in Saint Hill were actually treated with cruelty. They were assigned to the same 'Cadet Org' and did full production days. This entailed schooling from 9am until 3pm, followed by cleaning work at Walshe Manor or at Saint Hill between 4pm and, at earliest, 6pm. It would sometimes go on until 10pm. The shifts rotated and those off cleaning duties would have to study for the same gruelling hours. I hated the Hubbard teaching that children are actually 'adults in small bodies' and are responsible for any condition that they find themselves in.

I bought time on my job and I began working with the Cadet School. I would take the 15 kids who were there at that time out on day trips. I became very fond of them, like a big brother really. One beautiful June Sunday morning, I was on my official hygiene time and I noticed that all the Cadets looked unusually down and upset. They were dejectedly mopping floors and dusting around inside the Manor. Outside the grass was green, the sun shone and the world looked beautiful.

I asked the kids what was going on and they told me they were doing 'lower conditions'. These were kids as young as eight years old and no older than twelve who should have been running around outside, having fun. Most were already traumatised due to the long months, and in one case, two years, of enforced separation from their parents. Now they were being put on lower conditions! This was a system of mental introversion, self-criticism, oppression and physical confinement. I suddenly got really angry – actually furious.

I marched up to the school where Angela, the Cadet School In Charge and a qualified teacher, was brow-beating a child into some kind of acquiescence to Hubbard's dictates. Angela was a nice enough person, but lacked the warmth and empathy that's needed when working with children. I told her in no uncertain terms that I was taking all these kids with me to my riding centre. I said that these conditions were wrong for children and I was not going to tolerate such treatment. My own experiences of 'ethics' were too fresh. Angela looked startled but let me take them.

I actually paid for a guided hack for the group of them who were there at the time. This was the beginning of a very fulfilling 24 months of doing something positive with these kids. Their parents kindly helped towards the costs involved. They brought tears to my eyes one day when, after months of work, they preformed perfect canters in the arena. They were really working with and listening to their ponies. I often had to feed my 'pony club' kids after school as they were badly undernourished. Picking them up after school to take them riding, I noticed that they looked pinched and pale, so I used to give them healthy protein and granola bars. Through this work, I gained the necessary paperwork to be officially recognised as a part-time teacher and got the necessary police clearances required for working with children. I have this certificate with me to this day and it is probably the only thing in my Scientology career that I am proud of.

In Crowborough we were surrounded with wild life. I would often find wounded or ill wild animals on the road or in the forest: badgers, rabbits and once even a baby deer. I established a very proactive relationship with a local wildlife rescue centre and used it as a tool to broaden the children's world view. I would often get small groups to help to deliver 'first aid' to the animals I rescued before delivering them to the wild life centre. In the case of the baby deer, we found a special box to transport him. The kids had fun and their parents were very appreciative but the Advanced Organisation Saint Hill (AOSH) UK and the Hubbard Communications Office Personnel Dept were not. The Senior Personnel Control Officer was aiming to get these kids on almost full-time training as auditors, preparing them for careers in the Religious Technology Centre and Commodore's Messenger Organisation International. They were supposed to finish the legal minimum of schooling each day and then all go to Saint Hill and study, or if not to study, then to clean and do other work. I would often swing around at the Castle as late as 10pm and pick up stressed out, almost psychotic, pale-faced and exhausted children from AOSH, after they had done five hours on Training Routines and such like. I had two fights with Personnel Control Office people over it but eventually worked out a compromise where I would get a batch of kids one day and they the same batch the next.

One of the saddest experiences I had was when 'my' kids joined a barbeque at the riding centre with pupils, parents and teachers from a local private school.

My batch of kids refused to join the other children and hung around me. The little ones were actually clinging to me. They were frightened because these 'wog' kids actually scared them. The children had never actually spent any time outside the confines of the weird world of Scientology.

I was keeping very busy and feeling in control for the first extended period of time in years. The Pony Club filled both my Sunday mornings and mid-week afternoons and I grabbed any time I could to go riding myself. Transport was running like a dream so I had plenty of time to myself out in the countryside. I had also adopted a half-mad, six-month-old Collie that a very senior executive needed help looking after. The dog was great fun and I enjoyed training him to heel and sit. Thoughts of leaving gradually slipped further and further away. Although I still raged against management, I felt that I could not just abandon the Scientology 'technology' without giving it a real test on its own. I wanted to try it away from the often idiotic and literal interpretations of senior and local management. It could be that Hubbard was right but RTC and Miscavige were wrong. I felt compelled to find out and could only do so by applying it to what I was doing.

October 2004 came around with the usual sense of dread across the whole Sea Org base, as the annual International Association of Scientologists Gala Ball loomed. Held at Saint Hill every year since 1984, it was dreaded because it involved a full two months of 'Condition 1' for the whole base. As well as working our own posts and functions, we all had to help make the base ready for an influx of around 5,000 people over the weekend and an additional 100 or so Sea Org staff arriving from Hemet, Los Angeles, Australia and Copenhagen. The event also meant that the Chairman of the Board would be in residence for at least two weeks. You could cut the executive tension with a knife when he was around. People spent weeks in advance getting 'ethics clean ups'. Any 'out-point' recruits were either off-loaded or put on the RPF. All Commanding Officers had to have full Security Checks as Miscavige would pick up on the slightest thing. My routing out had more or less been forgotten by everyone, including myself at this stage, but others who were on the scheme were either quickly kicked out or shifted to another base. Every year's ball had to be bigger, and better, than the one before and each year the IAS had to raise more money. That meant bigger marquees and a lot more Scientologists. In 2004, the 'tent' was big enough to comfortably house a Jumbo 747 and the accompanying 'service tents' made Saint Hill look like a huge refugee camp. We soon found why this was not just bigger, but also more grand than any previous year. Tom Cruise and John Travolta would both be in residence for at least two days.

A few weeks before the big night, I witnessed and colluded in something that, to this day, cuts to the bone whenever my thoughts stray back there. Earlier that year, a girl I knew quite well had been assigned to the Rehabilitation Project Force. Alice had been brought up in Scientology from childhood and been with the Sea Organisation for three years. When I knew her, she was working as a Public Relations Officer for the Jive Aces. Her crime had been sleeping with a guy she was attracted to. She was assigned to the UK RPF and her fiancé was sent to the RPF in Australia. Alice decided to leave the Church and so was put on the even harsher regime, the RPF's RPF. Six months on and subjected to a course of daily intensive interrogations, she decided to kill herself.

One afternoon, at the beginning of October, I had just arrived back at Walsh Manor; I saw an ambulance and people running around. I soon heard that Alice had walked out of the RPF course room, gone to the workshop and found a tin of paint thinner. She had swallowed it and climbed up on top of the gym roof, a 15-foot high structure, surrounded by concrete. Then she jumped.

Alice lived but will be crippled for life and her lower intestine is ruined. She also had to have a colostomy bag fitted. She was a very attractive energetic 19-year-old at the time.

We were instructed to say that she had fallen down the steps; so that there would be no health and safety enquiry. I don't know how they explained the paint thinner to the medics. It all ended well for the Church. Alice was sent home to Italy, an invalid for life, to be cared for by her mother, an OT Level V 'up-statistic' Italian Scientologist. To date, to the best of my knowledge, she has never said anything to sully the lily-white image of the Sea Org.

Instead of being utterly horrified by what had happened, I looked to Hubbard's 'philosophy' and tech for my reaction. It had long been drummed into us that a person is responsible for their own condition. If you are put on RPF it is your own fault; if you choose to kill yourself that is because you have put yourself in that position. Alice was considered, and we all adopted this view, a Degraded Being, as is anyone who leaves the Sea Org or fails to make it up The Bridge. That a Being is totally responsible for one's own condition absolves all outside influences, like Scientology, totally. I am ashamed to admit that at the time that is how I felt about Alice and her misfortune. As Hubbard teaches us in his 1967 policy letter, reissued in 1982, 'Keeping Scientology Working' "Never let them be half-minded about being Scientologists... rather have you dead than incapable... It is a tough universe, only the tigers survive..."

Alice's demise hardly impacted on us at all and back at the Manor there was still a lot of primping and preening to be done. I watched as the executive vehicles were delivered. For the Chairman of the Board there was both a black BMW X5 jeep and a silver Mercedes SLK. Cruise had the same but additionally had a jet-black Range Rover, with blacked-out windows. Security was incredibly tight. A 24-hour dog patrol, with vicious looking Alsatians, patrolled the wooded perimeter, as they were worried about paparazzi. Security guys in Land Rover Discoveries were parked on various routes, up to and around the grounds. Five very dangerous looking guards accompanied Miscavige everywhere. I watched Tom Cruise arrive at the Manor with a tall brunette and his two adopted children.

On the night of the ball I saw Cruise sitting next to John Travolta while a recorded interview of him played on the huge screen. On it, Tom, in a black roll neck sweater, extolled the absolute indispensability to humankind of Scientology. He insisted on the rigid application of Hubbard's policy, 'Keeping Scientology Working'. "At the scene of an accident, only a Scientologist can really help," he said, beaming that million dollar smile.

The interview ended with fast moving clips of Cruise on talk shows, meeting statesmen and shaking hands with adoring fans on red carpets. Then Miscavige came up to the podium and announced; "To the most

dedicated Scientologist I have ever met, please give
your applause to Tom Cruise!"

Cruise bounded up onto the stage and saluted
Miscavige to rapturous applause as he was handed a
Medal of Valor.

Like most people watching, I had no idea of
the impact this interview was going to have when
it was unleashed on the real world on YouTube in
January 2008. It was subsequently removed after legal
submissions made by the Church. It is still available
thanks to a New York based online celebrity web-blog,
which managed to download it before its removal. On
the night, I just took it all in with mixed feelings and
of course, fully agreed with the fact that Scientologists
were the only people who could help at the scene of
an accident!

On the way home I thought how remarkable it
was that Cruise had actually 'come out' and publicly
proclaimed his dedication to the religion. He had been
in the Church since 1986, the same year that I finished
my EPF, but he had never previously been so vocal.
I later found out it was because he was ecstatic after
completing OT Level VII, under the direct tutelage of
David Miscavige.

As I thought about the medal he'd received, I
was taken aback that Cruise, who after all lived an
incredibly privileged life and had never had to suffer
the indignity of being a Sea Org or Staff member, could
gain such aplomb only because he had a lot of money
and had the eyes of the world on him. We had lived on
so little, had no privacy, no time to chill out; we were
in fear or under stress all the time and we were not as
dedicated as Cruise?

That hurt.

TEN

SURFING FOR THE TRUTH

After the ball there was the usual huge clean-up and re-organisation at Saint Hill in November 2004. Although I was in Transport my workload was upped accordingly. I was often out until the early hours bringing workers and executives to and from the Castle. Once the clean-up was complete, it was business as usual and I went back to my normal routine.

I became close friends with Esther, the Deputy Commanding Officer in the Commodore's Messenger Organisation. She would be on demanding duties right through the day and night, and as she could not drive, would call me from Saint Hill, begging me to drive out and bring her home to her husband at the Sea Org berthing in Walshe Manor. I often stopped at the top of the Ashdown Forest just as the sun rose. I would make her get out and look around, breathe in some of the beautiful fresh, country air and at least take a few minutes to stop and be still. She appreciated this so much and later wrote to thank me for that time.

When I'd started routing out, I was initially adamant that I was not going to work with management ever again. I liked the simplicity of Transport and the life I had built up around it. But then, following the IAS ball, Miscavige decided to visit the Celebrity Centre in Leinster Gardens in London in the hope that he could bring Tom Cruise there and everything changed. No doubt the receptionist was as over-worked as the rest of us but when she didn't recognise the Chairman of the Board there was hell to pay. The incident resulted in the entire executive structure being removed from their posts. It also heralded the demise of Bruce Perry. In the end he had to go through vicious security checking and vetting as he completed his routing out forms, while working for me cleaning vans.

I had spent nearly three relatively happy years in Transport and had applied Hubbard's tech to the job in as many ways as possible. It had worked for me in the inner world of Scientology and I was anxious to see if it worked out there in the real world. The flurry of promotions that followed Miscavige's upheaval saw one of my best mates, Richard, given the hefty job of Finance Director, United Kingdom. He was soon on my case to get back on the lines and take a proper executive role as one of his team. Meanwhile, the Church had also purchased a building on Fitzroy Street and another on Victoria Street in London. This meant I was driving bus-loads of Sea Org renovations' crews into the city in the mornings and back again at night. The time seemed right to make the jump back up to senior level and I told Richard so.

A huge collection of Hubbard recordings, called The Clearing Congress Lectures, was about to be unleashed on the Scientology world. Miscavige, who had invested something like $8 million in it, wanted costs recouped in the first week and profits to start rolling in by the second. A team of Sea Org officers was being assembled to go out to every Class V Organisation on the planet, under the title of Deputy Flag Banking Officer for Org Resources and Exchange – D/FBO MORE – to make sure that the CDs sold like hot cakes. This new release contained ten boxes of beautifully packaged CDs, each containing six to ten lectures. They covered Hubbard's 'Congress Lectures' delivered in London, Washington and Johannesburg between 1952 and 1962. Most Scientologists already had some or all of them – but these were digitally re-mastered! The brief meant that every staff and public Scientologist was to buy their very own set at the cost of just under Stg£1,600. Directions were also coming from the top for a massive new drive to up-grade the Scientology image in the UK.

I was selected as one of the new breed of D/FBO MOREs.

I asked to go to Birmingham, as it was the most independent and prosperous Scientology Org outside Saint Hill. I chose it because I was damned if I was going to end up living on five quid a week again. Before I agreed to take on the job, I demanded that I would do it my way and not live under the constant threat of statistics and ethics. Richard and I went way back and he knew that whatever else, once I took up a posting, I gave it my all. He was happy enough to verbally agree to my demands.

After almost 20 years in the organisation I wanted to achieve something for myself. It had dawned on me that the Church had not, despite all the management

hype, grown or expanded that much since I signed
up. Miscavige had told us as far back as 1989 that we
were going to take over the field of mental healing. I
couldn't see how, as a church, we were achieving our
goals. Scientology had been my whole life and without
it, I had nothing else.

The night I was to leave Saint Hill I had a little
conversation, prayer if you will, with Hubbard, in my
mind. I told him that I wanted to give my new job my
all and test it to its limits, but if I found that he was
lying to me, well, I would not take it lightly.

In Birmingham, I started by throwing out all the
ridiculous programmes that had come in from the US
which were supposed to make the organisation boom.
I found them to be utter rubbish. There was no sense
that the writer had any idea what life was like down
on the ground for frontline Scientology staff members.
Then I took a look at the facts. Birmingham was the
most successful Class V Organisation in the UK, but
it had a total active participating public of not more
than 40 people and a staff of 30 who worked mainly
part-time. My job was to use marketing and PR to
drive business into the operation and make it grow. I
went back to what I had learned in LA, on my original
marketing course, and looked to Hubbard's books as a
starting point. Back in 1988, Central Marketing drove
business worth millions into the Church by selling and
marketing books in big volume. I decided that I could
apply that strategy to Birmingham too.

New Era publishes all Scientology books and an old
friend of mine, Maggie, was based there. I called her
up and got her to agree to furnish me with 2,500 copies
of 'Dianetics: the Modern Science of Mental Health'. I
hoped to get prominent placing in a chain of discount

bookstores around the Midlands. I was up and down to Saint Hill for high-level meetings about the project and everyone was mighty pleased with me. It was only at the 11th hour that a manager at one of the bookstores realised he was dealing with Scientologists and pulled the plug. I was gutted but picked myself up, brushed myself down, and put my thinking cap on again.

The book deal told me one thing – the public image of Scientology was as bad as, if not worse than, it ever was. I dug up some of my opinion survey work from the '90s and started doing some market research and very quickly realised why. The Church in Birmingham was viewed as being cultish as it offered no outreach whatsoever to the community. It had built up barriers and constantly saw itself as under attack, particularly from the City Council. The staff were paranoid but with a move on the cards, I saw an opportunity to tear down the barriers. I wanted to turn it into an inclusive Church. Reports from the US showed how Boston Org had used this tactic. By the small gesture of allowing the local Baptist Church have Sunday Services at their premises they had positively changed public perception. Tampa, Florida, too had done something similar and had begun working with community groups to their advantage.

I decided that we needed to use a drive from the Home Office to encourage inclusion and fight discrimination, using it to our advantage. While it was aimed at the Muslim community, I decided we could involve ourselves too. If anyone criticised my belief I could simply shout 'religious discrimination' and they would have to shut up or face fines and prosecution. Marie, the local Scientology Director of Special Affairs representative in Birmingham, was assigned to me and as a former Olympic swimming champion she was good at opening up meetings with public, multi-faith and community groups. I had high hopes for my project and wanted the Church of Scientology Birmingham to become a major player in the affairs of the city. Hubbard had claimed expertise in the philosophic secrets behind governance and power. This was from insights that he gleaned from galactic civilisations that had lasted for 98 million years. I intended to follow his advice.

I studied reams of marketing and public relations surveys and research. Spending time in the library was very revealing. One survey showed that in the UK the most respected people were those who volunteered their time for good causes. I studied the demographics for the area and identified key ethnic and religious groupings that I would need to target. With Marie, I began developing links with the Hindu and Afro-Caribbean communities that were so largely represented in Birmingham. We began by attending multi-faith days and it still makes me laugh to recall how wonderfully cynical the Buddhists were of us. We gave Scientology a friendly face and brought and distributed our magazines to try to show people what we were about. I turned my attention to voluntary work and was astonished to see how incredibly inwardly focused our Church was. Just like my revelation with the children, it was something I had always known about Scientology but had simply never acknowledged. After all, Hubbard had stated in his Principal of Exchange that you never get something for nothing and giving to charity or helping 'down stat people' would be 'Out Exchange'.

At Birmingham Community Voluntary Services, I put my name down for two programmes. One was with the Neighbourhood Forum for Hockley, the area I was living in, and secondly as a mentor with the Aston Villa 'Playing for Success' programme. I had already received a Police Enhanced Disclosure to qualify me to work with the cadet children, for my pony club, and this was valid for several years. The programme was aimed at kids who were failing in the school system and who had been identified as not engaging in the classroom. They were bussed down to Aston Villa football grounds one day a week and given education projects to try to increase their interest in schooling. Ultimately the aim was to keep them in the system until they had completed second level. I mentored by helping with small groups, teaching basic computer skills, animation and art. I decided that I would not reveal my involvement with Scientology to the people running the programme.

I gained another recruit, Julia. She had been a Scientology staff member in the Birmingham office but due to pressure from her anti-Scientology mother, Julia had been laid off. She was seen as presenting a security risk as a Potential Trouble Source. She was still committed to the Church and when I asked her to work for me as a 'volunteer' she was eager and enthusiastic to do so. Julia was hoping her mother would come around to the idea that Scientology was doing positive voluntary work. With her energy and great communication skills, we approached several key local government projects in the Handsworth area. We volunteered our services and the delivery of our 'educational programmes' to the people in charge. We were accepted and I got very busy indeed. The work gave us access to important counsellors and officials who held positions of real prominence in Birmingham and the Midlands. I wanted to start a dialogue with

Clare Short, MP for the Ladywood district. I researched projects that she supported and began to get involved in those specific fields. This was just like I had been trained to do in the Public Relations and intelligence courses that I had attended. I actually found the voluntary work fulfilling and I was interacting on a very positive level with 'wogs' for the first time in 20 years.

The CDs arrived a few days before the big release event. I made a deal with the Organisation that they would concentrate on making a successful release, so I could focus on this front line voluntary activity.

Julia and I began working to deliver a programme called Youth for Human Rights. This was a Scientology-sponsored programme geared at children between 10 and 15 years old. It taught them about the UN Charter for Children's Rights and came with a great rap song and DVD. The Scientology message was hidden. Among the great humanitarians described in the booklet, including Martin Luther King and Mandela, was the great humanitarian and adventurer, L Ron Hubbard.

There were also teaching packs available from the Church so we got them sent to us. We used them as the basis for workshops we were delivering in the various community activities. Again the message was cloaked.

I actually felt that I was making a difference while substantially improving the image of Scientology. I was making good friends too in the different communities, such as my Sikh friend Mohan, Chairman of the Mathew Bolton Neighbourhood Forum. I became his Marketing and Public relations man. I somehow knew that no matter what would happen in the future, they would stand by me.

By October 2005, I was deeply involved with my work. While the Annual IAS event for 2005 at Saint Hill was fast approaching I was a member of a whole host of forums, carrying out different lobbying work with the Council. Although I didn't think that my projects would get recognition that year, I definitely wanted to gain a mention by 2006. Of course the huge gala event had to build on the previous year, when Tom Cruise received the Medal of Valor, so I knew that it was going to be pretty powerful. But just a few nights prior to it, on October 22, an explosion of inter-racial violence, just across the road from where I lived, would change everything. It would irreversibly alter the way that I perceived my world.

On two consecutive nights in the Lozells area of Birmingham, racial tensions erupted between the Black and Asian communities. The clashes were horrendous, as hatred spilled out onto the streets. The place was turned into a warzone of burning cars and broken windows. Over 150 riot police were called in to try to restore the peace. I saw it as an opportunity for me to put my intentions for this inward looking, self-serving Church into action and to get it interested in what was happening in the real world around it. It must have been around 8pm, when I was in my office listening to the events unfold on BBC radio. I jumped up, gathered my distinctive yellow Scientology Volunteer Minister windcheater and back pack loaded with 100 copies of the Church free handout, 'The Way To Happiness', and tried to round up at least five staff to go with me.

Some of the comments I was hit with were deeply racist and they shocked me. As expected, my colleagues were also calling these people 'Degraded Beings' and 'Criminal Wogs'. Nobody would come with me and they didn't care about the riots. Julia was away that week but I know she would have been there in a snap. I decided I would go in alone and, in the name of my Church, I headed down to the centre of the tension. I spent about 48 hours there just talking to all those poor people whose communities were being ruled by fear. I was trying to find a way that we, as a Church, could help out with some sort of multi-denominational education for the children or something that could end the awful hatred.

I planned to go up to Saint Hill to have a meeting about getting some backing for my plan, but before I could set it up, I got a call. I was told I needed to help make the IAS target of $16 million by that weekend. An order had gone out to every Org across the planet to raise funds and get the money rolling in. I knew better than to ask for funding when we were, yet again, being told to raise more money.

Less than a week later, I was standing in the opulence of Saint Hill at the October 28, 2005, Gala. I was in my rented black-tie suit, surrounded by the good and the great of Scientology. The patrons were all there, all of whom have to donate a minimum of $40,000 for the honour. Tom Cruise was there, as always, at Miscavige's side. Travolta was there, as was Nancy Cartwright and the style and the wealth was remarkable. The event really was beginning to look like the Oscars, with expensive limousines and golden-coloured goody bags for the rich and famous. While the Ball is billed as the annual conference, the actual purpose of it is to make money. That night we celebrated the fact that we had reached the IAS target of $16 million.

After the opening video, Miscavige came out on

stage, wearing his crisp, perfectly fitting tuxedo. He soaked up the thunderous applause we, his adoring followers, gave. We hadn't a clue but 2005 had been harsh on Scientology. There had been the 'South Park' cartoon poking fun at Cruise and Travolta. Cruise had then upset Brooke Shields on national television, and mothers everywhere, by claiming that there was no such thing as post-natal depression. After that, he had appeared on another national TV talk show, hosted by Matt Lauer, and shocked the world with his wild-eyed, fanatical rant against the psychiatric profession. The icing on the cake had come that June, with Oprah Winfrey and the infamous couch-jumping incident. While I knew about 'South Park', I didn't know anything about Cruise and the other stuff. We were not allowed to watch television and I certainly wasn't going to engage in any conversation about Tom Cruise or Scientology with any of the 'wogs' I was dealing with. As always I was living in a bubble and to us, Cruise was a hero, on par with Miscavige.

Whenever there was applause, the cameras would pan the front row and showcase the stars, wearing their 'Freedom Medals'. These medals are awarded to people who have done big press relations activity and mentioned Scientology or who have struck a major blow against psychiatry. That night, flanking Tom Cruise, was his pregnant girlfriend Katie Holmes.

Mike Rinder, the Commanding Officer of OSA International who was the overall Head of Church intelligence, security and PR, then walked on stage. He honoured the work of Tom Cruise. We hadn't a clue Cruise had been a public relations disaster. As the praise was heaped upon him, we were told that as a result of Tom's tirades about 'psych drugs', there were now hundreds of thousands fewer children taking drugs for ADHD. Later, Rinder gave more of Tom's statistics. He said that the day after one of Tom's 'anti-psych' interviews, the Federal Drugs Administration (FDA) called for a black box warning on one drug. Two days later, after another of Tom's interviews, the FDA called for a black box warning on a second drug. There were two standing ovations for Tom.

He grinned and punched the air.

Then Miscavige came back on and said that the 'interest' there was in Scientology on the Internet was the highest that it had ever been in history – mainly due to Tom Cruise of course. Finally the last two Freedom Medal Winners were announced. They were given to two women from Venezuela, one a major celebrity.

I looked at Miscavige in all his finery. He had his usual armed security entourage with him. He and Cruise were, as always, staying at Saint Hill while the real power behind the Church, the attorneys and lawyers, were staying in a number of beautifully opulent five star hotels that dot that area of West Sussex. I sat there that night and I looked around me at all the money that was being thrown around and how much they had made that evening. I thought about all the staff in all the Orgs around the world and how much money they were raising. I dwelt on how much pressure they were under to constantly make money and how then, exactly as commanded, they had to go out and make even more money. I thought about how little we workers were paid and how hard we worked and how dedicated we were to this cause. And yet there was nothing for us. I had no pension scheme, no security, and no back-up. And I wondered – I really wondered for the first time – where the money went. I certainly wasn't being given any to go into the Lozells and try to do some good in a community ravaged by prejudice. Wasn't that the kind of thing a Church was supposed to do?

I went home with a heavy feeling in my heart. I couldn't stop questioning what it was all about. I came down with a bug for a week and had to go to Saint Hill for a Potential Trouble Source check and some auditing when I got better. I told my auditor that I was upset by the IAS event, and the lack of acknowledgement of people like myself, who had been manning the parapets and fighting in the trenches for so long. It must have been a fairly common sentiment because I heard nothing back at all.

Passing a bookshop days later, I bought myself a copy of 'The First Circle' by Alexander Solzhenitsyn. It is a novel detailing life for the occupants of a prison camp in Stalin's Russia. I started to see startling parallels between the specific camp he described and the Sea Org that I had come to know so well.

Internet access remained forbidden for all Sea Org members and Scientology staff. But I had some questions that needed to be answered. I began looking for information on the computer in the house where I was living. I started surfing the net for hours, firstly trying to verify what Miscavige had told us about the increasing interest in Scientology but I could find no evidence of it. What I did find was increasingly critical comments about the Church, particularly by the ever-swelling numbers of ex-members. I read some of them and did feel some sympathy for certain stories that rang true with me, like long working hours, low pay and abuse and harassment at the hands of senior executives.

I was particularly interested in material I came across on the Larry Wollersheim case I'd been involved with all those years before in LA. I read that despite all our tactics, Wollersheim had won his case. He was awarded a total of $30 million – $5 million in compensation damages and $25 million to punish Scientology for intentional 'infliction of emotional distress'.

Miscavige vowed never to pay a cent of the money and rallied the troops again. This time it was under the slogan: 'Not one thin dime for Wollersheim.' On Appeal, damages were reduced to $2.5 million but still Miscavaige swore not to pay up. The Church had continued to fight him through the courts for years. In 2002, they'd finally agreed to pay $8.7 million. I read quotes from Wollersheim, who had become one of the most vocal opponents to Scientology. He is behind the FACTnet site, an internet cult watchdog.

I actively avoided the sites which purported to contain the information about the contents of the OT levels. I knew that that would mark the end of my journey and I was not quite ready. I joined the Belief Net community and argued the case for the Religious Technology Centre and Scientology. Many were being critical about the practices used by the Church. Alan in Minnesota referred me to some sociological studies about cults and one about Scientology. I read them with suspicion.

Daily life continued. I began writing articles for community newsletters and slowly began building my reputation as a community activist. I was elected to several Voluntary bodies including the Voluntary Community Services Panel. This had the potential to be the breakthrough I needed to integrate myself with key players in the City Council. I began a project to upgrade a little overgrown park in Hockley. We raised money and got the plans drawn up. It was something for the community and the Council was pleased. At night though, the Internet had become an obsession.

By March 2006, I was on it every night. And every night I would look that little bit further, dig that little bit deeper.

I read that Hubbard was described in a Californian Court in 1984 as a 'pathological liar' and a brief look into his background proved just that. Born in 1911 in the US, I had been told he was a gifted child who could ride a horse before he could walk and read and write by the age of three and a half. As one of his followers, I knew that he had spent five years from the age of 14 travelling alone in China, Mongolia and Tibet, studying holy men. In reality I discovered that two visits to China were holidays with his mother. At 19 he entered George Washington University where he tried to major at Civil Engineering but failed to qualify for third year. He also failed a short course in molecular and atomic physics. As a Scientologist, I had accepted his claim to hold degrees in both civil engineering and mathematics and be one of America's first nuclear physicists.

While I had been told that upon leaving college he was, within two months, established as a major fiction writer on a pay level that was 'astronomical', I was now reading that he actually struggled to sell his work. In 1941, he signed up to the US Navy. This had led to more outlandish claims about his achievements, including that he was awarded 27 medals for bravery, when he only received four routine service ones. At the end of World War II, he claimed to be 'blinded' and 'lame', saying his service record stated 'permanently disabled physically'. While recovering for two years at

Oak Knoll Naval Hospital California he claimed to have developed Dianetics and cured his injuries through its use. The Internet revealed that he spent the last months of the war as an outpatient at Oakland Naval Hospital where his chief complaint was an ulcer.

One biography I found explained that two years after 'Dianetics' was published, Hubbard was financially ruined. Although his book had sold tens of thousands of copies, the American Psychological Association lambasted it, saying that there was no scientific evidence whatsoever for its claims. The fact that the book rubbishes 200 years of neurological, psychological and psychiatric research hadn't seemed to register with me when I first read it. Penniless, he decided to give college lectures and created a whole new subject called Scientology. It included sprinklings of his friend Aleister Crowley's 'magical' ideas, mixed in with large helpings of his own science fiction. Hubbard had apparently long hankered to start a religion, believing that that was where the real money can be made, so in 1953 he set up the Church of Scientology. By the time of his death, 33 years later, it is alleged that he held a personal fortune of over $640 million.

I was really rocked by this because whatever problems I had had with management over the years I had never questioned Hubbard. The fact that his background was all too human really disturbed me. I was extremely tense as I clicked on to information about auditing.

It appeared that even Scientology auditing was not, as it had been sold to me back then, the findings of our great and masterful founder, L Ron Hubbard. Instead I read that it was essentially one-on-one regression therapy – mostly stolen from Freud, Jung and even the

New Thought movement of the 1920s and 1930s. I had been told it was a system that Hubbard and Hubbard alone had evolved. It is a controversial therapy that has often come under severe criticism for the way it can merge reality and something else, be that the imagination or the mind's ability to work beyond its own understanding.

Past Life Therapy has been studied and practiced in the Western Hemisphere since at least 1875, when H M Blavatsky founded The Theosophical Society. Even before that, in 1857, Kardec wrote 'Book of The Spirit', which was primarily a study of Past Life experiences. Much later during the 1920s and 1930s the author of the Sherlock Holmes novels, Arthur Conan Doyle, founded the British Psychic Society and studied the life after death phenomenon. A hugely influential phenomena, called 'the New Thought Movement', swept across Western Europe and the United States, between 1900 and 1938, opening up limitless vistas of human spiritual potential for millions. From 1930 onwards, Alfred Korzybski was responsible for much of the groundwork that became 'Gestalt Therapy'. Korzybski's book 'General Semantics' fundamentally changed the way people approached the mind. Dr Carl Jung's seminal findings in the area of symbology and the psychic archetype, changed the way that we approach psychology. In 1950 Andrew Canon wrote 'The Power Within' a hugely popular and well-researched study of the 'past life concept'.

Hubbard 'borrowed' ideas, quotes and even people from all of these movements, but he disguised the origins of his 'research', mainly through the feint of inventing his own language. Jung's 'Collective Unconsciousness' became 'Group Bank Agreement', an identical concept, but with a new name and a typically 'Hubbardian' twist.

I looked up from the computer one night and tried to gather my thoughts. Over the past few months I had become more and more disenchanted with auditing. Scientologists are never allowed to discuss their case outside auditing sessions, so there is no hope of sitting down and having a logical discussion with a friend about it. Having read what I had on the Internet, I could now see why we were banned from discussing cases. It was vital to ensure the success of the auditing process that I had undergone for years. We were undergoing the same experience, so isolating us was crucial because, as I learned on the web, back in the 1970s, before the non-discussion rule, Scientologists talking about their auditing sessions caused major problems. There were lots of incidents of four Julius Caesars or three Marie Antoinettes finding each other during a Scientology night out. In my own case, during one session I'd had a full recall of standing on a hill, overlooking a deep river valley with ships tied, side by side, to create a bridge across the river. While feeling an acute sense of isolation from the people around I just knew that I was Alexander the Great. As I took on board what I had just read I thought how much I would love to know now how many other people, like myself, found themselves to have been Alexander.

Of course, they needed to isolate us – we had to believe that everything Hubbard said was true. We had to believe he was right about heightening IQ and spatial awareness. We had to believe he was right about the engrams, the auditing and the 'State of Clear', which for years had become my only goal and ambition. Most importantly, we had to think he was right about the past lives because if he was right about that, then he was right about everything. As I logged off for the night, I thought about that memory I had of being on military patrol in the Tunisian desert 8,000 years ago and realised that if I really believed that, I would believe just about anything.

Throughout April, under orders from senior management, I was also spending hours every day listening to the Clearing Congress CD set. All staff and all public had to attest to having listened to the whole set by Easter. The recordings were the consecutive lectures given by Hubbard as he developed the whole 'Theory of Clearing'. I wasn't just listening to the material, I was analysing it. Firstly I noticed that Hubbard was repeating himself a lot. He had initially claimed in 1955 that he had found the key to 'Clearing' but on listening more, I discovered that he said the same thing in 1957, 1959, 1963 and 1965. I listened as he spoke about 'synthetic clear' – gained through extensive and tough training on the 'Upper Level Indoctrination TR's' courses which meant we could Clear fellow Scientologists. But instead of just accepting it, I now realised that it was a cheap solution to the expense of training up auditors. 'Synthetic Clear' was an invention to serve a purpose and cut costs. In another lecture Hubbard warned us not to try to 'understand insanity because it is insane'. Instead of beating myself up about not comprehending this, I recognised it for the witless statement it is. In the final recording I listened as Hubbard himself gave away what is supposed to be a major Scientology secret 'The Clear Cognition'. While getting to Clear is supposed to be the time that this secret is revealed, Hubbard just blurted it out in the lecture series, revealing that we can 'create or uncreate' our reactive minds.

By the middle of May another promotion was looming for me. This time it was to Hemet and into the inner circle of David Miscavige. It was due to the fact that over the previous two years almost 200 skilled staff had been sent to the RPF or Declared Suppressive Persons. Hemet was beginning to suffer an acute lack of personnel. I had to travel back to Saint Hill for auditing. This was geared to repair earlier auditing sessions, which had been confirmed as having caused me the problems that led to me wanting out. I needed to move up to the 'State of Clear' before I could be sent to California.

I didn't want to go to California. The story Tom had told me back in 1995 during my stay in Vancouver was still fresh in my mind. I was becoming pretty certain that I didn't even want to stay in Scientology any more. But I had more to find out and if I was going to leave, then I was going to have to plan my exit very carefully indeed. Now that I could see things more clearly I knew, for a fact, that I was not going to be allowed simply leave. I had so much information on the workings of the Church that I was like a time-bomb to them. I was at a senior enough level that I was being asked to work at the very top of the Scientology Organisation. If I left it would be a totally different matter than the average disgruntled staff member routing out. I had years of information on marketing techniques and the structure of the Church. I had also, over my time, seen the bizarre financial web of bank accounts that seemed to filter money away from the Church into nowhere. And I had seen people held against their will on the RPF, sometimes for years. There was no way I was going to be allowed route out. I now knew for certain that I was running out of time and I needed a plan.

Since my run-in with the Religious Technology Centre investigators after my trip to Dublin, I had somehow learned how to manipulate the E-Meter. Initially my blasé attitude had caused the needle to stop moving at all but soon I'd discovered that if I thought about a particular object, as innocuous as a lampshade, while answering a question, I was able to cause the needle to float quite easily. As I was doing this on a regular basis, my auditors reckoned I was on the verge of reaching Clear.

In all the time I had been a Scientologist I had been working towards Clear and a move to the OT levels. Reaching the 'State of Clear' would mark a significant point in my Scientology career. It would be a major achievement. I should have been elated. I was not. Instead, I was becoming more and more cynical about the whole business of Scientology.

My Internet research became more intense as I realised that the time had come to face the truth. I found Hubbard's death certificate and the Coroner's report from the San Louis Obispo Sheriff's Office. The actual facts of Hubbard's death were a lot more prosaic than the fiction I had swallowed so willingly at the Hollywood Palladium all those years before. After suffering a massive stroke, Hubbard had actually died a week later. He was in poor health and mentally incompetent. The autopsy report described the poor physical state of his body and how the psychiatric drug Vistaril was found in his system. The drug, which is used to calm frantic or overly anxious patients, had been injected into his right buttock.

I thought it was ironic that Hubbard had a psychiatric drug in his system when he died. Much

of the hold that the Church of Scientology has on its
followers is the vehement hatred, horror and terror it
inculcates in them towards the subject and professions
of psychology, psychiatry and psychiatric drugs.
Since the release of 'Dianetics' in 1950, Hubbard had
condemned these subjects. He claimed to be the sole
agent of the solution to all mental illness, in any form.
However, instead of his body being 'sound and strong
and fully capable of serving this mighty Thetan', as
Cooley had informed us, Hubbard was clearly very
poorly when he died.

My Web research revealed that Cooley had tried
to arrange a speedy cremation at Reis Chapel at San
Luis Obispo but officers there became suspicious when
they heard whose body it was. They had contacted
the San Luis Obispo County Coroner who halted the
cremation. It couldn't go ahead until he had carried
out an examination and blood tests, during which the
Vistaril showed up.

I read another theory that pointed to the possibility
that Hubbard was in fact murdered, as he had become
a dangerous liability to the highly lucrative Scientology
operation.

I came across and avidly read Jesse Prince's online
testimony of life at the very top of the Church's
executive structure. He had been the number two in
the international corporation and the only black man
to get himself so high up within the structure. He left
after his wife underwent a forced abortion. Prince
mentioned a name I hadn't heard since the Hollywood
Palladium, Pat Broeker. Prince described how Broeker
had looked after the daily care of Hubbard and got
Miscavige to bring suitcases full of cash to fund his
every whim. In a statement on the anti-cult site factnet.

org, he described how Broeker and Miscavige would often meet in Las Vegas where they would go to a casino and gamble away thousands of dollars. Prince told how he was ordered to investigate Miscavige around 1983 as Hubbard felt his hold on the Church weakening. Prince said Miscavige freely admitted his dalliances in the casinos of Vegas but was adamant that if he was going down he was bringing Broeker with him. He went on to describe how Miscavige had eventually 'Declared' Broeker and in a Machiavellian coup, had taken over the full power structure of the Church. His reports were another eye-opener into Hubbard who he said spent millions freely under the guise of 'research' and even bought exotic animals like llamas and buffalo for the ranch.

Prince's blogs brought me deeper into the Internet and the various forums ex-scientologists host in the hopes of helping people like myself. I read about LRH's increasing paranoia, which by 1980 had extended to mistrust of his most dedicated and loyal followers, the Sea Org crew surrounding him on the Hemet Base. This was why he'd had Pat Broeker, whom he trusted more than Miscavige, locate and purchase the San Luis Obispo property. Pat Broeker had loved cloak and dagger so much that he had been nicknamed 007. In concluding the deal, Broeker had stated that Hubbard was a wealthy retiree, and his wife Annie's elderly father. Once installed, LRH had the ranch house completely re-designed and restored to his exacting speficiations. He ordered the building of a race track and miles of fencing. His every whim was looked after by Sea Org personnel and he had a crew of full-time painters just to look after the fencing. As it took six months to completely white-wash the full length of the fence, once done they would start all over again at the beginning to keep the place looking pristine and immaculate.

On the ranch Hubbard had poured millions into renovating the old house. He lived, meanwhile, in a motor home on the land. He acted oddly and displayed traits of obsessive compulsive disorder. The renovations on the house were never completed. Hubbard would view renovations and have work redone constantly. The fireplace alone was built and stripped out ten times because Hubbard was never satisfied with the result. He never moved into the ranch house.

While officially retired from all management involvement with the Church corporations since 1967, he actually ran all aspects of the Church through what were termed 'LRH advices'. He had also tried to keep a tight grip on top Church executives. The 'advices', in writing or on tape, were handed to Broeker. He then drove, with boxes of this material, to a pre-arranged meeting point a long way from both Hubbard's ranch and the Hemet base. He then passed them to Miscavige.

This all tied in with Prince's own testimony and I had no reason to doubt it was true.

I soon realised that the one piece of the Internet puzzle that I had been purposely avoiding since I started my late night computer sessions would complete the picture for me.

One weekend, with my housemates Helen and Bernard away, I decided that it was finally time to have a look at the OTIII materials on factnet.org. It was the most difficult thing I have ever done in my life, typing in the two letters and three Roman numerals; I knew it would be a defining moment for me.

Within seconds I was looking at a copy of Hubbard's own hand-writing. It looked like a scrawl and was partially illegible. It was followed by the transcript of this great secret that I had waited so many years to read.

I could tell it was set to bring my world crashing about my feet.

OT Level III told of Lord Xenu, the master of the galactic confederacy, who 75 million years ago reckoned this part of the universe was over-populated. He figured out how to bulk kill people's bodies and freeze their spirits in blocks of ice. Using a space-craft, that looked exactly like a DC 8 airliner, he transported their spirits or 'thetans' to planet Earth. The spirits of these dead people, contained in these ice cubes were dropped into volcanoes. These were then atom-bombed in order to 'cluster the spirits together'. Then they were brought, in a badly disorientated state, to huge cinemas, hidden in the mountains in Las Palmas and the Andes. They were implanted with the story of Christ, the Prophet Mohamed and the future history of the world. He said then they were dumped in 'clusters' into the bodies of primitive man. According to Hubbard and Scientology, there are millions of these spirits in each person and they have to keep being addressed and banished with auditing all the way through to OT Level VIII.

I just sat there utterly stunned.

This was the secret.

Hubbard hadn't even tried to link his story to any kind of pre-historic evidence or data. I was expecting something solid, something I could get a grip on, something that would explain the origins of the universe. Instead it was just pure fiction with no basis in reality; it was not even a good fiction story.

I don't know if I even blinked as I stared at the screen. Not only was the story ludicrous and nonsense but, as I tried to catch my breath, I realised that it was likely it was taken directly from a science fiction story that Hubbard had failed to get published.

When the shock abated I felt rage and anger as I realised that I had been taken for a ride – big time. I was furious with myself too. Why didn't people like scientology? Not because of any campaign by psychiatrists but because it is a scam. All the little warning signs and pointers had been there but I had ignored them. Now I couldn't turn away any more.

There was absolutely no way back and from that moment Scientology was over for me.

It was Earth-shattering.

I had held out a vague hope that in reading OTIII I would see something tangible that would make sense. But this was the end of the road and it was a bitter pill to swallow after 22 years. At 42 years of age I should have been married with children and have a career. Instead, I had absolutely nothing.

In deep shock I read on through the rest of the OT levels and all the way up to OT Level VIII where Hubbard really loses it. He basically describes himself as being the beast 666, Lucifer, bringer of light, and described by Christians as the anti-Christ.

All this time I had lived and breathed Scientology, worked for nothing for the Church and lived like a pauper in shared dormitories. I had undergone self-deprecating, soul destroying auditing sessions, shunned my family and friends and it was all for nothing.

There in front of me in black and white were the secrets that the Sea Org had been formed to 'protect'.

This was what had kept me and my many good friends enslaved as we worked so hard to carry out our 'Proud Sea Org Duty, the only force for good left in this sector of the Universe'. Here they were, so goddamn secret that they were all over the Internet, which funnily enough, we Scientologists were banned from using!

If it wasn't so serious I could have almost laughed.

I started to do the sums in my head. In order to reach the Operating Thetan levels, a dedicated Scientologist will spend in the region of €50,000 on auditing, courses, books and materials before he or she is declared to have reached the 'State of Clear'. The secret upper levels beyond 'Clear' ranging from OT Level I through to OT Level VIII become progressively more expensive as one moves up. OT I through to OT IV will cost around €40,000 each. To reach OT VIII, it is unlikely that a Scientologist will get much change from having spent €300,000, although some have been known to spend over a million attempting to attain this spiritual pinnacle – all that money for a science fiction story. A story that was free for all to see online.

But how come we are all taken in? Then it started to sink in just how clever and how dangerous my so-called Church was. In order to get a person to believe that science fiction is true you have to really mess with that part of the mind that distinguishes fiction from reality. You read the OTIII stuff as a rational person and you can see it for what it is but you read it as a Scientologist, who is being heavily audited and hypnotised, and you believe it. That scared me now. If I had gone on to the 'State of Clear' and studied OT Level I and OT Level II, with all the conditioning and hours of auditing and heavy hypnosis that goes with it, I would have believed it too.

I read on and found an online piece by Robert Kaufman who had completed OT III in 1967. Kaufman detailed the mental torture that you have to go through before you can read the material, the bizarre exercises designed to induce LSD-like trips, the countless hours of mind numbing training routines and the hypnotic auditing. He described how he had to envision cherubs riding on chariots pulled by horses, explosions and blackness that all pointed to Hubbard's links to occultism. He noted that several people had committed suicide during the process, while others had gone quite nutty. Anyone who had actually taken LSD appeared to get psychotic breaks. I had wondered why that had happened to my dear friend Effie back in the late 1980s as she was on the brink of OTIII. She had utterly flipped and ended up locked away for months, under watch, barred from any medical inspection or intervention. She recovered but was never the same person and always appeared to be in a different world. The hypnosis-induced psychosis, coupled with massive doses of Vitamins that Kaufmann described, made sense to me now.

I thought about Noel, an Irishman who had been a very wealthy property developer in Bermuda during the 1970s. Noel had reached OTVII and then he had flipped too and lost absolutely everything. Every time he got out of the mental hospital he was in back in Ireland, he used to show up in the London Org. He was an embarrassment to the Church and so he was taken to a remote location, a little hotel owned by Scientologists up on the Firth of Soloway. I was his minder for three months at one stage and I nearly went mad myself. I used to take him for little walks, during which he would

Mike personally because I had been up against him in a previous role as the senior executive over the Irish branch of the Church. Initially he didn't believe I was serious but eventually he took on board what I was saying. He put me in touch with his equivalent in the UK, a man called Christian who gave me great advice over the phone.

When the couple I was renting a room from, Helen and Bernard, went to Belgium for a week I 'went home to my Uncle's funeral'. No questions were asked. My last Sunday service consisted of a reading of Hubbard's scriptures. It was all about blood and death and vengeance and what wasn going to happen to non-Scientologists. It was like something from an Ian Paisley sermon from the 1970s, all fire and brimstone. I just thought 'Oh My God'. I was seeing it all in a completely new light. I had heard this same lecture a thousand times before but I had never actually listened to it. Hubbard was absolutely mad. I was troubled by how I had insulated myself for so long from the actual meaning of the words our Founder was spouting out.

I went home, packed, contacted my friend Mohan, the elderly Indian gentleman from the neighbourhood forum, and told him what the story was. He was fantastic and a great support but he did say he wasn't surprised by my admission. He knew all about Scientology and his friends on the Council had been watching my every move. They never trusted Scientology and hadn't been won over like I thought. I was relieved to hear it.

I sorted some documents and gave him a briefcase of material to mind for me. Then I went back to the house and I did what I could to wipe the computer. There is no way of actually clearing a hard drive but I needed to hide all the stuff I had been looking at. I just dumped loads of stuff onto the computer, pages about cars and other innocuous material and then deleted them. I wiped the histories and up-loaded new ones, then I wiped them again so that anyone trying to trace my steps would have to work bloody hard to do so.

Mike Garde also put me in touch with Dermot Fortune, whose brother Odhran had made headlines back in Ireland in the 1990s. Odhran was a fellow Sea Org member who had been based in Copenhagen. When he went home to visit his family during Christmas 1997 they were horrified by his emaciated appearance. His family got in touch with an exit counsellor and Odhran had agreed to stay at home and leave behind his life in Scientology. But just when they thought he was doing really well he disappeared one night. He had been in the family pub, in the company of a group of Irish Scientologists and has never been seen by his family since. The police managed to trace him back to England where he issued a statement, supposedly of his own volition, saying he didn't want anything to do with his family. In 'Freedom' magazine, the Scientology in-house monthly, he wrote an article implying that a large team of 'deprogrammers' had held him captive for days without his consent. I remembered that Odhran Fortune story because at the time it was used to keep us at arms' length from our own families. Dermot was fantastic, absolutely fantastic. He was just right there for me and he understood what lay ahead and knew how carefully I had to tread. He was the only other person who fully understood the danger I was in.

Dermot provided me with some money so I had enough to get me by for a short time until I decided which way to jump. I picked up my small holdall bag, that contained my entire worldly possessions, and I walked out the door. I made my way down to Digbeth, a run-down part of Birmingham near the National Express bus station, where I took a room above a pub. I bought a bunch of black jeans, t-shirts and baseball caps and in the small en-suite bathroom I shaved my head.

Over the first few days, I contacted the social services and housing departments and told them that I had been in a cult, was coming out and needed to have a social security card issued. I went down to the job centre and put myself on their books. In my innocence I really thought that I could just start a new life there in Birmingham. I felt a desperate urgency to set myself up in some way, so I woiuld be free of Scientology. I had no idea how impossible it would be.

At night, I would sit looking out the window of my room trying to see if anyone was watching me. I ate nothing but crackers and smoked constantly.

After five days chasing up various social services and trying to make some kind of headway in building my new life, money was getting tight. I moved to a truck stop motel in Tisley, where I got a room for 120 quid a week. My fictional week in Ireland came to an end and of course when I failed to show up in the Birmingham office, my mobile phone started ringing. Then came the texts and I realised that I would have to make my big announcement.

I made my way to an Internet cafe, sat down and placed my fingers on the keyboard. I dated a blank mail 10 July 2006. Then I wrote to Graham Wilson, the Church PR and Disinformation expert in the UK:

'Please communicate this message below to all concerned individuals. I have resigned from The Church of Scientology. Since 2001, and with the minimum wage legislation taking effect in the UK, to avoid huge expense OSA had our original Sea Org and staff 'contracts shredded. We had to sign new sets called 'Voluntary Commitments'. My position became, legally, that of a volunteer, and I have, with this writing, un-volunteered.

'Quite frankly I have been lied to. Spending time with my family and being made aware of the truth about Hubbard, I now know: his lies about his war record, his lies about his 'adventures', his lies about his 'doctorate', his untruthful statements with regard to his actual agenda, his paranoia, his megalomania and his disdain for others. If the man lied about himself, he could not possibly come up with any truth with regard to mankind.

'I was directed to some very interesting data on OT III, IV, V, VII and VIII. I read testimonials of people who had done these levels and since abandoned the operation. I have to agree, poor and badly written science fiction is an accurate description.

'I have volunteered 22 years of my life to an operation that was not frank and honest with me. I gave my trust, I gave my energy and I gave my hopes and aspirations. I have been conned and I am deeply enraged.

'I am putting this behind me now. I do not want any contact from the Church, I do not want to hear anything about the Church and any attempts to reach me will be considered as harassment and will be treated as such. I am taking legal advice on this matter.

'Please delete my name from any and all mailing lists, records of employment and any statement mentioning me as a church member.

'Do not reply to this email.

'John A Duignan.'

As I had been so senior in the organisation, I knew exactly the reaction that my e-mail was going to provoke. This was a Scientology code red.

In the past I had worked as part of a Scientology security team charged with returning a member to the fold. I knew what they were capable of. Ultimately, if they found me, I would be kidnapped and brought back to Saint Hill where I would be sectioned to the RPF and its brutal regime of 24-hour watch and forced labour. I remembered all those times I had been called in to assist on a 'watch' of someone who had blown. I had shadowed escapees in Gatwick and Heathrow airports in the past and had stood for hours in train stations in London waiting to report any sighting of an absconder.

I remember once being sent to a house in Sussex where I had to park outside all night, every night, for a week. I had to report any movements I saw and describe any people entering or leaving. I had a hired car, parked close to a bushy hedge and I was dressed in a watchman's cap and black clothes. I 'hunkered down' and remained so still that I would not be spotted. I would send status reports with a quick squeeze of the walkie-talkie's trigger. I noted movements at the house and this allowed security to build up a picture of the person's routine so they could identify the perfect time to pounce. This was usually when the subject was alone, and in the case of Odhran, it was calculated to coincide with a point when he would be feeling isolated and vulnerable. Often a person who had blown from the RPF would be surrounded by up to 15 Scientologists. Dressed in civilian attire, they could crowd the target, even in a public place. Then there'd maybe be a hint as to what OSA had in terms of information in pre-Clear and ethics files and then they would be walked with no resistance to a waiting car.

Over the next few days, I operated on pure adrenaline. I registered for housing and got my National Insurance Card. I spent another week in Tisley in the truck stop motel. I was stressed out and began getting severe asthma attacks; I had to go to A & E a couple of times. Despite my attempts to build a new life for myself in Birmingham it was beginning to dawn on me that this was not going to fly for many reasons. I had to face up to the fact that if I stayed there I would be on the run all the time. A quick assessment of my mental state showed me that I was operating on nerves, running on fumes and something was going to break in very near future. I needed a safe place.

Back home the pressure was already on. When I got in touch with my Aunt Cath she told me there were two men sitting in a car outside Kilmony. They had knocked on the door and identified themselves as close friends of mine, Rupert and Eoin. Rupert was Head of all UK security operations and Eoin, a County Monaghan man, was a Security Watch Chief. They said they were trying to get in touch with me and asked had she heard from me. They had been parked just up the road, in view of the house, ever since. Cath suspected that they had a listening device and were monitoring her phone calls. She warned me not to call the house.

I phoned Christian, the anti-Scientology Dialogue contact in Britain. He agreed to come and meet me in a pub. At the arranged time I sat on a wall opposite the pub, mobile phone in hand. I watched a stocky grey-haired man stop at the entrance to the pub, this fitted the description he had given me. I phoned his number. The man answered his phone and I knew it was Christian and he was alone. I told him to come across the street to a different pub. I watched him cross the road to make sure no one was shadowing him. He was reassuring. He understood the danger I was in and and the stress I was under. He strongly advised me to go back to Ireland, saying I needed the emotional support of my family and the sense of being on home turf. I agreed and the decision was made.

I was going home.

I knew I needed to be clever if I was going to shake the guys that were camped outside the house in Kilmony. The following morning, I rose early, shaved off my beard and dressed in my familiar grey suit. I packed up my bag and settled my bill. I then left my luggage with the manager and caught the train to Moor Street Station.

I crossed over to the Selfridges Centre that swallowed up the far end of New Street in Central Birmingham. Roger, the Registrar at the Org, was a creature of habit. In all the time I had lived there he had never changed his daily routine, and sometimes I had accompanied him so I knew his habits. At lunch-time he got up from his desk, walked to a nearby bookshop, checking on his own titles as he is a well-known British crime writer. Then he would make his way up the escalators to a sandwich place overlooking Moor Street Station, for a coffee. Dressed in my suit, I was easily recognisable despite my shaved head. I stood at the top of the escalator waiting for him to make his way upstairs and, sure enough, at about a quarter past one, I spotted him.

As Roger stepped onto the bottom of the escalator to go up, I stepped onto the one going down. I watched his momentary confusion as he became aware that he was being watched. He shook his head as he came out of his daydream, casting around to find the source. He had a look of utter disbelief on his face as we glided past one another. It was too crowded for him to do anything but get to the top and then try to follow me. I rushed through the crowds towards the doors but as I stepped off the pavement I caught a glimpse of him following me down. I dashed across to Moor Street Station. The concourse was quite busy so I was able to get lost in the crowds before crossing over the bridge onto Platform 4 where a train was due to depart for Tisley.

By the time I got back to my motel to pick up my bags, I was almost certain that the Office of Special Affairs would have been informed of my presence in Birmingham. I knew they would then pull their men out of Cork and concentrate their efforts on my last known whereabouts. Back at the motel, I collected my bags and headed to a phone booth to arrange a taxi. I found a skip. Not sure if they could actually track phones, I took no chances and dumped my mobile in it.

The taxi driver who brought me to Birmingham airport was a really nice Islamic guy who showed me real kindness. Dermot had my BMI flight to Dublin pre-paid and had booked me on a connecting Aer Arann flight to Cork. A friend of my Auntie Julia's was due to meet me there.

Back in Ireland everyone was to act as normal. None of my immediate family could be seen to be heading for the airport, in case they were being watched and followed.

All I had to do now was keep it together, for a few more hours, until I got to Cork.

ELEVEN

BUILDING A BRAND NEW LIFE

In Dublin Airport I made my way to internal departures. I scanned the area and sat in a corner. From that position I had a wide view of the all entrances and exits to the departure lounge. My flight to Cork had been delayed by an hour and I could have done without it.

I was sure that my Birmingham ruse had worked, but I was not taking any chances.

I concentrated on the crowds, scrutinising faces, and watching body language. I was looking for 'out points' – a Scientology term but really an application used in fields as varied as intelligence gathering and management training. In an airport, people waiting for delayed flights usually look bored and sip from coffees or bottles of water. They write on laptops or look through magazines and newspapers. I was interested in what people were doing with their eyes, were they scanning crowds? Were they looking at people? Were they directed outwards, searching? I noted body language, looking for movements that did not fit.

The flight was eventually called at 10.30pm. As I took my seat I felt a huge sense of relief wash over me. Nobody had followed me and as far as I knew, the coast was clear in Cork. I was pretty convinced Eoin and Rupert were now back in Birmingham, scouring all the train stations between Moor Street and Tisley.

Shortly before midnight, my flight landed in Cork. We were walked through both the new and old terminals, before arriving at the baggage carousel. Our bags seemed to take an eternity to emerge.

Mary, a friend of my Auntie Julia, had agreed to collect me. She would be unknown to the Church and it was a safer option. As I walked into the arrivals hall I spotted a middle-aged woman with a low-key sign. It had 'John' written on it.

I was greeted with hugs when we got to Iona, Auntie Julia's house in Douglas. The coiled tension in my body began to ease up. I knew this old house so well. It had practically been a second home to me in my teens when it belonged to my Granny. I would drop in after my German classes in town and my Granny Cotter would make me cheese toasties. She would also help me with difficult pronunciation and grammar. I felt her presence there that evening. On the lounge floor was the beautiful hand-made rug that had belonged to my mother. I knelt down and touched it and remembered lying on it as a young child, playing with Jeremy. It was such a long time ago.

Auntie Julia called us into the kitchen where a supper of sandwiches and tea were spread on the table. She came over to me and stroked my face. "God would ya look at 'ye? Eat up."

I tried to hold back tears.

We finished our supper and Maurice and I went out to the car. We drove to Passage West, five miles down the estuary, to an old terraced house he was renting.

I didn't even look around when we got in the door. Maurice showed me to my attic room, which had a big Velux window and said: "Get into bed. You need a bit of sleep mate."

I thanked him and threw my bags on the floor. Pushing the window open, I leaned out and listened to the sounds of the night and I watched the lights of a big freighter pass below as it headed out to sea. I was too tired to think anymore and fell into a fitful sleep.

I woke with a start at around five in morning. I could not get back to sleep and decided to go for a walk. I followed the pathway along the estuary, as far as Monkstown, and watched as the night gradually gave way to dawn. I would become very familiar with insomnia and that two mile walk, as the weeks stretched ahead of me.

For the first few days my body ached and every muscle told me that the stress of the past few weeks had taken its toll. I was under-weight and sleeping badly. Some people commented on how haggard I looked and how bony my face had become, others just looked away and said nothing. When I was alone I began to feel very alienated and wondered if anyone would ever understand what I had been through. The anger was always there but buried, just below the surface.

Once we knew that I had successfully shaken off the Scientology watchers, I moved out to Kilmony for a few weeks. I took Frank and Cath's daft Alsatian on long walks through the woods and breathed in the smells of summer. Later I spent a couple of weekends sailing the south coast between Kinsale and Crookhaven and visited Cape Clear and the Sherkin Islands. I stayed for a while up in a little cottage in the hills outside Skull, and later spent some time up on the rugged and remote Mayo coast with my sisters Kate and Christine.

In my mind I was taking a holiday. I did not want to look at the reality of the state I was in.

I had nothing.

I was desperately clinging onto the idea of taking up a place I'd been offered in a teaching degree course in Birmingham. It served as an anchor, a reason for living and I was terrified of loosing that. But by August I realised that I was being very unrealistic.

A friend helped me to see that I was in no state to embark on that kind of adventure. Instead, I needed to heal myself and rebuild the part of me that had been destroyed. I began to make plans to stay on in Cork.

Since I had returned to Ireland, I had been pretty much living off my brother, Maurice. My lack of financial independence wasn't helping my confidence. Once I decided to stay, I began the long drawn out process of registering with social services. I started learning how to navigate the system that I so badly needed to help me get on my feet. I was impatient, if not frantic, as I went through the frustrating and lengthy process and dealt with endless queries over my habitual residency. I hadn't really lived in Ireland since the 1970s and was only briefly back in '84, before my fateful trip to Germany. The only documentation I had to confirm my origins was my passport. I had no employment records, no medical records and no social insurance details. None of this helped my case.

Maurice was great. He was very gentle and careful with me and never made me feel like I was a burden. In the evenings when he came in he would always ask had I enough money to buy some tobacco and ask me if I wanted anything to eat.

Toward the end of September, Maurice and I packed up our few belongings and moved to a newly built apartment in Blarney. My stuff pretty much fit into one case and I was struck by how little I had to show for my life. The endless tussle with the Social Services continued and I was not in any condition to work. I was grateful that the Society of St Vincent de Paul gave us food vouchers, but I was also feeling angry and demeaned. I was becoming the most scorned of Hubbard's whipping boys – the charity case – and my self-esteem crashed to new lows daily.

By October, with no alleviation in my circumstances, I became very depressed. I would wake up in a black mood and I was quite brutal about beating myself up with the harsh reality of where I was at. Here I was, 42 years old and with absolutely no qualifications. I had no friends left and barely knew my family, although they were being hugely supportive to me. The entire 22 years I had spent in Scientology was absolutely useless. People around me could not possibly understand what it was like in there and the difficulty I was having in trying to re-adjust to the outside world. It was just so far outside the normal human experience. By leaving, I had lost all the friendships that I had built up over two decades. The shared experiences and common reality was wiped out overnight. I was now, in church terms, a 'Declared Suppressive Person', while in real world terms I was a washed-up, middle-aged, unqualified ex-cultie.

Every now and again I popped into an Internet cafe and checked my e-mails. One day I got an e-mail from a close former Sea Org friend, Esther, a senior

executive at Saint Hill base. She had been forwarded
the e-mail I had sent Graham in OSA and was writing
to me as 'a friend'. In reality it looked like a carefully
worded dictate from the Church. The communication
she wrote really shook me:

'You feel that you are being ripped away from your
family because of lies? I ask you now – who is telling
you the lies now that they have successfully ripped you
away from your friends? Have you honestly looked at
both sides, and discovered the truth and motivations?
Apparent facts can always be selected, distorted, in a
way to support a false agenda and lifted completely
out of context.'

The mail brought so much anger and rage to the
surface. I was trembling as I read it. It took me a week
before I could reply:

'Esther,

You have to understand something: I am no longer
a Scientologist; I no longer have any interest in the
subject; its goals and its objectives. I have started a new
life and am very happy with that.

I am not going to get into the circumstances leading
up to this decision; it is a private matter relating to me
and my relationship with my family.

You are an unusually good person, and I was only
too happy to be a friend to you, and I wish you well
– as I do all the good people I worked with while in
Scientology.

I asked that the church no longer contact me, and
that it respects my decision. I have to ask the same
of you, as the Church and its staff are not mutually
exclusive.

John.'

Writing such a curt response to someone I used to really care about was hard but I knew that it was something I had to do. I didn't want any of them to contact me because I knew how the Church could use people to manipulate me if they wanted. Reading between the lines it looked as if Esther was already doing that. I also didn't need to churn up more pain, as the dark tendrils of depression begin to envelop my mind.

There was no response and I reckoned she had got the message

As the next few weeks passed I felt an incredible sadness as the enormity of my exit began to sink in. I was becoming increasingly depressed and could feel myself sinking.

It was early one morning, around 3am and once more I was awake and restless while the world slept. I went for walk in a dark, rainy and deserted Blarney. From the old stone bridge the fast-flowing flood waters were deep, black and enticing. I longed for oblivion. The pain in me screamed for the solace of death, a place where I would feel nothing more.

I was standing, thinking maybe I could do it now.

A security guard patrolling across the river called out 'Are you alright?'

I suddenly felt stupid, self-indulgent and irritated. I walked home and called a suicide help line.

The guy on the other end was also called John and I found someone who understood. His warm and reassuring tones brought me back. My eyes burned. I went to sleep then but a little glimmer of hope got through to me.

John connected me up with Donald Coffey of LES, Local Employment Services, attached to FÁS, the Irish employment agency. He was also a Mediator on behalf of people like myself, who were having difficulty engaging with the system. He called me in and we sat down and had a chat.

By the end of that week he had resolved the issues with Social Services and a week later I was receiving Social Welfare as financial support. On his advice, I eventually switched to disability after I was assessed as suffering from depression related to trauma and stress.

It is hard to express just what it meant to me to be receiving money independently of that given to me by Maurice. I received my first cheque for €165 and I was elated. With my own money I felt a bit more independent and was able to get a hold of a very dilapidated '96 Ford Fiesta belonging to my cousin's girlfriend. She had parked it up at Kilmony a few months earlier. That same day I took the very long bus trip from Blarney to Carrigaline. There had been torrential rain for a quite a few weeks and it was still raining when I arrived late that dark October evening. Cath and Frank were away, but I got into the house and retrieved the car keys. The sorry looking little car was sitting in the field under a tree, with about an inch of water on the floor and leaves were scattered across the seats. But it started. The car limped back to Blarney, where I discovered it was in worse condition than I'd imagined. But I was thrilled and felt that I now owned something substantial.

Donald had recommended me for counselling at the Cork Counselling Centre on Father Matthew Street in the city and I attended an assessment session. I was slightly unnerved as there were quite some similarities to the auditing set up in the Scientology organisations. Part of me was terrified that I was going to see an E-

Meter. But I quickly found out that in the real world, counselling is a healing process.

As we got under way, I had no idea of the rage and despair that was bottled up within me. The counsellor asked me to describe what I was feeling and the lid came off.

Within minutes I was slamming the table, as tears welled in my eyes. It was like it was the first time I really realised how much I had been screwed with by Scientology and how much of my life they had stolen from me. As we closed the session my counsellor looked at me kindly and gave me an important piece of advice: "Be gentle with yourself!"

I listened to those words. Since I had returned to Ireland my mind had been working in overdrive. I was constantly berating myself over how blind and stupid I had been. Operating in a heightened state of worry and anxiety about my future, I had found it practically impossible to relax. Instead, I had manically immersed myself in tasks like getting the old Fiesta up and running. In fact, I had almost totally rebuilt it, mostly working from 9am through to 11pm at night. It was like I had the ghosts of the Commanding Officers in my head. Those simple words from the counsellor really got through to me

Donald assisted me in applying for a degree course at University College Cork as a mature student. Having to focus on the possibility of gaining a recognised qualification helped me slow down a bit. It got me through until I started weekly counselling sessions in January. In the meantime, I took a part-time job as a mobile security guard covering much of Cork City and its surrounding suburbs. I really enjoyed the work. I was more or less my own boss when doing my rounds and I enjoyed the variety and the odd challenge when I was called to help with violent drunks. I worked mostly at weekends and had the odd night shift.

Aunt Cath had me stay over in Kilmony for Christmas. Pretty much all the family was there and we had a lot of fun. For the first time in years I felt a sense of belonging and I also found out just how much I could drink before becoming quite stupidly drunk. Frankie was back from Los Angeles where he was finishing up his music Doctorate in UCLA. On St Stephen's Day he had to do his traditional climb up Ireland's tallest mountain, Carrauntuohil and he dragged me up there with him. It was a tough, beautiful climb and I was thrilled with my achievement.

That January in my counselling we started to talk through my time in the Sea Org. I began to see the self-demeaning and destructive, soul destroying tactics that had been used to control me there. I understood for the first time how Scientology had completely invalidated my own self-worth and changed the way I looked at the world. I saw how my sense of self had been subverted and replaced with what can only be described as an artificial Scientology personality. We spoke about my childhood and as I deconstructed my relationship with my father and my mother I could see how deeply I had been affected by their deaths. For the first time, I recognised how they had never been replaced and how I had always looked for that safe family unit. That is what had attracted me to the Covenant Players, that is why I had wanted to join the army when I was still a teenager and that is why I had ultimately been swallowed up by Scientology. I saw patterns of behaviour and thought that I had operated from and still do. I would often walk out after a session and just sit looking at the river, sometimes for an hour, running with the emotions of long suppressed grief and anger. Yet it was healthy, cleansing.

At home, I was reading the enlightenment philosophers, Rousseau, Descartes and Spinoza. I was reading the breakthroughs in sociology by Durkheim, trying to deconstruct Hubbard's 'tech' and everything that had been pounded into my brain for more than two decades. Hubbard had constantly knocked these great thinkers, giving the impression that he was familiar with their work. But as I read, I realised that he probably had only the sketchiest knowledge of their writings.

One late Sunday afternoon in February, I was doing my security round at the docks and Odlums Flour Mills. It was a lovely evening along by the Lee and there were a couple of big cargo ships tied up at the wharf. I have always liked boats and parked my van nearby. I strolled alongside them while taking a cigarette break. I felt very relaxed. Then as I looked across river the evening sun caught the buildings and the colours were quite lovely.

It was just a moment that should have been like any other. But for some reason, I suddenly realised that I was out and that I was free. That part of my life was over now. It was an incredibly powerful realisation. I felt elated and liberated. I somehow knew that I would never go back to that dark place again.

Slowly I began to feel more positive about life. I was emboldened by the counselling and gradually realised that Hubbard and his cult had no power over me. I was master of my own destiny now. I thought that it was about time that I shared my life with someone else. In the Sea Organisation, while I had many relationships, all of them were fraught with difficulties. To start

with, you could never fully trust your partner, due
to the ever present 'Knowledge Report' – a system
that saw everyone tell on everyone in detailed written
documents. Time too was a consideration. I could never
work out how to develop a meaningful relationship
when I worked seven days a week and sometimes 18
hours a day. Sexual repression was built into the system
by placing the harshest of penalties on any sexual
activities outside marriage. Rather than risk losing one's
place on the career ladder many, like myself, eventually
suppressed the sexual urge altogether. I had always
wanted my own children but that too was a dream that
Scientology suppressed due to Miscavige's 1980s decree
that Sea Org members could not have babies.

I started doing some Internet dating and signed
up to a few Irish dating sites. I was honest enough
and described myself as someone who had just been
through a traumatic period but who wanted to build
his life again. I listed my interests as philosophy,
history, literature, psychology and sociology. I also
put in sailing, horse riding and walking. Of course, I
didn't mention Scientology, as I didn't want to scare
any prospective dates away.

In April 2007, I met Rose. She had two kids from
a previous marriage. We talked a lot online and I told
her that I had been away somewhere for a long time
and was only starting to re-build my life. I reassured
her that I hadn't been in jail, nor in the priesthood. I
promised to explain if we decided to go somewhere
with the relationship. We met a few times and appeared
to be attracted to one another. Later that month, I was
told I had been accepted into UCC to start a degree
the coming September. While my life was definitely
moving forward and good things were happening to me

almost daily, I didn't trust it. In Scientology whenever
something good happened you knew that something
bad would follow on the back of it – the Church seemed
designed to pick you up only to smash you down again.
If you got good pay one week, you could be certain
that the next would be very low indeed. It was hard to
shake that cynicism.

The following month, I took an opportunity to go
out to Norway to help out on a job for my foster brother
Coleman's engineering firm. Rose and I kept in touch
via e-mail.

I flew back for a week at the end of the month and
because I had stood her up the week before, I took her
on a special date to Kinsale. We enjoyed a lovely meal
at my favourite pub overlooking the harbour. We really
connected at that point and I knew that I had found a
very special person indeed.

Then, just as everything seemed to be going so well
I was given crushing news – my work with the security
firm had caused problems for my Back to Education
Award and it looked like I wasn't going to be able to
get my place on the degree. Doing the BA had been my
total focus for months, ever since I had been called for
assessment at the university and then told I had been
accepted onto it. Everything I was doing was geared
toward September 29 and the start of the semester. I was
really looking forward to it and was devastated with
the news but Rose was a great encouragement. With a
bit of persuasion UCC agreed to defer my place until
2008. I signed up for a one-year journalism course in a
local college instead.

It was around this time that I felt confident enough
in Rose to tell her about my past. I didn't know how
she would react but when I did start to explain, she

was taken aback. She later told me that her friends and family were more worried than she was. Thankfully she decided to continue with our relationship.

As the months rolled on, Scientology and my previous life seemed to slip further and further away. I began to wonder how my former comrades were doing. To find out what was going on, I went online for the first time since I had left the Church. I was amazed to find a whole world of people just like myself. I started talking on some of the ex-scientology forums. Some people, like me, utterly rejected it. Others rejected the corporation but still believed Hubbard. It was interesting to see the mixture. Some were still Scientologists but were becoming more sceptical.

I found Mick Winlock on line. He was the guy I had gone to Dublin with in 1987. He is living in Colorado now, after he and his wife got 'Declared' during one of the late 1980s purges. Mick woke up to Scientology long before me but we enjoyed catching up and taking our former religion to pieces.

There were a whole bunch of people that Mick knew who had left too. Jeff Hawkins was one. He had been running all art directions at Central Marketing and was, at one point, designing Documercials with Paul Haggis, who would later direct the 'Crash' movies. When Marketing moved to Hemet, Jeff had been in charge of the production end but Miscavige had taken a dislike to him. Jeff was eventually put on the RPF and had left Scientology in 2001.

Rose began to worry that my online conversations were becoming an addiction and were shackling me to my past. I certainly had a hunger to know what was going on inside the Church but I didn't think it was unhealthy. I saw other people's stories on the Internet and realised that many had worse experiences than I'd had, particularly on the RPF. I thought about Alice a lot, the young girl who had tried to kill herself at Saint Hill, and I was deeply ashamed of my attitude at the time. When it happened I had fobbed her off as being 'out ethics'. But now, from a normal perspective, I could see exactly what had happened to her and how Scientology had destroyed her.

I was annoyed too when I came across a paper published by Professor Gordon Melton in 2001. It made the RPF look like a boy scouts camping adventure. I was around when Melton was at Saint Hill. He was given unprecedented access to the Sea Org and the UK RPF camp. It was a scam. I knew all the RPFers he'd interviewed and the conditions they lived under. During the two weeks or so running up to Melton's 'free access' interview, they'd all been treated like kings. They were fed, briefed and very carefully drilled on exactly what to say and how to say it. They were given little or no work details and loads of sleep. Professor Melton had certainly got a very good impression of the set up but had completely missed the point. His rosy description of the RPF is still used internationally to show just what a wonderful organisation the Church of Scientology is supposed to be.

The forums built a new anger within me. It was a more controlled one that I wanted to focus on using to the disadvantage of the Church. I attended a conference on radicalisation and extremism in Brussels where I submitted an essay on Scientology and its paramilitary arm, The Sea Organisation. I was asked to speak at a Dublin school for a Dialogue Ireland conference and I was pleasantly surprised by the reaction. I joined a debate on the subject at UCD, along with the long-term

Scientology critic, Professor Stephen Kent from the University of Alberta.

At the beginning of 2008 everything moved up a gear when Tom Cruise's controversial recruitment video was posted on YouTube and within days removed, thanks to legal action by the Church. It coincided with the release of Andrew Morton's book 'Tom Cruise, an Unauthorized Biography'. Across the world, headlines screamed the book's claims that the actor is now the number two in the organisation. After that happened, an article I had written on the web site Orato.com, got 50,000 hits and I was phoned by radio stations across the United States to talk about my experiences in the Church.

Scientology was firmly on the world agenda and as my confidence grew, an organisation called Anonymous emerged. Anonymous are really a viral marketing version of a human rights' movement. It is made up of regular people from all professions, creeds and religions across the world, who have decided to stand up and say 'this is enough'. I think this Internet-based group of wonderful activists will prove to be Scientology's nemesis. They believe in the right to freedom of speech and fight organisations that try to hide nefarious deeds behind the cloak of legal threats and 'public relations'. Anonymous run forums, print material, alert journalists and, since February 2008, have staged protests every single month outside every Scientology Centre in the world. Their mere existence has empowered me, and many others, to be even more vocal in exposing this abusive cult. They have given me huge strength and a new-found belief in the human race. The humanity and the sense of empathy I have gotten from these strangers, or as the Church of

Scientology has described them 'cyber-terrorists', has been just gut-wrenching for me. Each and every one of them who have contacted me, have expressed their disgust and shock at the conditions endured by staff and Sea Org members.

When I realised what the movement are doing and how powerful a force Anonymous have become I actually broke down and cried. They are taking a stand for me and for Scientology's victims like Alice and Lisa McPherson, and for the countless others whose stories have not been told but whose lives have been destroyed by this evil cult.

I face the future now with a growing sense of hope and with each day I try to gain a deeper understanding of the weird world of Scientology. What I have learned so far is how important it is for people not to get caught up in the celebrity of Scientology. We cannot write it off as a fad just because it has so many famous followers. The Church is run by very ignorant people. It has nurtured its own executive structure through the Commodore's Messenger Organisation, Hubbard's child soldiers. They are incubated under the harsh, and emotionally cold 'ethics' system, educated exclusively in Hubbard's distorted world view and have little, or no, exposure to historical or philosophical systems in the outside world. These are the zealots who have ended up managing the Church. I believe David Miscavige will eventually have to face the truth that he is as much a victim of Hubbard as I am.

Scientology does not thrive on scrutiny and the information age has damaged the Church. As a public Scientologist it is simply impossible to go through life and not come across critical material about the Church – largely thanks to Tom Cruise jumping up and down

on Oprah Winfrey's couch. Ok, so we forgive him that
and we might even forgive him for ripping into Brooke
Shields for taking anti-depressants after the birth of
her child. But when he goes out on YouTube saying
that at the scene of an accident only a Scientologist
can help, that doesn't communicate very well to the
rest of the world. That is Scientology preaching to the
rest of the world religions – to Muslims, Catholics or
Atheists. That is Tom Cruise morphing into David
Miscavige. It is also why the Church is haemorrhaging
Scientologists. Few are vocal about it; most are just
quietly slipping away, just not turning up for courses
or events anymore. When they are called up by frantic
organisation or Sea Org staff, they give an appropriate
excuse and then install an answering machine.

A cult can be described as a tightly controlled social
unit where all energies, be that money, people or
recognition, are focused inwards to a central figure at
its core. It cannot be argued that mainline religions are
cults. Most of them project huge efforts outwards to the
betterment of mankind, care of the ill and weak and in
attempts to enrich the quality of life where they operate.
Cults are dangerous because they operate, like criminal
gangs, outside of the law of the land and they have their
own 'solutions' for problems. In Scientology we refused
any kind of drug or psychiatric intervention, no matter
how ill the person was. This has proven disastrous in
several recent cases. In Boston, Jeremy Perkins, a young
man who had a bi-polar disorder, killed his mother
Ellie when she took him off his medication. They were
both Scientologists. In Australia, an almost identical
situation occurred, except in this case the young woman
killed both her Scientologist mother and father.

In April 2008 the Norwegian paper 'Aftenposten' reported that the daughter of a member of the country's parliament committed suicide. It happened hours after she received 'devastating' results from a personality test administered by the Church in Nice in France where she was studying. Kaja Bordevich Ballo was just 20 years old and had been invited into the Scientology Centre, near the student-housing complex where she lived. She killed herself a few hours later and left a note with the test results. The Church has said it is "deeply unfair" to link them with her death and have pointed to an eating disorder she suffered as a teenager. They have also suggested that she had a history of psychiatric problems.

I knew that the evaluation of the Free Personality Test could be quite vicious. The evaluator is supposed to 'cave you in', to make you realise that you really need the help that Scientology offers.

Some have argued that that a Scientologist has a right to freedom to practice his or her religion. But a Scientologist is not free. Scientology is not about freedom; it is about obedience and compliance. And it is not a religion. It costs a lot of money and it is not freely given, as most other religions are.

At its core, Scientology is, in fact, an unlicensed and unmonitored psychotherapeutic system, operating under the guise of religious practice. This way it avoids paying taxes and scrutiny by authorities in the medical field. The fact that it actually costs in the region of €50,000 to get to the OT levels, and about €10,000 for each level, should clear up the 'religious' argument straight away.

I do not believe that the Scientology cult will survive in its present form. I predict that we are going to witness something quite shocking with this operation. Right now, according to several recent escapees from the International Headquarters in Hemet, California, there about 30 former senior Scientology executives being illegally held in a locked room in a compound, surrounded by razor wire, fitted with almost 500 CCTV cameras, motion detectors and armed guards. I have not been there, but the numerous firsthand reports from people that I know from my Scientology years are surely alarming enough to warrant investigation by US authorities. In the United Kingdom, I have personally observed at least 20 people enduring prison-like conditions and forced manual labour. They receive a pittance and are allowed no privacy and no freedom.

Such activities are illegal, but the Church of Scientology gets away with it because it can control the thoughts and the expressions of its inmates. It controls them because the captives believe that it is not just this life but their future lifetimes that really matter. He or she is cowed by the fear of being born a cripple, a lunatic or a street kid, lifetime after lifetime. If a person does not make it in Scientology now, then that will certainly be their fate in future lifetimes. No human rights' legislation can beat that, so the RPFers or regular Sea Org members will carry on saying what they are told to say. Then, once the threat is gone, they will go back to their camps and enforced slave labour.

The Church claims membership of something like 8 million people worldwide but that is a lie. I estimate that it has no more than 50,000 members around the world. During my 22 years with the Church, I have visited almost all the Scientology Orgs. The absolute maximum staff numbers in even the largest centres are about 20 full-time dedicated staff. Sometimes it's five or ten people and the maximum public doing services at any time would be about 40 people.

Scientology is a 'pure' ideology and tolerates no other practices. One of the great lies that the Scientology PR machine touts is that 'you can be any religion and still be a Scientologist'. This bare-faced lie was exposed to me when I was attempting to get one of my staff members promoted. The senior executive, who had to approve the promotion request, sent it back, writing: 'This person prays to God, he needs to be handled in Ethics on both PTSness and involvement in other practices'.

In Scientology we were run on the vitally important goal of 'Clearing the Planet'. This essentially means the replacement of the existing social and political systems across the world with Hubbard's system. Hubbard described his vision of the 'Homo Novis' in 'Dianetics', and brings up the same theme in later lectures. Scientology has roots in the occult but carefully clouds them. It has a caste system. The 'Degraded Being' is the lowest caste and refers to people who are mentally incompetent, disabled people, homosexuals, communists, journalists and psychiatrists. Hubbard tells the Scientologist to dispose of homosexuals without remorse. He actually says that a disabled person is a 'Degraded Being' and should also be disposed of 'quietly and without remorse.' In a pure Scientology world, where the philosophy and the words are taken to their literal extreme, homosexuals, the disabled and communists have absolutely no place.

With the Sea Org, Hubbard created a fanatical, militarised, dedicated core for his empire. This is a group that take his word as holy writ, operate outside the law and can be described as a State within a State.

It has its own punitive system, prison-like camps and very own take on human rights. In the writings of Hubbard, the Sea Organisation's primary goal is to forward 'Command Intention'. It is motivated by 'Duty, which is the highest motivation that there is'. As an organisation, it trains children as young as ten in a fanatical militant manner. It views crying and emotion as weak. It views 'grief at the death of a loved one as 'down tone'.

The Totalitarian strain in Hubbard's teaching is clearly stated in one of the most important policies in Scientology. It is a policy that is so important that Tom Cruise quoted it in his video interview at the IAS event in 2005. The policy is called 'Keeping Scientology Working'. In it Hubbard says: "I don't see that popular measures, self-abnegation and democracy have done anything for Man but push him further into the mud."

I can attest to the fact that the Sea Org could be motivated to carry out any kind of programme devised by the Church. Had I been ordered at any point in my Sea Organisation career to find any business owned by our perceived opponents and intimidate them, maybe even smash up the shop windows in their premises, I would have done it, unquestioningly. If I had been told to go and grab them and lock them up, I probably would have done so too. If I was asked to kill them, I cannot, hand on heart, say I wouldn't have done that too.

Hubbard talks about releasing criminals and using them in a military capacity. Criminon, the Scientology front group, is operating all over the world, going into prisons and claiming to offer a rehabilitation service for criminals. In the past 10 years they were found to be attempting to set up in Arbour Hill Prison in Dublin which houses some of Ireland's most dangerous rapists and sex offenders. They claim to have operated in Portlaoise, Ireland's Maximum Security prison, where paramilitaries and major drug dealers are housed. In California they have been operating at the notorious Corcoran State Prison, which houses a high percentage of mentally ill inmates. In Mexico a major programme has been underway at Ensenada Prison. On its own website, Criminon cites prison programmes from Thailand to Indonesia, back to South Africa and all over South America and the US. Robert F Henderson, the Captain of the New York State Department of Correctional Services is quoted as saying: "The rehabilitative technology employed by Criminon represents the only truly workable means to handle the increasingly burdensome criminal populations." In the UK, Criminon claims to have carried out courses in 140 prisons, including Wormwood Scrubs and the top security Brixton jail.

Should Scientology be ignored? Should we still laugh the Church off as a celebrity fad? I don't think so.

I was recently invited by Ursela Caberta to attend a conference in Hamburg, Germany. I first met this wonderful woman at a conference in Pisa a few months earlier. Before that I had come across her many times in Scientology, where she is considered to be the very personification of evil. The Office of The Protection of the Constitution had appointed her in 1992 to investigate the activities of Scientology, a group the German judiciary system believes merits watching. Ursela had organised a three-day event during which a number of former Sea Org officers briefed, mixed

with and enlightened, a selection of European police
investigators, politicos and journalists. We were also
joined by about 20 young people from Anonymous.
I watched as investigators and officials from the
Belgian, German and French police took notes as we
talked. Security was very tight at the conference and
it was obvious that all these countries were taking the
potential risk posed by the Church seriously.

I am now a Suppressive Person and as a result I am Fair
Game. Just as Paulette Cooper and so many others have
discovered in the past, this means that any Scientologist
has the right to damage and even kill me without fear of
censure from any Church executive or committee. Most
Scientologists are law-abiding people, but not all of
them are and I know there is always a risk. The Church
of Scientology works on the principle of bullying and
instilling fear and threat. But I am no longer scared. I
have come through some extreme experiences and I
learned how to face them down.

Every day, even on my bad and dark days, I
experience a sense of tremendous liberty. I can, and
often do, drive into town on a whim, go to an expensive
restaurant and have an exquisite meal. I relish the
freedom I have to do this simple thing.

Sometimes I just get in my car and drive to the Kerry
Mountains, just because I can. I value this – it is called
freedom and I would protect and fight for this right for
me and for others.